INTO THE

RELIGIOUS EDUCATION IN THE LEAVING

Issues of Justice and Peace

John Murray

Series Editors
Eoin G. Cassidy and Patrick M. Devitt

VERITAS

First published 2005 by
Veritas Publications
7/8 Lower Abbey Street
Dublin 1
Ireland
Email publications@veritas.ie
Website www.veritas.ie

ISBN 1 85390 791 X

10 9 8 7 6 5 4 3 2 1

Copyright © John Murray, 2005

The material in this publication is protected by copyright law. Except as may be permitted by law, no part of the material may be reproduced (including by storage in a retrieval system) or transmitted in any form or by any means, adapted, rented or lent without the written permission of the copyright owners. Applications for permissions should be addressed to the publisher.

A catalogue record for this book is available from the British Library

Cover design by Bill Bolger
Printed in the Republic of Ireland by Betaprint Ltd, Dublin

Veritas books are printed on paper made from the wood pulp of managed forests. For every tree felled, at least one tree is planted, thereby renewing natural resources.

Contents

Acknowledgements		7
Series Introduction		9
Preface		19

PART 1	REFLECTING ON CONTEXT	32
1.1	Social Analysis	33
1.2	Social Analysis in Action	61
PART 2	THE CONCEPT OF JUSTICE AND PEACE	88
2.1	Visions of Justice	89
2.2	Visions of Peace	142
2.3	Religious Perspectives on Justice and Peace	152
2.4	Violence	203
PART 3	THE RELIGIOUS IMPERATIVE TO ACT FOR JUSTICE AND PEACE	239
3.1	Religion and the Environment	241
3.2	Religious Traditions and the Environment	257

APPENDIX ONE
Outline of the Course   317

APPENDIX TWO
Concerning the Use of Websites   320
and Other Resources

APPENDIX THREE   324
A Shorter Bibliography

*With love
for my wife
Sandra*

Acknowledgements

I'd like to thank the many people who gave me general encouragement or practical help in the writing of this book. The list includes the following: my editors, Frs Eoin Cassidy and Patrick Devitt, who kindly invited me to write the book and who gave me prudent advice for its successful completion, and also those in Veritas who carefully read over the book and offered specific suggestions for its improvement; my former colleagues in St David's Holy Faith Secondary School in Greystones, especially the stalwart RE team of Norma Keogh, Miriam Kane and Moya Bolger and the ever-inspirational Fr John McDonagh, former chaplain of St David's School and now PP of Dalkey; my present colleagues in Mater Dei Institute, especially Fr Paul Tighe, Gráinne Treanor, Sandra Cullen, and Fr Paddy Greene; my former classmate and present leading light in the Irish RE scene, Robert Dunne, who kindly read over an early draft of the introduction and chapter one and offered valuable advice; Frs Patrick Hannon, Michael Conway, Hugh Connolly and, in particular, Vincent Twomey of St Patrick's College, Maynooth, who helped me become somewhat more scholarly; Honor Fagan, of NUI Maynooth, who contributed ideas regarding conflict resolution websites; Annette Honan and the NCCA; Philip Barnes of University of Ulster, author of the book in this series on world religions. Very special thanks are due to Dr Yaakov Pearlman, Chief Rabbi of Ireland who contributed some information for the section on Judaism in chapter three; to Bruno Breathnach, MA HDE, Director of Rigpa Dublin, Tibetan Buddhist Meditation Centre, who sent me substantial material for the sections on Buddhism in chapters two and three; and to Seán Farrell of Trócaire, who sent me some of their very useful resources. I'd also like to thank John Murphy, one of my fellow organisors in the always-supportive Johnstown Family Mass group, whose political savvy was invaluable, and Fiona Hannon, a student in the same group, for encouragement and suggesting the war poetry idea; my friends, Fiona Gallagher, who gave me some initial pointers regarding conflict resolution, and Mícháel Murphy, who encouraged me both on and off the pitch each week. Thanks also to my father, Jim Murray, my late mother, Pat, my sisters Elaine and Shauna and brothers Ronan and Conor (and Jo), and all my extended family and friends, especially Paul Corcoran and Michael Hanly, who constantly wondered when the book would be finished. (Oh, and who all kept me going with their confidence and interest!) Finally, most importantly of all, I'd like to thank my wife, Sandra, and my children, Kevin and Rachel, who had to put up with me over the past year and a half in all my abstraction, distraction and subtraction! Sandra, especially, has embodied all the virtues to the highest degree in this regard, most particularly patience! The debt of gratitude I owe is great and I am glad to acknowledge it here (hoping I have left out nobody). How I have used the suggestions given by some, and responded to the encouragement given by all, is my own responsibility, as are any errors that remain.

Series Introduction

September 2003 saw the introduction of the Leaving Certificate Religious Education Syllabus by the Department of Education and Science. For those concerned to promote a religious sensibility in young Irish adults it is hard to exaggerate the importance of this event. It both represents a formal recognition by society of the value of religious education in the academic lives of second-level students, and it also reflects the importance which Irish society attaches to promoting the personal growth of students, including their spiritual and moral development. Religious education offers young people the opportunity to understand and interpret their experience in the light of a religious world-view. Furthermore, in and through an engagement with the RE Syllabus at Leaving Certificate level, students will learn a language that will enable them both to articulate their own faith experience and to dialogue with those of different faiths or non-theistic stances.

The Department of Education Syllabus is to be welcomed in that it gives recognition to the role that religious education plays in the human development of the young person. It is not an exaggeration to say that religious education is the capstone of the school's educational response to the young person's search for meaning and values. In this context, it encourages students to reflect upon their awareness of themselves as unique individuals with roots in a community network of family, friends and parish. Furthermore, it allows students to acknowledge and reflect upon their relationship to a God who cares for them and for the world in which we live. Finally, it gives students access to the universal nature of the quest for truth, beauty and goodness. Most of these themes are addressed sympathetically in the section entitled *The Search for Meaning and Values*. In particular, this section is to be welcomed because it offers the possibility for students to grapple with theistic and non-theistic world-views in a context that is hospitable to religious belief.

A critical dimension of the young person's educational journey is the growth in understanding of their own culture and the manner in which culture shapes their outlook on the world. The Religious Education Syllabus not only addresses the manner in which religion (and in particular Christianity) has shaped Irish culture over many centuries, but it also provides an extremely valuable platform from which to critique aspects of the relationship between faith and culture in the contemporary world. The section entitled *Religion: The Irish Experience* addresses the former concern by showing pupils the manner in which the Christian religion has contributed to the belief patterns and values of Irish society. It also alerts them to the depths of religious belief that predate by many centuries, even millennia, the arrival of Christianity in Ireland; and it also connects them to the cultural richness that links Ireland to the European continent. In this context, the devotional revolution that took place in Ireland (including the extraordinary growth in religious orders from 1850-1930) is a topic that could be expanded. The missionary outreach of the Catholic Church in Ireland in the last hundred years is worthy of special mention. Finally, students studying this section should be encouraged to acknowledge the ambiguities that have attended the presence of religion in Ireland over the centuries; to see on the one hand the image of an island of saints and scholars, and on the other hand to note how 'lilies that fester smell far worse than weeds'.

In examining the manner in which faith and culture interact, the sections entitled *Religion and Science* and *Religion and Gender* make a valuable contribution to the Syllabus. These sections address topical issues that were controversial in the past and continue to be problematical even today. In treating of these two topics it is obviously important to avoid stereotypes – the acceptance of unexamined assumptions that mask or oversimply the truth to such an extent as to do a disservice to the seriousness of the issues involved. Likewise, the section on *World Religions* should be taught in a manner that is sensitive to the dangers of cultural and religious stereotypes. This section not only gives students a valuable introduction to the main religions in the world, but it also provides a cultural context for an awareness of the fact that the phenomenon of religion and the experience of religious belief is something that shapes people's understanding of themselves and their lifestyles across all cultural boundaries. Furthermore, it should never be forgotten that if, as Christians believe, God's Spirit is present in and through these religions, there is a need to study these religions precisely in order to discover aspects of God's presence in the world that has the capability to continually surprise.

In the Irish cultural context, Catholicism shapes the religious sensibilities and practices of the majority of young people. The Syllabus offers a generous acknowledgement of the importance of Christianity in the Irish context by providing two sections that focus on core aspects of the Christian faith. These are: *Christianity: origins and contemporary expressions* and *The Bible: Literature and Sacred text*. In this context, the Syllabus section on the Bible is to be welcomed. However, greater attention could be given to the role and significance of the Prophets in the Old Testament and to Paul in the New Testament. Furthermore, in studying the Bible it should never be forgotten that the primary reality is not the 'book' but rather the person of Christ and the community tradition grappling with this reality that is revealed in and through the Bible.

What is often in danger of being forgotten in an academic context is the importance of the fostering of attitudes and practices that promote personal growth. Religious education cannot be focused only on knowledge and understanding, because religion is primarily a way of celebrating life and, in particular, the spiritual dimension of life in and through the practices of worship, ritual and prayer. The syllabus's recognition of this critical dimension of religious education through the section entitled *Worship, Ritual and Prayer* is to be welcomed. In addressing this section of the syllabus it would be important to alert students to the great variety of spiritualities, prayer forms, mysticisms, rituals and styles of music that are to be found within the Christian tradition in order that students may have the possibility of exploring the richness of the spiritual dimension of their own tradition.

A key remit of the educational process is the fostering of moral maturity through a syllabus that allows students to engage in moral education. Not only is religious education particularly suited to facilitating this educational imperative, but the ethical character of human life is a core feature of all religions. The importance of this dimension of religious education is recognised in the provision of two sections entitled *Moral Decision-Making* and *Issues of Justice and Peace*. There is nothing optional about the challenge to promote justice and peace. However, it is a topic that can all too easily be ideologically driven. Therefore, there is a special responsibility on those teaching this section to ensure that the instances of injustice cited, and the causes of injustice proposed, are grounded in solid research.

The challenges to Catholic religion teachers
Though religious education has been an integral part of Irish second-level schools long before the foundation of the state, it

has not until now been possible to assess this work under the State examination system. The reason for this anomaly is the Intermediate Education Act (1878) which allowed for the teaching but forbade the State examination of religious education. The removal of this legal constraint on State examination of RE has provided the impetus for the introduction of the Junior Certificate syllabus in September 2000 and the introduction of the Leaving Certificate syllabus in September 2003. These changes are to be welcomed but they provide a number of major challenges to Catholic religion teachers that should not be minimised.

In the *first* place, Catholic religion teachers have to attend to the danger that the new syllabus will lead to a weakening of a commitment to catechesis in second level schools. The catechetical project of faith formation is built around six key pillars: knowledge of the faith; liturgical/sacramental education; moral formation; learning to pray; education for community life, including a fostering of the ecumenical character of Christian community, and finally, missionary initiative and inter-religious dialogue. Clearly, the RE Leaving Certificate syllabus does give attention to many of the above themes, including the key catechetical concerns of attitude or value formation and the development of commitments. However, the emphasis in the syllabus is undoubtedly upon the acquiring of knowledge, understanding and knowledge-based skills, all of which undoubtedly place it under the rubric of religious education rather than catechesis. The religion teacher ought to value the distinctive approaches to religion reflected in both catechesis and religious education. Both are important because both contribute in distinctive ways to the religious development of the young person. Catechesis aims at maturity of faith whereas religious education aims at knowledge and understanding of the faith.

From the point of view of the religion teacher, the teaching can have a different tone at different times. On one occasion, it might have a 'showing how' or catechetical tone, one that assumes a shared faith experience and encourages active participation. At another time it can have an educational or 'explaining' tone that invites pupils to stand back from religion to a certain extent, so that they can gain a more objective understanding of what is being taught. The religious education syllabus should be taught in a manner that keeps both of these approaches in balance. In a similar vein, the presence of RE on the Leaving Certificate curriculum should not distract teachers from acknowledging that the religious development of young people happens in many contexts, which are distinct, though complementary. It can take place at home, in the parish, with friends as well as in school. Furthermore, even in the school it can take place at a whole series of levels including liturgy, prayer and projects that encourage an awareness of the need to care for those in most need.

In the *second* place, teachers have to attend to the scope and range of the aims of the syllabus, one that seeks both to introduce students to a broad range of religious traditions and to the non-religious interpretation of life as well as providing students with the opportunity to develop an informed and critical understanding of the Christian tradition. In this context, teachers have to balance the need to promote tolerance for and mutual understanding of those of other or no religious traditions, alongside the need to give explicit attention to the Christian faith claims that Jesus is the Son of God and that he died to save us and to unite us with God and one another. Similarly, in teaching Christianity, teachers need to give attention to the role and significance of the Church from a Catholic perspective. It should never be forgotten that the idea of the Church as 'people of God', 'body of Christ' and 'temple of the Holy Spirit' is one that is at the heart of Catholic self-understanding.

In a similar vein, the syllabus encourages students to engage critically with a wide variety of ethical codes with a view to the development of a moral maturity. Teachers will have to balance this approach with the way in which morality is viewed within the Christian tradition under the heading of discipleship – Jesus invites people to follow *him* rather than an ethical code or vision. Furthermore, from a Christian perspective, morality is never simply or even primarily concerned with a listing of moral prohibitions, rather it situates the ethical dimension of human nature within the context of a belief in a forgiving God. Finally, it should not be forgotten that it does not make sense to teach morality in too abstract a manner. Morality is something preeminently practical and at all times needs to be brought down to the level of real people – those who struggle with the demands of conscience in their lives. From a Catholic perspective, one has in the lives of the saints a multitude of examples of the manner in which people have attempted to follow the call to discipleship that is Christian morality.

Finally, nobody concerned with the seriousness of the challenge facing schools to promote moral maturity could be unaware of the importance of the contemporary challenge posed to the promotion of societal and religious values by the rise of a relativist and/or subjectivist ethos. In this context, the teaching of the broad variety of moral codes will have to be done in a manner that draws students' attention to the importance of acknowledging the objective nature of morality as opposed to accepting uncritically either a relativist or a subjectivist standpoint. In the light of the need to critique an exaggerated acceptance of pluralism, there is also a need to acknowledge that not all theories are equally valid, and moral decision-making is not simply a matter of applying one's own personal preference.

What is proposed in these commentaries

Given the breadth and scope of the syllabus it is undoubtedly true that teachers will have to attend to the wide variety of sections in the syllabus which demand a breadth of knowledge that some may find a little daunting. Even though it is not envisaged that teachers would attempt to teach all ten sections of the syllabus to any one group of students, nevertheless, the syllabus will make demands upon teachers that can only be met if there are support services in place. For example, apart from the need to ensure the publishing of good quality teaching and learning resources, the schools themselves will need to ensure that appropriate resources – books, CDs, internet and videos – are provided. Finally, teachers will need to be provided with appropriate in-service training. It is to furthering this goal of providing good quality teaching and learning resources that the present series of volumes is addressed.

The eleven volumes in this series of commentaries comprise an introductory volume (already published, *Willingly To School*) that reflects upon the challenge of RE as an examination subject, along with ten other volumes that mirror the ten sections in the syllabus. These commentaries on the syllabus have been published to address the critical issue of the need to provide resources for the teaching of the syllabus that are both academically rigorous and yet accessible to the educated general reader. Although primarily addressed to both specialist and general teachers of religion and third-level students studying to be religion teachers, the commentaries will be accessible to parents of Leaving Certificate pupils and, in addition, it is to be hoped that they will provide an important focus for adults in parish-based or other religious education or theology programmes. In the light of this focus, each of the volumes is structured in order to closely reflect the content of the syllabus and its order of presentation. Furthermore, they are written in clear, easily accessible language and each includes an explanation of new theological and philosophical perspectives.

The volumes offered in this series are as follows

Patrick M. Devitt:	*Willingly to School: Religious Education as an Examination Subject*
Eoin G. Cassidy:	*The Search for Meaning and Values*
Thomas Norris and Brendan Leahy:	*Christianity: Origins and Contemporary Expressions*
Philip Barnes:	*World Religions*
Patrick Hannon:	*Moral Decision Making*
Sandra Cullen:	*Religion and Gender*
John Murray:	*Issues of Justice and Peace*
Christopher O'Donnell:	*Worship, Prayer and Ritual*
Benedict Hegarty:	*The Bible: Literature and Sacred Text*
John Walsh:	*Religion: The Irish Experience*
Fachtna McCarthy and Joseph McCann:	*Religion and Science*

Thanks are due to the generosity of our contributors who so readily agreed to write a commentary on each of the sections in the new Leaving Certificate syllabus. Each of them brings to their commentary both academic expertise and a wealth of experience in the teaching of their particular area. In the light of this, one should not underestimate the contribution that they will make to the work of preparing teachers for this challenging project. Thanks are also due to our publishers, Veritas. Their unfailing encouragement and practical support has been of inestimable value to us and has ensured that these volumes saw the light of day. Finally, we hope that you the reader will find each of these commentaries helpful as you negotiate the paths of a new and challenging syllabus.

Eoin G. Cassidy
Patrick M. Devitt
Series Editors

Preface

Never really optional

Section F is an optional module in this syllabus, one that will probably be a popular choice.[1] It is a familiar topic, clearly significant for the lives of teachers and students. Issues of justice and peace are to be found everywhere: newspapers, news headlines, films and novels, the school curriculum, the professional concerns of teachers and the personal concerns of students, and throughout society. To be fully engaged in the real world as a morally aware person, one will inevitably face the challenge of understanding and interpreting fairly issues of justice and peace (and the central concepts involved). Issues of justice and peace are never really optional.

A controversial and complex area

The subject matter is controversial, unavoidably so if one is to be accurate and specific. This makes the area potentially very interesting, particularly at senior level where students can be expected to engage with complex and debatable issues in some depth. This is not a cut-and-dried syllabus module, presenting neat answers to every question and ready-made solutions for all problems. An approach that is simplistic is to be avoided, especially one that sees all issues of justice and peace as a battle between the 'good guys' and the 'bad guys' (as many popular films portray them). Often, the reality is that the opposing 'sides' in disputes disagree about the relevant facts and the appropriate interpretations of the situation, even though they are equally committed in good conscience to justice and peace as ideals. What is needed is the virtue to find and face the relevant facts, to interpret them in the light of a clear knowledge and understanding of 'justice' and 'peace', and to act justly for peace.

Accuracy and fairness are essential

The controversial nature of the material should not encourage vagueness to avoid offending anyone or 'disturbing the peace'. Some types of 'offence' can be socially responsible and some types of 'peace' ought to be disturbed. Needless controversy should be avoided, however, as a polemical approach tends to generate more heat than light. The study of justice and peace will come down to specifics at some stage and it is then that a good teacher will help students to become aware of personal biases and prejudices and how to deal with them. A concern for justice will entail a commitment to accuracy and objectivity in one's critical thinking, especially when dealing with points of view that differ from one's own. Anything that prevents us from being accurate or fair is a serious obstacle to the successful teaching or study of this section of the syllabus.

Some common errors to avoid

Another danger of stressing the controversial nature of the subject matter is found in the temptation to see 'justice and peace' as a totally subjective or relativistic moral area. We can be tempted to conclude illogically, from the fact that not everything in the area of justice is clear-cut, that nothing is clear-cut. We move from the true observation that we do not know everything in this area to the false conclusion that we cannot know anything. One of the most common expressions of this *non sequitur* category of logical fallacy is the idea that because morality is not always black or white, it is (always) grey. Another popular slogan is that there are no absolutes in morality, because not every element of morality is an absolute and because we can always learn more and improve. None of these conclusions are logical. We do not have to see everything in this section as totally clear-cut, known, black or white, or absolute; nor do we have to see everything as vague, unknowable, grey, or relative. Some things are not totally clear; some things are absolutely clear. Our aim is to work out which is which, or to at least show how we can go about doing this. We may not be able to specify all the possible answers to questions of justice and peace but we should be able to clarify *some* answers, to demonstrate and facilitate how to find further answers, and to explain how still other 'answers' are inadequate or even just wrong.

One cannot be totally neutral
I believe that it may be possible and useful for a teacher (or an author) to be a *temporarily* 'neutral' chairperson of the discussion of issues of justice and peace, to facilitate discussion and exploration by others, but I do not think one can be neutral ultimately or totally. One cannot 'do justice to justice' by always sitting on the fence: the reality of justice demands commitment at some point. Even though one is always ready in principle to revise one's position in the light of further knowledge or insight, one must take up a position of some sort. Pupils will often ask what the teacher thinks on a particular matter, and it will not always be appropriate to dodge the question or refuse to answer it. To claim to be 'neutral' is in fact to take up a position of sorts. Such 'neutrality' might even teach (falsely) that no position is correct, or that all are acceptable, or that one is as good as any other. None of these positions are adequate; each fails to grasp moral *truth*. Teaching is always concerned with truth.[2] Besides, any teacher teaches in a school with a

particular ethos or identity, and this ethos will never be neutral on the basic issues of justice and peace. Nor should it be. A teacher should always teach in harmony with the ethos of his or her particular school.

Though this is not the place to go into the matter in detail, I believe that there is a problem in the lack of explicit attention in this syllabus to the issue of truth, particularly religious truth. There exists a real, though unacknowledged, challenge in teaching coherently in a religious school a course in RE that does not directly treat the school's religious faith as true, that deals with the 'meanings' of various faiths and philosophies, but does not take any position on whether any one of these is better or more accurate than the others. In reality, no curriculum is ever entirely neutral, even if it aims to be. This book assumes that the new RE exam curriculum can be taught in a way that respects all faiths and philosophies and is fair in its investigation and presentation of them, whilst being faithful to the ethos of a school, which most often in Ireland will be of a Catholic ethos. How this can be done is not entirely clear to me and I have not addressed it directly in this book. It is an area that deserves and needs further attention from all concerned.

My approach
My approach is not neutral. This book, which is practically focused, will deal mainly with the teaching of this section within the context of a Catholic ethos. This is the tradition I know best and the one I accept as true. It is the tradition that most potential readers of this book will share. I believe that much of what I write should be readily acceptable to other traditions because the Catholic moral tradition is reasonable and open to the truth present in other traditions.

I write as a Roman Catholic who is committed to a 'natural law' approach to ethics, one always informed by Divine Revelation as understood and taught authoritatively by the Catholic Church. Natural law is examined in the other primarily moral section of the syllabus (Section C: *Moral Decision Making*), but it may be helpful to outline here the Catholic understanding of it.

Natural Law
By natural law, the Catholic tradition means our grasp of moral right and wrong *by reason*. Human persons are created in God's image (a truth that is foundational for much that will be examined in this book). This suggests we have a God-given ability to know moral truth by the light of our reason reflecting on what it means to be a human person living in community. We do not have to rely totally on our access to God's law through our faith-response to God's Revelation to know moral principles and norms. We can know them by thinking clearly about our human potential and the various goods at stake in living a human life as an individual in community with others (and in relationship with our natural environment).

Faith in God's Revelation is not superfluous, however, as the natural law is not always clearly known and it does not tell us all we need to know about God and his full plan for us. Though morality can be grasped by all rational persons in principle, we need God's specific guidance in Scripture and Tradition to enable us to be certain and confident about morality in practice.[3] The following is a prime example of this complimentary relationship of reason and faith. We can know the truth of the Golden Rule – 'In everything do to others as you would have them do to you'[4] – by reasoning about the common humanity that makes all humans equal. As a compliment to this essentially personal *rational* grasp, we can know the truth of this rule by our acceptance *in faith* of the Gospel and the authority of Jesus Christ as the Son of God who teaches us the truth about how to treat each other. In this case, faith backs up reason and strengthens its authority, but it does not supplant it or contradict it. The moral 'reasoning' referred to here is the characteristic feature of 'natural law'.

Even one who does not accept the theological explanation of natural law given above (referring to the human person as created in God's image) can know the reality of natural law. From a secular perspective, this is seen in understanding morality as essentially rational and objective. (I do not mean by this to neglect the very important emotional aspect of morality but to emphasise that morality is not purely emotional. It is always necessary to judge prudently and fairly whether our emotional reactions or responses are appropriate.) True principles of right and wrong, and consequent rules of behaviour, are not arbitrary impositions of the will of the stronger on the weaker (the State on the citizen, for example, or the school principal on the student). True morality is a matter of *reasonable* principles, norms and rules. We can discover what the principles, norms and rules should be by using our reason well. This enables us to know the rightness of the good laws and policies we already have and to be fully committed to them; it also enables us to criticise and reform those laws or policies that are faulty (that is, unreasonable). A natural law approach, at least in a general form that emphasises the reasonableness of morality, is implied in any kind of ethics that allow for a justified, reasoned critique of the existing society, or any subsection of it, and its laws, policies, customs and behaviour.

A natural law type of approach is very much in keeping with the spirit and letter of the present syllabus and this section in particular. One of the aims of the RE syllabus is to foster an appreciation of non-religious views as well as religious views[5] – natural law emphasises that a non-religious approach to morality can be compatible with a religious approach (and *vice versa*) insofar as both are reasonable. Natural law provides a kind of bridge between faiths and between all people of good will.

Not totally subjective
There are different views of what constitutes 'natural law'[6] and of what is 'reasonable': this is an area of some debate

amongst those who agree that morality is essentially reasonable. There are also some emotivist or intuitionist approaches to morality that leave out reason altogether. Such approaches seem plausible in the face of the wide-spread disagreements about ethical matters. It is extremely important, nevertheless, to emphasise the rational nature of ethics, rather than an ethics based on emotions or conventions or mere prudent avoidance of trouble. The obvious fact of disagreement on moral issues, or even on fundamental moral theory, does not prove, as many assume, that 'morality is subjective' (another example of a common fallacy in moral discussion and teaching). In fact, the more moral disagreement there is, the more we have to work at discovering the objective morality that will enable us to find, or at least work towards, unity and peace. Tolerance of pluralism is not enough in itself to build and maintain a community; there must be some shared values to ground a common basis for living in society with others.

'Justice' cannot be merely a totally individual idea inside each person's head. What is subjectively in one's head should match the objective reality outside one's head. This in turn should be reflected in the understanding of others so that we can share morality, at least at a basic level, and so live in peace as a community. Reference to 'justice' does not sit easily with a subjectivistic approach to morality – the common understanding of justice is that it is an appeal to *objective* standards, not merely individual preferences or claims. When one claims 'That's not fair' one is not referring to purely personal preference but to what one hopes will be accepted as an objective standard proving that the particular act or situation objected to is not actually fair.

Not totally relativistic
So justice is properly understood as not purely subjective, but objective. Nor can it be understood adequately as totally

relative. Justice is not a completely culture-based or society-based set of ideas or moral rules. A relativistic approach, seeing justice as a society or culture-bound set of conventions and opinions, does not allow for any justified critique of cultural injustice or society's injustices nor a more global view of a 'higher justice' transcending 'lower', local versions of justice. Unless we can agree on the basics of justice, we will not be able to address responsibly the many problems facing individual societies and the world, such as poverty and environmental degradation (which cannot be solved by mere tolerance or lack of discrimination). So we must avoid being drawn into any distorted or reductionistic view of justice. There must always remain the possibility of a shared search for, and agreement on, the 'common good'.[7]

This rejection of relativism does not deny that there can be some valuable diversity and an essential open-endedness in how a shared morality can be applied to various situations and societies in a plurality of ways. Such varying applications can be right and just. There may be more than one right answer to the questions of justice (and more than one wrong answer too). We will need to be committed to objective moral principles while being respectful of the plurality of potential ways to apply these principles. Before respect for pluralism, however, comes knowledge of, and commitment to, objective moral principles: this suggests how the teacher might approach this section of the syllabus.

My main aim
One of the most important things necessary for teaching this syllabus is a clear understanding of the key concepts and their interrelationships. Providing this understanding is the main aim of this book. It does not provide a 'one-stop' book containing everything needed for a teacher to teach the section. (This book may be teacher-friendly – but it's not *that* friendly!) This would make for a more unwieldy, much bigger book. It is hoped that

other authors, especially those from other religious traditions, will contribute further material for the syllabus. I have not tried to provide many examples from current affairs and analysis to illustrate and back-up my discussion. Examples given here are more typical than topical. Topical examples go out of date quickly. Students are not impressed by stories that are even a few years old. To the teacher they seem like only yesterday; to the student, they are ancient history! If a teacher knows what to look for, it will not be difficult to find up-to-the-minute examples and information to use in teaching about justice and peace. Some practical ideas regarding this are given throughout the text. Also, copious references will be made to specific websites and other sources to aid research.[8] (I have included a large number of such references to allow some choice to teachers and students and to show the breadth of material available on the various matters in the syllabus. I am not suggesting that teachers or students ought to read everything I mention; nor do I necessarily agree with everything in all the references I give. I expect all references will be used judiciously.)

The importance of the religious aspect
Justice has been a popular topic for religion teachers over the years. Unfortunately, the specifically *religious* aspect of the subject matter can be neglected. It can be tempting to teach the topic in a mainly (or even exclusively) 'secular' way, noting examples of various injustices and dealing with the definition of the central concepts in a generally moralistic way, without ever really dealing with what justice and peace have to do with faith in Christ (or with what Christian faith has to do with justice and peace). This secular approach might seem appealing because of fears that students will be hostile or apathetic towards explicitly religious material. Teaching this way, however, fails to integrate reason and faith, which is a major aim of good religious education. One also suggests to students by this non-religious approach that the secular approach is 'real

life', whereas the religious approach is not. section F of the senior RE syllabus is not exempt from this danger if it is read superficially or interpreted in a particularly narrow fashion, (focusing on the first half of the section, for example, which is quite non-religious in its language).[9] In order to facilitate the integration of the philosophical and the theological approaches to justice and peace, this book deals in extended detail with the five perspectives on justice (in part 2.1), the Judaeo-Christian vision of justice and peace (in part 2.3), with theological challenges in interpreting environmentalist arguments (in part 3.1) and with the concept of stewardship from a Christian perspective (in part 3.2).[10] It is worth mentioning in regard to the integration of the religious and the ethical, that a new book has just been published by the Pontifical Council for Justice and Peace, a book which should help to explain how justice, peace and Christian faith are linked. This is the *Compendium of the Social Doctrine of the Church* (Vatican City: Liberia Editrice Vaticana, 2004). Unfortunately, it appeared too late to be used much in the writing of this book, and I have referred to it directly only a couple of times. I would highly recommend it as a support for, and development of, what is presented here.[11]

Integrating this section with other sections

As well as the challenge of understanding the section as an integrated whole, rather than a set of separate bits about justice and peace issues and opinions, there is also the challenge of integrating this section into the senior cycle RE syllabus as a whole. This lies beyond the scope of this book but I will finish this introduction with a few remarks on how this section might link up with other sections (and with the respective books in the present series that deal with the sections).

The first section that immediately springs to mind is section C: *Moral Decision Making*. This section makes reference to ethical topics directly relevant to section F: *Issues of Justice and Peace*. These include human rights and their charters (part 1.2), the common good and individual rights (1.3), the relationship between morality and religion (2.1), the idea of 'right relationship' in the preaching of Jesus (2.2), social sin (2.3), moral conflict and debate (3.1), moral theories such as natural law and virtue ethics (3.2), the role of conscience (4.2), and various areas of moral decision making in action such as political and economic questions, crime and punishment, and medical ethics (4.3).

Section A, *The Search for Meaning and Values*, sets the context for the entire syllabus (and is therefore obligatory). The first and last parts of section A link up with section F. In particular, it is useful to deal with issues of justice and peace in a way that respects the transcendent questions of meaning and identity that give rise to the emergence of values, as studied in section A. Putting this in a simpler way, I would suggest that for a Christian the issue of justice and peace cannot be understood merely as a practical matter of finding some way of getting along with one another without trouble or harm. Though this is no mean challenge in itself, there is a further dimension than the immediately practical. Why be just? Why search for peace? The Christian answer will include reference to God and his plan for our happiness and fulfilment as human individuals in community. The Christian views morality not as an arbitrary set of conventions agreed by the majority, nor as only an application of reason or logic to human interrelationships; Christians see morality as a response to God. 'We love because he first loved us' (1 John 4:19). Our commitment to justice and peace arises out of our being created by God, saved by God and sanctified by God. It is hard to see how justice or peace could fully make sense in a meaningless world: God creates the meaning of our world and the 'sensibleness' of justice and peace.

Other sections deal with justice and peace issues. *Religion and Gender* and *Religion and Science* are the two that clearly specify topics with a definite justice angle – issues such as sexism and genetic engineering. One could also keep the themes of justice and peace in mind when treating the sections on the Bible, Christianity, and world religions.

There is plenty of scope for the teacher to combine elements of section F with other sections of the syllabus. One certainly should not see justice and peace concerns as confined to section F. As I said at the beginning, issues of justice and peace are not optional; they constitute an important dimension of virtually every human situation or topic.

Notes

1 An outline of section F is found in Appendix One. Readers can use this as a way of keeping track of the course as they read through this guide. The outline is my own; it is not intended as a substitute for the official text, which should be studied carefully.
2 It is appropriate in this regard that the publisher of this book is 'Veritas', a name which means 'truth'.
3 Various Protestant traditions emphasise Scripture over tradition and some would be very wary of 'natural law' because it seems overconfident, in the light of sin's effects on our intellects and wills, of our natural ability to know right and wrong. The well-known reference by St Paul in Romans 2:14-15 to the 'law written on the hearts' of the Gentiles has been understood by most Christians, nevertheless, as a warrant for accepting the possibility that all people can to some substantial degree grasp God's moral law by the natural use of reason, even though supernatural grace and truth are practically necessary for fully clear moral knowledge and the ability to live by this knowledge.
4 Matthew 7:12. All Bible quotations in this book are taken from *The Catholic Bible: New Revised Standard Version* (STL, 1993).
5 The fourth aim of the syllabus is this: 'To appreciate the richness of religious traditions and to acknowledge the non-religious interpretation of life', syllabus, p. 5. The syllabus in full is available online at www.education.ie/servlet/blobservlet/ lc_religion_sy.pdf and is published in hard-copy by The Stationary Office, 2003.
6 Some consider 'natural law' to be exclusively the simplistic approach of the Catholic Church behind its condemnation of contraception –

the view that what is artificial is wrong and that we must never intervene in natural processes. This is not the concept of natural law in the present work. Nor is it the view behind the Church's condemnation of contraception, nor her understanding of natural law in general. I deal in more detail with this in part 3.2 below.

7 See on this, and on other matters mentioned in this paragraph, the fine book by David Hollenbach, *The Common Good and Christian Ethics* (Cambridge: Cambridge University Press, 2001).

8 Please see Appendix Two for criteria for using web sites and other materials.

9 The third overall aim of section F in the syllabus is worth noting: 'To identify and analyse the links between religious belief and commitment and action for justice and peace', syllabus, p. 59.

10 Though the book does deal with some major issues of methodology, especially in chapter one, it does not attempt to gauge how much material should be taught at each stage of the course, nor how the various parts of the section should be proportioned to each other, nor how much time should be spent on each topic. In some cases, it may not be practical to refer in class to all that is explored in the present book, but it is hoped that all will be useful. It is also hoped that the treatment of issues here will be of interest to others outside the context of second-level schools.

11 There is a kind of compendium of Catholic Social Doctrine available online: *The Social Agenda*, by the Council for Justice and Peace, at www.thesocialagenda.org. The new *Compendium* is similar to this, though much more developed – it is more than five hundred pages long. It has an extensive index that will enable the reader to quickly find what the Church has to say on specific topics dealt with in this book (and on further important topics). Though the style is highly compact, and difficult to read and probably not suitable for any direct use in a classroom, it is a sound and comprehensive treatment of the main issues and its overall vision is very inspiring.

I

Reflecting on Context

Aims

The first and second general aims for the section (syllabus, p. 59) relate directly to the concerns of its first segment – *Part One: Reflecting on Context*. The first reads: 'To introduce the principles and skills of social analysis'. The second is: 'To encourage the application of these principles and skills in the local context, and in a selection of national and global contexts'. This chapter explains what these terms mean so that teacher and student can achieve the specific objectives listed in the areas of knowledge, understanding, skills and attitudes (syllabus, p. 60). 'Reflecting on Context' requires examination of the concrete social world with a critical eye in order to understand it better. The chapter does not engage in specific social analysis or make any detailed empirical claims about society or issues, but instead explains what social analysis is and how it can be done.

Overall structure of the course

Why does the section begin with social analysis, before one has studied the central concepts of justice and peace? Beginning in this way emphasises that 'Justice' and 'Peace' are not purely abstract or theoretical concepts; they arise out of, and apply to, specific situations and real people. Part 1 focuses our attention on concrete reality and questions will be raised by this initial analysis. Then part 2 (to be looked at in the next chapter) looks at the moral principles of justice and peace in order to shed light on the questions raised by the initial social analysis. One could revise one's initial social analysis in the light of the moral principles studied in the central part of the course. As written, however, the syllabus leads the student on to look at new issues (from part 2.4 and through part 3), namely violence and just war and environmental concerns, rather than looking backwards at the specific issues analysed in part 1.

- Part 1.1 deals with the central concepts of social analysis;
- Part 1.2 deals with applying social analysis to selected, specific contexts.

1.1 SOCIAL ANALYSIS

There are various ways one might go about analysing society. The syllabus indicates a particular approach and gives a brief outline to guide the process (syllabus, p. 61). This draws heavily, almost word for word, on a classic text by Joe Holland and Peter Henriot, *Social Analysis: Linking Faith and Justice* (1983).[1] Mention should also be made of two books, also published in the early 80s, by Irish writers Seán Healy and Brigid Reynolds, both well-known in the justice and peace movement in Ireland. These are *Social Analysis in the Light of the Gospel* (1983) and *Ireland Today: Reflecting in the Light of the Gospel* (1985).[2] The latter contains a detailed social analysis of Irish society at that time and would be very useful as an example of the kind of thing looked for in the syllabus, although it would have to be up-dated considerably in its reference to empirical observations and measurements. This chapter draws extensively from these three books in looking at part 1.1, although I have avoided frequent references in order to shorten the number of footnotes.

Social Analysis

Definition
Social analysis involves examining economic, political, cultural and social structures to gain a more complete understanding of social situations. The aim is to investigate the way things are and to ask why they are so. One explores issues, and, more importantly, one tries to get behind the issues to understand their causes. Holland and Henriot explain the importance here of moving *from the anecdotal to the analytical*: 'We must move from issues [...] to explanations of *why* things are the way they are. To stop with anecdotes, to concentrate only on issues, obscures the comprehensive systemic picture. If the picture is obscured, one becomes trapped in immediate *ad hoc* solutions.'[3] Second level students, and indeed many other people, express their views on issues such as the place of travellers in Irish society or the role of the Gardaí by way of stories or examples (sometimes at second or third hand). Social *analysis*, however, goes deeper than recounting stories of injustice. A clear focus on social analysis as a precise kind of investigation will help us to avoid mere conversation or casual discussion, mere 'sharing of ignorance'.

Structures

Definition
What is meant by 'structures'? The 'structures' metaphor refers to socially organised ways of behaving or being in relationship, the systems that shape the way we live in community with others. These include institutions, behaviour patterns, organisations (on the more objective side) and common values, prejudices and belief systems (on the more subjective side).

Structures are relatively stable, permanent and common, rather than temporary, ad hoc, random or individual.

Four types
Structures become more concrete when examined under the four headings given in the syllabus:[4]
- economic structures
- political structures
- cultural structures
- social structures

Each of the four types of structure is treated separately below. After an initial definition, various typical questions are listed to show how one can analyse society under each particular heading. These questions are not answered here; they are merely typical guides to what the specific structure refers to in concrete detail, mainly in the national context. It is not expected that all the questions will be answered whilst studying this syllabus. After each type of structure is defined and outlined by questions, some related matters are discussed, including some cross-curricular possibilities. When all four types of structure have been examined, some final remarks conclude the first half of this chapter – how there are different levels of structures and analysis, how the four structures are interconnected and related, and how a balance between Right and Left approaches is important for accurate analysis.

The four structures and four associated issues
The syllabus mentions looking at the four types of structure with four issues in mind: the availability and allocation of resources, the determining of power, the shaping of relationships and the according of meaning to people within specific contexts.. Holland/Henriot and Healy/Reynolds link each type of structure with an issue as follows:
- economic structures with *resources*
- political structures with *power*

- cultural structures with *values*
- social structures with *relationships*

Though the wording of the syllabus does not tie an issue to a type of structure as specifically as this, this way of making the links seems quite natural and is the approach I will take here. The links, however, are not meant to be seen as exclusive. The four types of structure are not totally separated from each other, but interact, and so, too, do the four issues. So, for example, political structures can influence the allocation of resources; this is not an exclusive area for economic structures alone.

(a) Economic Structures

Definition
'Economic structures' refer to the way in which resources are organised in society, or, in other words, how 'the availability and allocation of resources' are influenced or shaped.[5] In coming to understand how the economy is structured we need to look at its various sectors: business, commercial, agricultural and industrial. What are the natural (and other) resources of the country? We examine the processes of production, distribution, exchange and consumption. In other words, we ask:
- How are things made (or services rendered)?
- How are they made available to people?
- How do people access them?
- How do people use up the resources?

An area of weakness – wealth production neglected
The syllabus wording does not emphasise *production* as such. The wording seems to assume that there are resources that are simply available and then allocated. (It is assumed in the syllabus, however, that resource availability can be influenced

for better or worse by structures.) It has been observed, however, that resources are not simply 'there': wealth has to be produced. This issue features in the debate around whether to analyse society from the Left or the Right. The Right emphasises the importance of wealth *creation*; the Left focuses on wealth *distribution*. Both are important features of the economy and should be included in social analysis. It is an important theme of this book that both Right and Left approaches should be respected and combined whenever possible, rather than focusing on either one exclusively. The syllabus wording could lead one to focus on resource distribution and ignore or neglect wealth creation.

Typical questions regarding economic structures
One might continue to ask questions such as: Is the production highly technological or labour intensive? Are the centres of production concentrated in a few areas (to the detriment of others)? Is distribution dominated by monopolies or is it more widely dispersed? Is it a free-market, or a planned, or a mixed economy? If mixed, how is the 'mixture' proportioned? What kind of budgets are produced from year to year? What were the economic elements of the last budget? Is consumption wasteful or excessive? How do interest rates affect spending? How are interest rates set? What about inflation? What kind of labour force is there? Where is there poverty? What are its patterns? What is the income distribution in the nation? What is the employment/unemployment rate? What are the trends in these rates? This is not a comprehensive list of possible questions, but should give some idea of the range of relevant economic 'structures' to be scrutinised.

After many of these questions comes the further important question: Why? In other words, we ask why is it that the particular economic structures exist. Answering these questions leads us into the historical dimension of social analysis, where we examine how the various structures are created and maintained by people making choices over time. This will be looked at further under the heading of 'political structures' below.

A philosophical and methodological issue – Business or Religion?
One would need some knowledge of business studies or economics to understand the concepts fully and answer the questions accurately. Many religion teachers are not fully conversant with economics or business. Perhaps, like me, they went into teaching partly because they were not inclined towards business. How are such teachers to deal with this aspect of the syllabus? Not all students will be business or economic experts either.

This is a religious education course, not a business studies course. There is some overlap between the subjects, though each has its own autonomy. One of the lessons of this section is that religion has to do with all areas of life in society. Without meaning to deny the proper autonomy of the different subject areas, it is important to remind students and teachers (and society) that no subject is entirely value-free. There is a moral aspect to virtually everything and it is important to focus on this moral aspect in a sustained and explicit way in RE class. This calls for an integrated vision of education that allows teachers and students to see the various subjects as parts of a greater whole. The subjects are not in separate 'boxes', sealed off from one another, as might be suggested by the structure of a school timetable. So the student can learn in RE class that there is a moral dimension to economics, although in economics class the emphasis is rightly on the more technical aspects of that area. (I presume this is not doing an injustice here to the ethical concerns of economics teachers!)

The value of religious knowledge
As well as a moral aspect, there is also a religious or theological aspect to many subjects, including economics. God is the

creator of all people and all subjects of study. The central concepts of the dignity of all human persons, the social nature of the human person, the priority of the common good, the need for solidarity and subsidiarity, the value of all created things and nature as a unified whole, and more, all flow from a religious perspective and are strongly supported by religious faith. A religious aspect is not alluded to in section F, part 1; it is noted explicitly only at part 2.3. However, it cannot be left only until part 2.3 to mention religious concerns, not least because, if we leave religion out of the picture for the first few weeks, many students will quickly wonder why they are doing sociology or economics or geography in religion class! It is unwise to bring religion into RE only at the end, as a kind of imaginative colouring or optional extra. This would not do justice to the nature of a religious education course, which focuses primarily on religion and speaks from within a religious tradition, even when teaching ethical issues that are open to natural rational analysis. In a Catholic school, this religious perspective will be specifically Catholic, in line with the school ethos and philosophy (though not in a narrowly, exclusive fashion).

Further issues – Religious or Sociological? Partisan or impartial?
How might social analysis in a RE class differ from that in a sociology class? As well as religion's shaping of one's understanding of human life and ethical principles, as mentioned above, there is another possible difference concerning commitment to action. It could be said that social analysis as the first part of a justice and peace course in a RE syllabus is concerned with diagnosing social problems with a view to seeing how justice can be done and peace made, whereas in an exclusively sociological course, social analysis would be more an end in itself, an exercise in scientific description for the sake of understanding, rather than action as such. Nevertheless, social analysis in RE must seek to be as

scientific as that in sociology. We ought not to let our concern with social action for justice and peace interfere with a scholarly, honest, impartial pursuit of the truth about society and its structures. Our religious and moral commitments are to truth and honesty and, particularly in the school context, to scholarship. We must, in other words, be ready to follow the evidence wherever it leads us. We must not be afraid to revise our conclusions in the light of criticism (or even abandon them, if they are completely mistaken). Although we will probably come to a justice and peace course with religious and moral concerns for the improvement of society, we ought not let ourselves be controlled by partisan attitudes that blind us to bias and prejudice.

Some would argue against this view, claiming that social analysis is *necessarily* partisan. I think, however, that this first part of the section must strive for the most impartial approach possible to finding out the facts about society without letting ourselves be overly influenced by ideological interpretations of the facts. It is easy to fall into a 'goodies and baddies' approach to social analysis and justice and peace teaching. This simplistic kind of approach occurs, for example, when the Right 'demonises' those who hold socialist views as merely woolly idealists or worshippers of the state, and when the Left 'demonises' those who hold liberal economic views as essentially greedy and selfish individualists. Though sometimes there may be some truth in these criticisms, the reality is usually more complex. We must be fair towards the complexity, or else we will misjudge people and their views, not to mention failing to analyse society well. Also, we will miss the opportunity of learning from those who differ from us, and combining the best of both 'sides' in the justice and peace debate. Often the differences between Right and Left are not primarily ethical as such, but technical – they disagree over the interpretation of the data and over what to do to improve matters, rather than the ethical requirement to do good and avoid evil. One important sign of openness to the evidence and an attitude of strict impartiality will be our willingness to seek out diverse authoritative sources of information and interpretation of the social facts and figures and to try various techniques and approaches to teaching and learning. If we read only the authors we like and look at only the arguments we already agree with, we will never really test our convictions and sharpen our grasp of the truth.

Cross-curricular possibilities – the value of economic knowledge
It has been said that much of the Catholic Church's social teaching is weak on the realities of business and economic life: bishops and socially-focused theologians are idealistic and moralistic but not realistic![6] This criticism could perhaps be levelled at religious and philosophical approaches in general. There may be some truth in such criticism. There is an important distinction, for example, between the more abstract level of religious and ethical principle and the more concrete level of particular application to historical circumstances. This suggests that the teacher should study the area of economics, to some extent at least, to teach this specific part of the course well, and not confine him- or herself to the purely religious and moral areas. This book cannot go into any great detail in this regard, unfortunately. In every school there will be a business teacher or two who will no doubt be more than willing to share knowledge with the humble religion teacher! Indeed, there is great scope (and need) for cross-curricular consultation and team-work in teaching the whole of 'Issues of Justice and Peace', and not just in relation to business studies/economics. The religion teacher should view the challenges arising out of trying to teach this topic as an opportunity to widen his or her knowledge. Why not look over the text-book or teacher-book for business studies (or the syllabus for the subject); chat with the teacher(s); and/or get students who have studied the subject to talk to the RE class or make a formal presentation

about the specific concepts and processes mentioned in the RE syllabus or arising in social analysis itself?

There can be a tendency in religious circles to look on the free-market and profit as evil and this is something that the RE teacher should think critically about in teaching this part and the section as a whole. Knowledge of economics will help the teacher to gain a realistic understanding of how markets actually work, and their true strengths and weaknesses. Teaching ethical principles that do not make sense will help no-one. So, for example, it is best to avoid teaching that profit is always evil or that competition is always wrong or that the real national economic success of recent years is an illusion (because it is not completely perfect), and so on. Accurate economic knowledge will help the RE teacher and student to avoid falling into naïve or simplistic assumptions or assertions, while enabling fair criticisms to be made confidently and persuasively.

Not for experts only – informed citizenship
Having said all that, there is another important point to make, one that may seem to contradict the emphasis on knowing accurately the economic area, and other areas, by consulting the experts. And the point is this: social analysis is not something exclusively for experts. In fact, one of the aims of promoting the importance of social analysis for *all* students and teachers, even those who have little experience in specialised areas such as economics, is to break out of an attitude that sees society as too complex for ordinary citizens to understand (and so criticise). This is an attitude of passivity that allows others to interpret social realities and policies for us, rather than being more 'pro-active' ourselves. We cannot rightly avoid the responsibility of making *some* personal judgment at some stage, even if only to decide if what particular experts say is reasonable or plausible, so why not work at making our judgement as accurate and informed as possible? We ought not

be put off by the difficulty of understanding everything totally before we start – or else we will never start!

It is hoped that the promotion of social analysis as part of this new syllabus will contribute to the idea and reality of all young (and not-so-young) citizens taking responsibility in examining their society, trying to understand how it has come to be the way it is, appreciating the good aspects of how it works, and working out ways it ought to be, and can be, improved. An elitist attitude is to be avoided. Healthy democracy calls for the involvement of informed citizens, not just an elite or a class of specialists. The mention of democracy brings us to our next heading: political structures.

(b) Political Structures

Definition
'Political structures' refer to the various ways society organises power. Here we draw attention particularly to the institutions which shape society, which create the economic structures just looked at and the social and cultural structures to be examined below. Such institutions include government parties but not only these. Areas to investigate include:
- Political parties
- The Government
- Democracy and its procedures
- The legal system
- Other 'lobby groups' in society (for example, trade unions, farming organisations)
- Social partnership

A central issue to analyse is how democratic society really is, or, in other words, how widely-distributed power is in society.

Typical questions
Who has power? Who does not have power? In other words, who makes the decisions? Who influences or decides what will

be done? What procedures are set up to facilitate the organisation of the various sub-sections of society and society as a whole? What forms of government are there? What philosophies of governance are there? Which forms and philosophies influence or shape the politics of this country? What are the political parties? What size are they? What distinguishes them from each other? Who joins them? How do they do their work? How is power 'distributed' among them?

Another area of political structure is law. This is a particularly important area of concern in a course on justice and peace. Any analysis of a society or social issue should include an examination of its legal system dimension. Questions to be asked include: What is the legislative body for this society? How are the laws decided? What is the system of courts? Who is involved in running the court system? Who goes through the system? How is the law enforced? How is the law itself monitored and regulated? Is there any structure for reform included in the system?

More informal, less obvious, types of power structure will include trade unions, churches, lobby groups, and so on. How do each of these influence the decisions made for our society? How many of the citizens are involved in the application of power in our society for our society? How democratic is our society? A very important point here is the recent development in Ireland of 'social partnership', which involves farming organisations, trade unions, community and voluntary organisations, and employer and business organisations coming together to discuss and agree economic and social policy.

Again, this is not meant as a comprehensive list, but a method of making clear the meaning of the concept and its concrete reference.

The historical dimension to social analysis
And again, after many of the questions above one must ask: Why? This question points to the fact that things are not 'just

the way they are'. Things have developed over time. As noted above in looking at economic structures, there is an historical dimension to all social analysis. When we look at how things were in the past, we notice that things were often quite different from today. This is a reminder that things are not set in stone, but can change or be changed. It is also a reminder to look at the structures of today (economic, cultural and social, as well as political) as *caused*. They did not simply arrive or appear out of thin air. They arose out of specific circumstances and were shaped by particular individuals and their choices. What we do now will shape the structures of tomorrow.

Further cross-curricular possibilities
There is an obvious link between this part of the RE syllabus and the subject of History, especially as it focuses on political concepts and issues. Many of us learned our political education from history class. Recently, a new subject devoted to political and social topics has been introduced at Junior Level: CSPE (Civil, Social and Political Education). As even its name makes clear, this is a very close relative of this section of the RE syllabus. Many RE teachers have experience of teaching CSPE and will be at an advantage teaching the new syllabus because of this. For those who have not had the joy of teaching it, it would help to talk with the relevant teacher(s), look over the text-books, and familiarise oneself with the concepts and examples therein. One textbook for example, divides up the course into seven key concepts: Rights and Responsibilities; Human Dignity; Stewardship; Development; Democracy; Law; Interdependence. Obviously, this overlaps considerably with the RE syllabus. The RE teacher should build on what has been done already.

However, one needs to avoid the danger of mere repetition. Students can get tired of hearing the same 'moralistic stuff' over and over. So, RE at senior level will need to be more sophisticated and more intellectually demanding than RE (and other overlapping subjects) at the junior level, clearly adverting to the more controversial aspects of the area of justice and peace and examining the more complex depth and breadth of the debates and conflicts. RE will need, most importantly, to emphasise and clarify the *religious* aspects of understanding and working to solve issues of justice and peace, aspects that will not be explicitly central in CSPE or history or other related subjects, though they may rightly shape the values that guide the teaching of all subjects in a religious school.

(c) Social structures

Definition
'Social structures' refers to how society organises relationships. Social analysis in this area will include looking at how society is divided into relatively stable and distinct groups or sections and how these are related. These groupings include:
- Social classes
- The family
- The sexes/gender
- Youth and the elderly
- Educational categories
- Urban and rural communities
- Ethnic and non-national groups
- Religious organisations
- Sports groups

Typical questions – class
The first area to examine here is division into social classes. Is the society stratified? How? Is it accurate to mention upper, middle and lower or working classes?[7] All know that there are differences in people's opportunities and welfare depending on such things as socio-economic background and level of education. Social analysis also examines how much social mobility there is between classes over time. A particularly difficult area is that of so-called 'class warfare'. Are the classes

REFLECTING ON CONTEXT

in conflict? Is one class winning this war? Marxist social analysis has been and still is an influence on how people see society and its structures. Such analysis places great emphasis on the notion of class war. Some might view reference to, and emphasis on, social structures, and especially social classes, as somewhat socialist, or even Marxist, though it is not necessarily so. Further study of this highly debated area is advisable.[8]

Questions – family
Another important social structure is the family, often referred to as the basic unit of society. What kinds of family are there? How are families structured? What size are families typically? What about the extended family – is it a factor in how families work? What level of family stability is there? What is the situation of marriage in the society? What is the average age for marriage? What is the level of separation, divorce, annulment, remarriage? What is the rate of cohabitation?

Of course, these two areas of social structure can be interrelated. So, we can ask how the class a family belongs to influences the answers to the questions above. And, also, we can ask how the family one belongs to can influence the questions related to class! These are highly contentious and sensitive issues.

Questions – sex/gender
Gender is another area that is highly debated and sensitive. The very term 'gender' suggests a perspective that claims most or all of the differences between male and female are socially constructed, not naturally given. The few natural differences are biological differences of 'sex', not socially constructed differences of 'gender'. The exact proportion between social 'constructions' and natural 'givens' is not fully known or agreed, but one strong trend is to see most of the differences as changeable social structures (that is, as 'gender').

Social analysis begins with a descriptive approach. How are the relationships between men and women structured in society? Which of the two has more power, money, prestige? Which makes the decisions in public life? Which in private life? Is the relationship between the sexes peaceful or not? Again, we can bring in class and family aspects too and ask how reference to these areas influences the answers to the previous questions. Feminist social analysis places great emphasis on this area and interprets many of the problems of society in terms of the discrepancy in the status and power held by women and men, and the way that this alleged conflict is embodied and perpetuated by 'patriarchal' social structures that grant privileged status and power to males.[9]

Questions – youth and elderly (including education)
Other group divisions in society as a whole include that between youth and the elderly. How are each of these 'groups' structured? Are they structured? How does society treat the young as a subsection of society? Here, a major consideration is the educational system. This can also be looked at under the heading of 'cultural structures' (see below). However, the schooling system is a major *social* structure in itself, and it includes political and economic aspects too. One major area here is that concerning the various 'partners' in education. How is education a matter of co-operation between teachers, students, parents, the local community/parish, the Church and/or the state? To what extent is each of these groups involved in the system? How does the Board of Management structure work? Are there student councils? What other groups are catered for by the educational system? Is education a life-long reality for all society? Is education accessible and available for all? A great deal of society's money is spent on the young (though, as all teachers and parents, including myself, will claim, not enough). After focusing on the young in society, we can ask:

How does society treat the elderly? Are they neglected? Are they involved in society? Who looks after them when they are unable to do so themselves?

Questions – other groupings
Urban and rural dwellers are another set of groups that society can be seen to divide into. What proportion of the society is urban and what proportion rural? What are the trends here?

A very important focus in relation to social structures will be ethnic groups and non-nationals in society. How are these a part of society? Or are they apart from society? What are the structures of each of these groups? How are they situated in relation to the other groupings in society?

Focusing on other subsections of society, one notices the various religious groups that constitute much of Irish society. What is the proportionality of these religions? How are they structured? How do they interact with the other social structures and political structures?

What are the other sub-groups that make up this society? Sports groups will have to be looked at. Many of our students structure their lives around sport, and especially around the sports clubs they belong to. How are sports clubs a part of society? How are they financed? Who joins and why? Who does not join and why not?

There are many other sub-groups in society. One way to visualise social structures is to ask what there is between the individual member of society and the state (the main political structure). This area constitutes the 'social' arena as such, a very important arena, one that can be neglected in an overly political focus on social analysis. What other social structures affect one's opportunities and one's participation in social living?

(d) Cultural structures

Definition
'Cultural structures' refer to the way that we organise meaning in society. Cultural structures are the stable and common ways that we shape and communicate the assumptions and values we all live by. Social analysis describes these common values and asks where they come from and how they are maintained. Significant areas in this regard include
- The education system
- Mass media
- Religions
- Other elements of culture

Typical questions – the education system
The education system can be examined in terms of the passing on of culture, engagement with culture and transformation of culture. What is the educational 'system'? What is the philosophy of the educational system? What are the values being transmitted by its structures? What values are being neglected? Who runs the system? What is the input of the Deptartment of Education and Science? The NCCA? The teacher's unions? The churches? Employers? Third level colleges? Parents? Students? Whose interests are served by the system? What is the denominational aspect of it? What about the multi- and non-denominational aspects?

Questions – the media
Another hugely influential area is the media. This includes several sub-sections. Perhaps the most dominant influence is television. What messages or values are communicated by television? What kind of diversity, if any, is there in the range of these messages and values? Who runs the television system? Who decides what we will watch? Who decides how much we will watch? What do we watch? How does the medium of

television itself shape what is communicated? What about the other channels of culture, the other media? How do they compare to television in terms of power, diversity, content? Radio is one example. What stations are popular and why? What values are embodied in 'talk radio', for instance? Why is so much radio dominated by pop music? Newspapers are important too. Many students do not read them (except for the sport, gossip, or television). Why is this? What kinds of newspapers are available? What kinds sell? Why? What values are communicated by the press? What are the dominant values passed on by advertisements? What effect do they have? How does the notion of 'fashion' influence how we think and feel and act? Who decides on the content and style of adverts? Magazines are read by many young people and should be included in social analysis. Again, the questions are similar to those above, focusing on the values communicated and the people who decide 'what' and 'how'. Linked to television and magazines, but an area in its own right, is music. What are the dominant values passed on by the various types of music? To some students, this will seem like a stupid question. 'What are you talking about?' they will ask. 'It's only music!' This suggests that music frequently sells itself as a kind of mindless entertainment. Is there a political aspect to this? A religious aspect? Are young people, and the not so young, being manipulated by the music industry?

Questions – religions
The area of religion is central to social analysis of cultural structures. When we are talking about the values we live by, then religion will have to be acknowledged as one of the most important sources of meaning and value we have. In fact, this is the central insight behind the new RE syllabus. We must inquire into the kinds and range of meanings and values that the various religious elements of society communicate. How does religion influence our society? What helps religion to have

an influence, and what hinders it from having one? How do particular religions and religious bodies influence how we see politics, economics, and social divisions in our society and in our world? Is there a dominant religion in the society and how does this fact shape the kind of society that exists?

Other elements of culture
Culture includes a vast number of elements. I have not mentioned art, or serious music, or traditional music, or theatre, or architecture, or languages (think of the place of the Irish language in Irish society). These may be important elements of any thorough analysis of a specific issue, and will certainly be part of any full picture of a society.

Individuals and organisations can influence society by shaping the philosophies that structure our understanding of things. Political ideologies, for instance, can shape the questions we ask and the evidence we look at in deciding about political and economic issues, including the ones central to this syllabus. Think of how nationalism has influenced Irish politics and society in more general terms.

Cross-curricular possibilities
Direct cross-curricular possibilities in relation to analysis of either social or cultural structures have not been mentioned yet. It is not as easy in their regard, compared to economic and political structures, to see school subjects that clearly overlap. Some schools will include Media Studies, especially in Transition Year, and this would be a good link with cultural analysis. Perhaps the best link of all is Home Economics, in particular the social side. RE teachers should find out what is in HE text-books, talk to the teachers, and so on. It would also be advisable for the RE teacher to consult with the Teacher Union Rep. and the teacher members of the Board of Management too for information regarding some of the issues raised above.

Structures – some overall issues

Levels of analysis

One could look at a local issue, or at the regional level, or at the nation as a whole, or at the nation as part of an international grouping, or at the international scene itself, or at the global level. Economic, political, social and cultural structures will operate and influence in various ways at all these levels.

I have posed the questions above with regard to the national level mainly, though even still, I have simplified somewhat: I have not alluded to the very important dimension of Northern Ireland in our national political life. One cannot understand the political structures of the Republic, without understanding Northern Ireland and the various issues connected with it. Obviously, issues of justice and peace are central to the whole debate around Northern Ireland and its problems and potential solutions.

One cannot get an accurate social picture without adverting to the international level, too. The European influence on Ireland is very strong and should be understood and integrated in any social analysis. We are members of the European Union – this affects us economically, politically, socially and culturally. The EU is expanding. which will affect us in times to come. As well as the European connection, we have an interesting affinity with the USA. Our economic policy is sometimes spoken of in terms of a contrast, or contest even, 'between Boston and Berlin'. Boston stands for the free-market style of American economics and politics, with minimum government, low taxes, and an emphasis on personal initiative and freedom; Berlin stands for the European social welfare type of economics and politics, with a more active government, higher taxes, and an emphasis on social responsibility and equality. It is a matter of some debate whether Ireland is closer to Boston than to Berlin.

Globalisation matters
We live in an increasingly globalised world, so the interrelationships between countries and continents are very much part of the full picture of any level of analysis, even the most local. Looking at Ireland, or any country, in isolation from the global scene will give a seriously inaccurate picture. To make sense of the data on economic or political policy, for example, one ought to take into account the fact that Ireland is a vulnerable open economy in an increasingly competitive world. In making decisions, governments bear in mind what the likely effect will be on foreign investment, on which we rely heavily for our economic and social progress. Numbers employed could be adversely affected if a policy were adopted to tackle poverty by raising taxes so substantially that it put foreign investors off coming to Ireland (or causing those who are already here to go elsewhere to find more profitable conditions). This is one reason given to explain why governments are often cautious about particular strategies to achieve social justice, even though the end in view is entirely laudable. Of course, there may be other, less noble, reasons why governments fail to tackle poverty, other than fear of adverse effects of raising taxes in an increasingly globalised world. Perhaps poverty is not being tackled because of weak political will or laziness or lack of vision and virtue. Taking a global perspective is not an excuse for governments or others to do nothing or do too little to help eradicate poverty.

The various structures interact
The four types of structure – economic, political, social and cultural – cannot be properly understood as separate, even though it is helpful to begin studying them one at a time. Some connections between the four areas have already been mentioned above as we looked at each one. Economic policies will be heavily influenced by political interests; political outcomes will be influenced by cultural factors; social divisions will influence economic outcomes, and so on.

There are ongoing debates about which of the four areas is most important in understanding a society and its problems.[10] Some see *economics* as dominant. 'It's the economy, stupid!', a slogan written on a poster on the main office wall during Bill Clinton's first presidential election campaign, is a pithy expression of this point of view. Historically, Karl Marx regarded the economic as *the* determining factor for all the other areas. Marxism is not the view of the majority, but it is interesting to observe how often social and political issues in Ireland and elsewhere are seen in primarily economic terms. When asked how the country is doing, most of us think first of how the economy is doing. Marxism also emphasises the importance of the *social* structures of socio-economic classes that are engaged in a class war (as noted above). A feminist analysis would stress the overall importance of the social structure of 'patriarchy' as the dominant factor in society. Still others see the *political* as the most important of the four structures, especially if one is concerned with social action involving the state, which has the most power. Recently, the possibilities of a unified and organised international or global political power has been discussed, in relation to finding world peace through non-violent political means rather than through war. This can lead to a statist approach, one that expects the state to solve every social problem. Those who do not agree with putting all this stress on the state and political structures have emphasised the *social* or *cultural* areas as most important. Rather than focusing only or mainly on the central government, the emphasis should include the intermediate groups such as families, community organisations and religious groups. Non-Governmental Organisations (NGOs) have become a major part of the social discussion in recent years.

The value of values
It can be strongly argued, especially in a RE context, that the most important area is that of *culture*. Behind all our social

discussions will lie our values. These affect our priorities, our ability to work together and make sacrifices, and many other things that shape our economics, politics and social structures. It is important, then, that we value what is truly worth our admiration, commitment and respect. Central in the Christian vision is the belief that economic progress or growth alone cannot be seen as the ultimate value; nor can political power. Only a firm commitment to the common good, including a deep respect for human dignity, human rights, responsibilities and freedoms, can create an adequate ethical standard for how we are to evaluate the various types of social structure. Such commitment and respect is grounded in our personal and social goodness, given to us by God, who is our origin and destiny.

There is more to society than structures
Too much social analysis can be bad. This may seem like a strange assertion, coming after everything above! My concern is that an emphasis on social analysis may lead us to neglect or even miss the most important element of ethics, namely individual free will (and the personal responsibility that it grounds). If we analyse society only through the lens of structural analysis, without an understanding and appreciation of individuals' freedom and responsibility, we cannot correctly understand the person or accurately analyse society.

Structures and personal responsibility: an illustration from teaching
This point may be illustrated by looking at a typical experience of teachers in second level schools. Frequently teachers have to deal with students who are not achieving their potential or who are misbehaving. In doing this, they engage in a kind of social analysis in trying to understand these students, although they may not see it as 'social analysis' at the time. This analysis tries to consider all the influences on the student that cause the student to fail in work or to behave badly. Sometimes it becomes known that a student's family is going through a bad

time – sickness, unemployment, marriage break-up, violence, drink problems, moving house, or bereavement, and so on. Perhaps the student has to get a part-time job to contribute to the family finances. Maybe the student lives in a small house with several brothers and sisters and hardly ever has time or space to study. Many things can influence the work or behaviour of a student. A student can be affected by the group he hangs around with, by the area he lives in, even by the distance he has to travel each day.

These kinds of concerns characterise a type of social analysis focused on educational purposes. Teachers try to 'diagnose' the student, to understand the causes behind the scenes that are influencing a lack of work and/or misbehaviour. Insofar as one focuses on the background influences, one can more easily be patient towards the student and perhaps lenient concerning misbehaviour. One does not hold the student *fully* responsible for his situation and 'failings'.

The problem is: would the teacher be tempted not to hold the student responsible at all? To see the student as a victim of circumstances? If serious reference to the student's own free will and personal responsibility is neglected, then the answer to these two questions would be yes. In other words, too much social analysis may lead to an over-emphasis on the determining causation of 'structures', thereby losing sight of personal moral agency. The social sciences, by virtue of their being sciences treating large-scale realities and patterns of behaviour, may lead people to see social matters as mainly, or even merely, outcomes of large impersonal structures or forces or causes. Thus, we would overlook the fact that we can make free choices that are to a significant degree independent of other causes. (If a 'choice' is fully dependent on outside influences, it is by definition not a free choice at all.) This emphasis on free will is not only philosophically sound, it is also the Christian way of understanding the human individual in the light of faith.

Teachers need to balance understanding of the determining factors of students' behaviour with a clear understanding of their personal potential and their corresponding personal responsibility. Even though a student has a difficult home situation, for example, the teacher might still encourage him to try harder and work more skilfully to rise above the negative influences, thereby holding him responsible for his behaviour. One might even punish him for disturbing the class and causing the other students to miss out on their education. Not to do so would be to fail to see the student as a responsible individual.

This is not to deny for a second that some students are so strongly influenced by realities outside their own control, that they are not responsible for their lack of work or their misbehaviour. Some students have such difficult social circumstances limiting their chances to do well that you can only stand back in admiration for what they actually *do* manage to achieve! Nevertheless, not all students are so badly off that they have no control over their work and behaviour. Judging the extent of personal responsibility is a difficult task. It is a central challenge of the virtues of prudence and justice. At their best, teachers try to take all the relevant facts into account. Nevertheless, one should not over-emphasise the social structures and so fail to see that students as individuals can make good or bad choices and should be taught to accept this and develop their personal initiative and potential. We should not treat all students as essentially victims of society's weakness and immorality; nor should we overlook how each student lives in a social context that influences the degree of freedom and responsibility he or she can exercise. The challenge is to find the wise balance between being understanding about personal limitations and being firm about personal responsibility.

Application to the wider scene – Right versus Left?
The illustration sketched above is not just a reality in the classroom or school situation. It mirrors the wider social scene.

It contains elements found in many debates on justice and peace issues. It illustrates an apparent dualism or division that haunts much of the discussion.

The basic division seen in the school context above, and in the wider social scene too, is sometimes seen as a divide between Liberal (Right) and Socialist (Left). The former emphasises personal and institutional freedom and initiative and responsibility; the latter stresses equality and compassion for the poor and social assistance for the vulnerable. Politics and economics have been understood by many as a battle between these two approaches. It has been said that a kind of basic dualism is found all around the world in the area of politics.[11] There can be a tendency in many Christian authors to side broadly with the Left, which is not surprising considering the centrality of love and compassion in the Gospel. Many Christians find it more natural to identify with compassion for the poor and concern for the vulnerable (as seen by the Left) than with economic freedom and personal initiative (stressed by the Right). Are we faced with an inevitable choice between these two 'sides'? It is a theme of this book that we are not faced with a choice of either the Right or the Left, but should combine their strengths.

The division into two rigid categories is something we should question. It is itself a kind of 'political-cultural structure' of thought that may not be very accurate or helpful. It arises, I would argue, at least partly out of the necessity for political competition among parties in a democracy or between nations or ideologies. In such a context, it can seem natural to label one party as x and the other as y, with the assumption that the two are poles apart. In the heat of political battle, it is to be expected that one side will exaggerate the other side's differences and may demonise the opposition as greedy or selfish or corrupt. The policies of the other side are thereby dismissed as worthless or even evil. The idea gains ground that one must choose only one or the other side: One must be either *x* or *y*. One must be either 'Right' or 'Left'. One must be either for the individual or for the community. One must be for freedom or for equality. One must be for private property or for social ownership. One must be for wealth creation or for wealth (re)distribution. One must be for the totally free market or for a planned economy. One must be a capitalist or a socialist. One must be for the rich or for the poor.

Right and Left can combine
The simple model of 'Right versus Left' does not do justice to the complexity of reality. It does not allow for a substantial overlap in moral commitment and even in practical ideas. It can be seen in practice from the example of Ireland that politics can include elements from both Right *and* Left, in an attempt to harmonise the strengths of the two perspectives and avoid their weaknesses. Think of the famous image of the scales of justice – the challenge is to get the balance right, not to go to extremes. Nor is it necessary to demonise or defeat the other side.

One Christian author puts it like this:

> Since in actual practice it has been found that neither the theoretical model of socialism nor of capitalism can actually be realized in practice, but that a combination of both forms of regulation must be used to make a society efficiently productive, the ideological struggle between socialism and capitalism is of little real interest. The real interest of societies is to find an appropriate mix of these two forms of regulation which have a common objective, namely to produce and distribute an abundance of economic goods to all members of the society in such a way that at least the basic needs of all are met and an effective division of labor is maintained.[12]

How this is to be done in practical terms is an ongoing debate. Section F, *Issues of Justice and Peace*, invites us to become participants in this debate. It is a complex debate that requires clear thinking, honest communication, patience with the inevitable difficulties and an attitude of respect for different ideas and approaches.

1.2 SOCIAL ANALYSIS IN ACTION

The second half of part 1 requires the student to apply their knowledge and skills from studying social analysis in theory to one or two very concrete, specific issues. Ordinary-level students have to tackle one area; higher-level students must research and compare and contrast two areas. The three areas are:

- World Hunger,
- Poverty in Ireland,
- Discrimination in Ireland.

Students are invited to look into various experiences of, and causes of, these realities. The four headings – economic, political, social and cultural structures – and the four concerns with resources, power, relationships and values are to be the guiding principles for their study.

SOME PRELIMINARY METHODOLOGICAL SUGGESTIONS

Initially, the teacher might demonstrate the principles of social analysis by doing some specific analysis, applying it to an issue such as industrial relations in Ireland (to mention a nice easy one to begin with!) or the recent development of 'social partnership' in Ireland or the European Union or education in Ireland or the media in Ireland. Alternatively, the teacher may decide to concentrate at the start on a more general analysis of the Irish and international contexts to prepare for the more specific analysis of the three topics of 1.2. This general analysis could use the typical questions listed above as a guide, adapting them to the international scene as necessary. Or the teacher might decide to do some brief introductory examples of how to analyse the three specific topics that belong strictly to 1.2.

One way to begin would be to brainstorm the three topics, without any teacher input at first. This would highlight certain issues such as whether the concepts and principles taught in part 1.1 (above) have been learned. Importantly, the values or assumptions the students bring to their investigation will also become more evident. It is important that one learns to acknowledge the personal bias one brings to one's study of society and justice issues.

The teacher could reflect with the class on what is discovered through the brainstorm exercise(s). In particular, the specific challenges and possible difficulties in the study of the topics can be clarified and encouragement and direction given. It may become evident, for example, that the class or members of it are very negative towards 'the poor' or sub-sections of 'the poor'. Maybe they assume that there is no discrimination in Ireland. Or it could be that they think all world hunger is caused by the poor having too many children for their own good. They may think these areas are too complex to understand or too simple to need analysis at all. They may wonder what this has to do with religion. All these issues should be addressed if they arise, at least in a preliminary way. A more in-depth look at the issues forms the substance of the second part of the section, 'The concept of justice and peace'. The students will probably need to revise their social analysis later in light of their study of parts 2 and 3 of the section. They should be reassured that their social analysis at the start is not expected to be definitive. It is a start, not an end.

Another task is to decide what topic (ordinary-level) or topics (higher-level) students will study. The brainstorm may have helped some students to decide this. The teacher may have to be more or less directive in this regard, depending on the kind of students one has to deal with and the school context. If the school already has some connection with the developing world, for example, then one might decide to concentrate on world hunger as the main topic. Of course, the two Irish topics could form a neat pairing for honours students, but the danger is that they will be confused with each other, especially as they are actually linked in ways. So, one might decide it is safer and more interesting to take one global and one national issue for higher level.

Finding the information
'Where will we get the information?' This is bound to be a major concern for many teachers and students. This chapter points out some practical ideas about how and where to find up-to-date information and highlights some of the most important issues in looking at the three areas, without intending to say the final word. The emphasis is on developing the skills of social analysis, rather than on presenting actual analysis.

The main sources of information are those we all use in building up our picture of society, but they will be used more systematically and critically in the classroom setting. They include:

a   *Newspapers*: Both reports and more discursive articles can be used to inform the study of world hunger, Irish poverty and Irish discrimination. The teacher and students could build up personal files of suitable cuttings. The teacher could encourage students to pool information fairly, so that no students will be unjustly disadvantaged, though avoiding allowing some students to neglect their own personal responsibility by letting others do all the work. (The availability of public libraries and the Internet might help in this regard.) The teacher should direct the students to read a variety of papers, and also to become aware of the possible bias in particular editorial policies, reporters' angles, columnists' opinions and arguments. Substantial book reviews may be of use, particularly if they summarise relevant scholarly investigations of the relevant areas. End-of-year analyses and pre- and post-budget features will be of particular value. Look at letters to the editor too. Local papers may contain valuable material. So, too, may the religious press. *The Irish Catholic* of 27 November 2003, for example, printed a very interesting 'double': a kind of debate between Barry Andrews TD defending the Government's record in dealing with the economy, especially in relation to the needs of the poor, and a strong criticism of the Government by Fr Seán Healy of CORI (Conference of Religious of Ireland) Justice office. Such a juxtaposition is very useful and can get students thinking critically about the issues.

b *Magazines*: These may furnish information on social matters and articles on discrimination and poverty. *Time, Newsweek, New Internationalist, The Economist*, to mention a variety of the most well-known titles, will often have articles on global issues.

c *Television*: Documentaries, interviews and discussions will be most useful here, but drama extracts may have some value too, because they can imaginatively portray realities such as living in a slum or being discriminated against. It is important to see the research (or social analysis) as more than just statistical or quantitative. Qualitative research is also valuable. This can include programmes that try to give us a feel for the subjects of famine and poverty and other social issues. Recently, the BBC showed a powerful documentary by Michael Buerk about Ethiopia, in which he revisited the country to see how it had fared since his last documentary on the famine there in the mid-1980s. This

programme and the accompanying web pages are an example of a great resource for student and teacher alike to use in examining the topic of world hunger.[13]
d *Radio*: Though not as popular as television, radio can provide some excellent programmes about social issues, and is better at analysis in many cases. Teachers could encourage students to listen more to current affair programmes, especially at budget times or when particular events focus attention on relevant topics. Radio programme extracts could be used as part of a class, and would be an exercise in listening well, a skill much needed in the areas of justice and peace.
e *Internet*: A number of useful sites are listed at the end of the chapter and in footnotes. Criteria to be followed in using the Internet safely and accurately are suggested in Appendix 2. Students should be carefully briefed about how to research using the net. Because there is so much material to be found, the teacher could explain to students how to set aside a certain period of time for such research and stick to it, making sure not to be overwhelmed by the amount of content and not to be side-tracked by unimportant material. Students could set themselves specific targets before they go online to research a topic, to avoid 'drowning' in information.
f *Books*: A number of useful books are listed at the end of the chapter. These can be hard to get and expensive, so public libraries should not be forgotten in this regard. Over time a school or RE deptartment could build up a library of its own. As already mentioned, texts from other school subjects can contain pertinent information. Students should be taught how to scan a book to find what is relevant, and to become aware of who the author is, what organisation he or she works for, what bias might be operating, what sources are being used, how old the information is, what areas are left out, and so on.

g *Textbooks*: At the time of writing, there are no textbooks for this section, but one hopes some will be written soon. This book is not a textbook. Some of the material in previous texts may be useful. (Avoid simply following the older books, however, as they were not written to match the new syllabus, and so may not cover its requirements.) The lack of textbooks will not unduly worry teachers of senior-level RE as they have been used to finding and making their own resources for years! The lack of a textbook may encourage true research, rather than simply regurgitating what a single textbook says.

h *Speakers*: You cannot beat the power of personal experience and observation, so, where possible, schools should try to engage a speaker or speakers with some knowledge or expertise in the areas of world hunger, discrimination or poverty. This may be relatively easily done by schools that already have a connection with the developing world, such as a teacher or ex-teacher who is working or has worked in a developing country, or a teacher who has visited one. Schools that organise annual fasts or other fund-raising activities may have some links with organisations that can facilitate finding a speaker. Some organisations dealing with refugees or immigrants may have an outreach to schools, which would highlight the issue of discrimination.

i *Surveys*: There may be some value in encouraging students to do their own local research, but this could be more trouble than it's worth. Such work would have to be done very sensitively and accurately. The risk is that one will only gain uncertain 'information' because the number of people surveyed was too small and/or the range of the survey was too narrow. Still, it may be a possibility that some survey or such method could be tried, perhaps to get some limited idea of what is going on locally or what real people feel or have concerns about. One could find out, for example, what percentage of the student cohort have experienced

discrimination. (See p.77 and following for a full analysis of discrimination.)
j *Simulations*: This might seem an odd idea for a source of information. It has its uses, however, in helping students to get an idea of what it might be like to experience hunger, poverty, or, as the most likely candidate for this method, unjust discrimination. Role plays and dramas and games can be devised to open up the topics imaginatively.

These are not the only sources of information. There are others, including personal experience. One should look at several sources and not rely on only one or two. Students need to be encouraged to be as accurate, fair, and comprehensive as they can be in investigating what are complex and emotionally-charged topics. The teacher should model this attitude of fair critical reflection in presenting material and organising discussion.

THREE SPECIFIC ISSUES

This book does not analyse fully the three specified areas but suggests some ideas on how they could be approached and what difficulties might arise. The following sections are not meant to be read as comprehensive or the final word on these complex topics.

(i) World hunger
One 'trap' to avoid in this area is to exclusively blame the poor for their plight. 'It's all their fault for having so many children!' is one variation on this theme. This over-population accusation is relevant both here and in part 3 (regarding environmental justice) and my main treatment of the ethical issues is found in chapter three below. For the moment, let it be noted briefly that, though the issue is hotly debated, it has been argued

strongly that the problem of world hunger is not one caused by too little food for too many people. There is food to feed people – what is lacking is justice in food distribution and peace to enable resources to be shared fairly. 'They are uneducated/lazy/inferior' are other accusations sometimes aimed at the peoples of the developing world to blame them for their hunger. These accusations are kinds of racism or stereotyping (see the treatment of the concept of 'discrimination' below).

Another 'trap' is the opposite mistake of exclusively blaming the rich. 'They are poor/hungry because we are rich.' Variations on this accusation include blaming the capitalists, the multinational corporations, the World Bank, the International Monetary Fund, and other large international bodies for the state of the 'Third World'.

There is *some* truth in these two mistaken approaches. The people of the developing countries can be to some degree responsible for their plight, or at least their governments can be; the people of the developed world, on the other hand, can be selfish and unjust in their treatment of people in 'the majority world' (one of several ways to refer to the poorest countries), or at least their governments can be. It is worth noting here, however, that an important moral principle states that those who are in a position of power are the ones most responsible for the well-being of the community.[14] It is undoubtedly true that most people in the developing countries who suffer from hunger are in a position of powerlessness relative to the developed countries and to the powerful elites in their own countries. Therefore, it is the powerful countries of the world, and the power elites in each nation, who have the greater share of responsibility to work for the well-being of the community, including the most basic need for food.

Blaming the poor or the rich exclusively is something to avoid also in that it is problematic to lump large numbers of diverse people into single categories, such as 'the rich' and 'the poor'. There are problems, too, in explaining a large-scale phenomenon, such as world hunger, by a single cause. One suspects simple explanations are in fact simplistic.

To understand world hunger, one needs to know the facts about hunger and its causes. These can be difficult to discover, especially as the causes are somewhat complex and debated. One way to provoke and encourage critical thinking about these issues would be to find a variety of views on these issues, not confining oneself to the anti-capitalist, left-leaning approaches or, indeed, their opposite. (The books by Lappé and Legrain listed in the text below would be a useful contrast – the former criticising globalisation and free-trade and the latter defending them.)[15]

One very useful source of materials for this part of the course is Trócaire. Teachers could familiarise themselves with its most recent brochure, especially the materials suitable for senior level students (and the background reading matter for teachers). Trócaire provides country profiles that are appropriate for the 'specific country' aspect of this section, where students are required to look at the experiences of a particular country. Other places to find information on specific countries are the BBC website and the Development Gateway website (listed at the end of the chapter). I would also advise liaising with your nearest friendly geography teacher.

It might be possible to combine the teaching of this section on world hunger with catechetical work on Lent in Catholic schools. There is a clear connection with the *zakat* (almsgiving) of Islam too. World hunger as an issue is closely connected with justice towards the environment, which we will look at in chapter three.

Structures

One of the most important structural questions to examine in studying world hunger, an issue that combines features of all four types of structure, is whether the stronger countries of the world treat the weaker as equals or as inferiors. It has been argued by many that the developing nations are in a disadvantaged position (or unequal relationship) from the start. This may put them off even trying to compete on the world market, even though an insular approach is hardly effective or appropriate in the modern globalised world. It is important in this regard to research such organisations as the World Trade Organisation and the United Nations, and their conferences, as well as the rules and customs shaping international trade. Some of the developed countries protect their own producers by subsidising them, often heavily, and thereby make it harder for developing countries to export their own produce and so improve their lot by trade.[16] In addition, economies focused on a narrow range of products are vulnerable to all sorts of calamities, including natural disasters such as drought and flooding, (though it would be wrong to blame world hunger on natural causes alone).

War, both civil and international, is one of the biggest factors causing world hunger. War is a matter of politics but it can be affected strongly by social and cultural factors too. Social divisions, especially tribal tensions, can contribute to the outbreak of war, especially if there is a power struggle between groups. A culture that puts too high a value on tribal or even national security can lead to precious wealth being used for purposes of war rather than feeding the hungry.

The weaknesses of various national governments of particular developing countries and their problems of corruption and inefficiency lead to major problems in wealth creation and resource allocation, and ultimately to widespread hunger. Unless countries have stable political systems and a clear rule of law creating favourable conditions for business and commerce, national and foreign capital will be tempted to go elsewhere to invest.

In many countries, power is concentrated in the hands of a few people, or a few families, to the detriment of the many.

Probably the worst situation is that of dictatorship. Dictators are usually very wealthy. Great wealth can co-exist beside the most appalling squalor. Often, attempts to remedy the situation of famine and poverty are resisted by those who are in power because they are afraid of losing their comfortable positions and their status. Also, there may be fear of social unrest and even revolution if powerful positions are given up or social control weakened. It is clear that honest and efficient political, economic and legal institutions are essential for countries to achieve integral development and so escape poverty.

In some situations, a culture of fatalism may be exacerbated by religious beliefs or the legacy of colonialism. People may feel that things are meant to be as they are, that suffering is inevitable, that it is God's will. People may lack the self-confidence to solve their problems and improve their lot.

These are just some of the structural issues to be considered in social analysis of world hunger. The additional factor of individual human choice should not be neglected, however, as social structures alone cannot explain why so many people die of hunger in a world of plenty. Only human sinfulness and people's sinful choices can fully explain why the evil of world hunger persists. Individual sinful choices contribute to social structures and maintain them, making them 'sinful social structures'. Thus, sin is not entirely an individual matter, but also a social matter, so that it is right to talk of 'social sin', a category of sin emphasised in recent moral theology and Church teaching.[17] This point is also relevant to the other two issues in this section.

(ii) Poverty in Ireland
Again, as with world hunger, there are quite divergent approaches to this area, with regard to its meaning, its causes and its solution.

Defining poverty

The meaning of 'poverty' might seem simple but there are some complexities to this issue too. One way to get a clear idea of the difficulties is to clarify the concepts of 'absolute' and 'relative' poverty, as the syllabus specifies. First, however, we must look at 'the poverty line'.

The Poverty Line – mean or median?

What is it to be poor? This question can be answered by comparing a particular income with the *average* income (or the *mean*). Anyone with an income below a particular percentage of the average income is below the povety line, (that is, 'poor'). Typical 'lines' used in assessing poverty are 40 per cent, 50 per cent or 60 per cent of average income, usually 50 per cent. So, anyone below 50 per cent of average or mean income is poor. Sometimes *median* income levels are used instead of average incomes to decide the poverty line. Median refers to the mid-point between the highest income and the lowest, which may not be the exact same as the average income. Once again, poverty is seen as lying below a line, which is usually set at 60 per cent of the median.

Official Irish analysts use the 50 per cent of mean (average) income line, which is similar to the 60 per cent line of median income. According to CORI's analysis this means that, at the time of writing, there is:

> a relative income poverty line of €180.30 [per week] for a single person. In 2004, any adult below this weekly income level will be counted as being in poverty ... For each additional adult in the household this minimum income figure is increased by €119 (66 per cent of the poverty line figure) and for each child in the household the minimum income figure is increased by €59.50 (33 per cent of the poverty line).[18]

The reality in Ireland in 2004 is that 'Over 700,000 now live in poverty, an increase of almost 84,000 since 1994 [...] Of these, more than 250,000 are children.'[19]

Relative poverty and absolute poverty
When poverty is measured like this by comparing or contrasting incomes, one is making a relative comparison, rather than looking at the amount of wealth in itself (in absolute terms). Examining relative or absolute types of poverty are different ways of deciding if someone is poor. Some people's incomes can be going down relative to the average or median incomes of those around them, but increasing in absolute terms. What this means is that people can be becoming better off in terms of the amount of money or wealth they have (adjusted for inflation), but worse off compared to the majority of those around them and the expectations and assumptions of their culture. This is the same as saying that there can be a decrease in absolute poverty and an increase in relative poverty, both happening simultaneously to the same people. (In the worst cases, people may be in the very unhappy position of becoming poorer in both absolute and relative terms.) In Ireland and the world in recent times, the proportion of people with little or no wealth has decreased and many have improved their lot (though certainly not all have), whilst the gap between the 'haves' and the 'have-nots' has increased greatly.

Relative poverty is a serious matter and it is the primary focus of much social analysis in Ireland today. People can feel poorer even though they may be better off than they used to be and better off than most poor people of past times. Poverty has a very important relative dimension – people do not die if they cannot afford a television and video in Ireland, but they certainly feel very poor. They feel inadequate, inferior and marginalised, even if they were better off than they had been fifteen or twenty-five years ago. And for many people in poverty it is not a matter of simply lacking a television or video, but of persistently serious hardship and deprivation, particularly affecting health care, education and family life. Very useful sources of detailed information and comment on the reality of poverty in Ireland today can be found at the CORI and Combat Poverty websites and publications (see below for details).

There exists a rather confusing situation in modern social analysis where some people point to the decrease in absolute poverty and say that we are basically doing things right to end poverty and should keep on doing what we've been doing (though perhaps with some improvements), whilst others claim that relative poverty has increased and so we should substantially reform or even revolutionise what we are doing to end poverty finally.

Causes of poverty

The causes of poverty are also somewhat controversial, with some people blaming the poor for their lot and others blaming society or some part of society. This is another aspect of the Right/Left split already mentioned several times. The important thing here is to avoid simplistic analyses and answers, especially ones that merely follow an ideological Right or Left approach, and to test everything against the criteria of reason and faith. Poor people are not totally to blame for their poverty; neither are society or the government.

There is a complex set of causes of poverty, including human choices and mistakes that are hard to quantify or measure by sociological or other means. People can become poor because of very diverse factors, which can include such things as serious or long-term illness, unemployment, poor educational attainment, drug addiction, bad money management, bad luck, violence suffered, teenage pregnancy and having to look after a dependent or dependents without enough resources, for example. These factors can affect individuals or families and can affect people badly in various combinations (for example, poor educational attainment with unemployment or drug addiction or crime).

As well as factors that cause poverty, there are others that exacerbate it or maintain it. Some of the factors just listed would not cause poverty, or at least would cause less poverty, if the state or society in general (including families) gave appropriate help to the people who suffer from the causal factors. Illness will not cause poverty if there is an adequate public health service, for example, and carers will not be made poor by their responsibilities if the state respects their right to adequate recognition and support and meets their needs. There can be little doubt that in these areas and others the state has, in the immortal words of many a school report, 'plenty of room to improve'.

In examining the causes of poverty, it is probably better to avoid apportioning blame, but to focus instead on *responsibility* for doing something about it. As already noted above, it is an ethical principle that whoever is in a position of power in a community has the main responsibility to set things right, to improve things, to make the first move. This is one reason for emphasising the responsibility of government for improving the lot of those people who live in poverty, even if the state is not always necessarily the cause of the poverty in the first instance. This can be done in a way that is not patronising towards those who are poor, treating them as objects of pity or mere passive victims, but which respects people who are poor and allows them a measure of self-respect and autonomy. Just how this can or should be done, and to what degree, and what the appropriate balance between the contribution of state and society should be, are hotly debated topics.

We ought to be fair and accurate in our finding out the facts and assessing them. In this regard, teachers should make themselves familiar with the ***National Anti-Poverty Strategy*** **(NAPS):** The 10 year plan of the Irish Government aimed at tackling poverty which involves consultation, target setting and poverty proofing. NAPS aims to achieve better understanding of the structural causes of poverty such as unemployment, low income and educational disadvantage.'[20] The recently published CORI Justice Commission's 'Socio-Economic Review 2004: Priorities For Fairness: Choosing Policies to Ensure Economic Development, Social Equity and Sustainability'[21] and the July 2004 Policy Briefing, already quoted, are essential reading for a thorough analysis of the Irish situation.

Structures

The following are some brief final comments on how structural analysis applies to this topic. Economic structures to examine include the employment/unemployment situation, the taxation system, and the social welfare system, all of which have a huge affect on people's welfare and ability to cope with challenges such as low wages or illness. Careful note should be taken of budget day details and debates.

Political structures are involved here too as it is the politicians who decide economic budgets and the details of economic systems. One additional area to look at here is whether those who are poor have a say in the running of society, and whether their concerns matter in our system of democracy. Does Social Partnership, for example, enable those who are poor to substantially shape decisions that will affect their situation?

Social structures matter here too. Poverty is more prevalent in certain social groups – those not in the labour force especially, including carers and the elderly, and women too. It is worth remembering, however, that even those who have a job can be poor, if that job is badly paid, as can happen too often. (One very interesting economic question is what causes low wages.)

Finally, regarding cultural structures, one very important issue is whether the recent affluence in Ireland created by the Celtic Tiger has caused economic progress for the majority and profit-making to be valued so highly that the needs of the significant minority who are poor are neglected or ignored.[22]

(iii) Discrimination in Ireland

Discrimination is another of those concepts that seem simple at first but reveals complexities on further examination. The easiest mistake to make here is to see discrimination simply as 'judgement' and therefore immoral – because all judgement is considered immoral. Sometimes the teaching of Jesus in the Sermon on the Mount (his command to 'Judge not' in Matthew 7) is referred to in this regard. 'Judgementalism' is regarded by many as the major sin now. Is 'discrimination' always immoral? Is it always wrong to judge others? The answer is that logically all judgement cannot be claimed to be wrong. Judgement is part of being an intelligent and responsible human being. Discrimination and judgement are important concepts to understand well so that one's teaching of morality in general will not be illogical or vague, and this applies very directly to section F of the syllabus. Accurate judgement is an essential aspect of justice itself. The important point is to make sure that one's judgement is always warranted, appropriate and fair.

Definition of discrimination
'Discrimination' is not in itself a pejorative term. It refers to picking out details or relevant facts about something. It could be said that to help students to become persons of discrimination is an aim of all good education. 'Unjust' should be used as a prefix before 'discrimination' to make its pejorative character clear. However, in common usage, the word 'discrimination' in itself refers to unjust judgement of people based on irrelevant features or inaccurate information or impressions.

The Equality Authority
An excellent place to find out how to judge whether unjust discrimination has taken place and to research its prevalence in

Ireland is the Equality Authority website and its links. Here is what it says about the actual grounds for a claim that unjust discrimination has taken place:

> The Employment Equality Act, 1998 and the Equal Status Act, 2000 outlaw discrimination in employment, vocational training, advertising, collective agreements, the provision of goods and services and other opportunities to which the public generally have access on nine distinct grounds. These are gender; marital status; family status; age; disability; race; sexual orientation; religious belief; and membership of the Traveller Community... Discrimination is described in the Act as the treatment of a person in a less favourable way than another person is, has been or would be treated on any of the above grounds.[23]

Teachers and students should research the two Acts mentioned here. Information about the extent of discrimination in Ireland will be found following up the links on the Equality Authority site (and in articles in the press and items on television).

The nine grounds mentioned in the laws against discrimination are:
1 Gender
2 Marital status
3 Family status
4 Age
5 Disability
6 Race
7 Sexual orientation
8 Religious belief
9 Membership of the Traveller Community

Many aspects of discrimination are simply matters of unfairness, of bias and prejudice. Examples are not difficult to find, explain and judge. There are some interesting, controversial aspects, however, to the nine grounds listed above. Difficulties can arise in working out whether a particular aspect of a person is relevant or irrelevant for a fair judgement. One example of this difficulty is whether a person's faith is considered relevant for judging suitability for a teaching post in a religious school. As things stand, the Acts allow denominational schools to 'discriminate' on religious grounds if it is necessary to protect and promote their religious character. Thus, a Catholic school could choose not to employ a person for a teaching post if it was reasonable to expect that his particular religious beliefs and practice (or lack of same) would be detrimental to the ethos of the school. Some who disagree with this position would regard any reference to one's faith in the context of a job application as always unwarranted, and thus always grounds for a claim of unjust discrimination. It is certainly a controversial case to judge. Another controversial issue that is frequently in the news at the moment is whether or not it is discriminatory to refuse to grant same-sex relationships the status and rights of marriage. It is not only in relation to religious belief or sexual orientation that difficulties in interpretation and application can arise. It is worth noting how a complex justice system is necessary to adjudicate fairly on disputed cases.

Having said all that, it should be mentioned that unjust discrimination is not always complex or difficult to judge. There are simple cases of unfair dismissal, for example, or victimisation of a person or group on racist grounds. It would be wrong to complicate matters unnecessarily when the issues are straightforward and the challenge to be just is clear. Often, an honest and direct application of the Golden Rule ('Do unto others as you would have them do unto you')[24] will uncover unjust discrimination in a situation. In other words, if we ask, 'Would *I* like to be treated in this way if the respective roles were reversed?', the answer will tell us if we are in danger of discriminating unjustly against a person or group. The points raised in this paragraph also apply to any attempt to avoid our obligations or responsibilities in analysing world hunger and poverty in Ireland. Although there are real complexities in these areas, we should not let that be an excuse for us to hide behind mere rationalisation rather than face the truth of how we or our society are unjust and need to seek greater social justice. There is always the risk that people can call an issue 'controversial' merely to continue to feel comfortable while doing little or nothing to accept responsibility to reform structures that contribute to the injustice (and to change one's individual thinking and behaviour too).

Structures

It is easy to see how social structures are relevant when analysing discrimination, as it often involves one social grouping being looked down on by others. The Travellers are mentioned explicitly in the Act, for instance, though one could also mention non-nationals as another example of a vulnerable group in our society that might easily become victims of unjust discrimination. Many of the nine grounds have to do with social status or position.

Cultural structures are important too, as these embody and communicate the values by which we judge others. Are there any deeply ingrained prejudices in Irish society that can lead to unjust discrimination? Where do these prejudices come from and how are they perpetuated?

Economic structural analysis is not as easy to apply here, but one might mention such questions as whether the taxation system discriminates against married people who work in the home, whether those who are disabled and those who care for them are given a fair social allowance, and whether women are paid equally to men for equal work.

Finally, political structures are important in that it is always those in some position of power who can inflict discrimination on others. And so the questions are: who has the power? How is it used or abused?

Further Reading

Abercrombie, N., S. Hill and B. S. Turner, *The Penguin Dictionary of Sociology* fourth edition (London: Penguin, 2000).

Ashley, B. *Living the Truth in Love: A Biblical Introduction to Moral Theology* (New York: Alba House, 1996).

Bruce, S. *Sociology: A Very Short Introduction* (Oxford, UK: Oxford University Press, 1999).

Combat Poverty Agency, *Annual Report 2002* (Dublin: Combat Poverty Agency, 2003).

Dorr, D. *The Social Justice Agenda* (Dublin: Gill and MacMillan, 1991).

Drumm, M. *Famine, Christian Perspectives on Development Issues* (Trocaire, Veritas, Cafod, 1998).

Dunne, J., A. Ingram and F. Litton, (eds.), *Questioning Ireland: Debates in Political Philosophy and Public Policy* (Dublin: Institute of Public Administration, 2000).

80:20 Development in an Unequal World (England: Teachers in Development Education, 2002).

Eoin G. Cassidy (ed.), *Prosperity with a Purpose: What Purpose?* (Dublin: Veritas, 2000).

Ferguson, N. *Colossus: The Rise and Fall of the American Empire* (London: Penguin, 2004).

Gula, R.M. *Ethics in Pastoral Ministry* (New York/Mahweh, New Jersey: Paulist Press, 1996).

Healy, S. and B. Reynolds, *Social Analysis in the Light of the Gospel* (Dublin: Conference of Major Religious Superiors /Folens, 1983)

Healy, S. and B. Reynolds, *Ireland Today: Reflecting in the Light of the Gospel* (Dublin: Conference of Major Religious Superiors /Folens, 1985).

Healy, S. and B. Reynolds, (eds.), *Social Policy in Ireland: Principles, Practice and Problems* (Dublin: Oak Tree Press, 1998).
Heywood, A. *Politics* (London: McMillan Press, 1997).
Holland, J. and P. Henriot *Social Analysis: Linking Faith and Justice*, revised and enlarged edition, (Washington, DC: Orbis Books/The Center of Concern, 1983).
Irish Episcopal Conference, *Prosperity with a Purpose* (1999) (available online at www.catholiccommunications.ie following 'pastoral letters' index.).
Joseph, J. *Food, Christian Perspectives on Development Issues* (Dublin: Trocaire, Veritas, Cafod, 1999).
Kay, J. *The Truth About Markets: Why some nations are rich, but most remain poor*, updated edition (London: Penguin, 2004).
Kirby, P. *The Celtic Tiger In Distress: Growth with Inequality in Ireland* (Basingstoke, Hampshire: Palgrave MacMillan, 2002).
Lane, D. (ed.) *New Century, New Society: Christian Perspectives* (Dublin: Columba, 1999).
Lappé, F.M., J. Collins, and P. Rosset, Institute for Food and Development Policy/Food First, *World Hunger – Twelve Myths*, second edition (Oakland, California: Grove Publications, 1998).
Legrain, P. *Open World: The Truth About Globalisation* (London: Abacus, 2002).
Lentin, R. and R. McVeigh (eds.), *Racism and Anti-racism in Ireland* (Belfast: Beyond the Pale Publications, 2002).
McVerry, P. *The Meaning is in the Shadows* (Dublin: Veritas, 2003).
Minogue, K. *Politics: A Very Short Introduction* (Oxford, UK: Oxford University Press, 1995).
O'Riain, S. *Solidarity with Travellers* (Dublin: Roadside Books, 2000).
Singer, P. (ed.) *A Companion to Ethics*, Blackwell Companions to Philosophy, (Oxford: Blackwell, 1993).
Singer, P. *Marx: A Very Short Introduction* (Oxford, UK: Oxford University Press, 2000).

Smith, D. *Free Lunch: Easily Digestible Economics* (London: Profile Books, 2003).

Trigg, R. *Ideas of Human Nature: An Historical Introduction*, second edition (Oxford, UK; Blackwell Publishing Ltd., 1999).

Whelen, T.R. (ed.) *The Stranger in our Midst: Refugees in Ireland: Causes, Experiences, Responses*, Kimmage Explorations in Faith and Culture (Dublin: Kimmage Institute of Theology and Cultures, 2001).

White, S. and R. Tiongco, *Doing Theology and Development: Meeting the Challenge of Poverty* (Edinburgh: St. Andrew's Press, 1997).

Web Sites
Artists against racism: www.vrx.net/aar/
Bread for the World Institute: www.bread.org/
Cafod: www.cafod.org.uk/
Central Statistics Office: www.cso.ie/
[Its school page is at www.cso.ie/schools/schoolindex.html]
Combat Poverty Organisation: www.cpa.ie/
Combat Poverty fact sheets on poverty:
www.combatpoverty.ie/facts_jargon.html
Comhlámh site: www.comhlamh.org/
Concern: www.concern.ie/index.php
CORI (Conference of Religious of Ireland) Justice site: www.cori.ie/justice.
CORI Justice Commission Policy Briefing on Poverty (July 2004): www.cori.ie/justice/index.htm
Department of Social Welfare site on NAPS: www.welfare.ie/publications/naps/index.html
Development Education Ireland: www.developmenteducation.ie/home.php
Equality Authority official site: www.equality.ie/
Economic and Social Research Institute (ESRI): www.esri.ie/index.cfm

Food First - Institute for Food and Development Policy:
www.foodfirst.org/progs/
Global Express: www.cdu.mic.ul.ie/global/default.htm
Government of Ireland: www.irlgov.ie/
Human Development Reports: http://hdr.undp.org/
Institute for Liberal Values: www.liberalvalues.org.nz/
Lappé et al. 12 Myths about World Hunger website summary:
www.foodfirst.org/pubs/backgrdrs/1998/s98v5n3.html.
Legrain website: www.philippelegrain.com/
National Economic and Social Council (NESC) [note its publications link]: www.nesc.ie/
National Consultative Committee on Racism and Interculturalism: www.nccri.com/
National 'Know Racism' site: www.knowracism.ie/
Office of Director of Equality Investigations: www.odei.ie/
Oz Spirit: promoting spirituality, social justice and global education: http://ozspirit.info/index.html
Pontifical Council for Justice and Peace, The Social Agenda (2000): www.thesocialagenda.com/article4.htm#11
Traidcraft: www.traidcraft.co.uk/
Travellers' website: www.paveepoint.ie/pav_home_a.html
Trócaire: www.trocaire.org.
United Nations Cyber School Bus:
www.un.org/Pubs/CyberSchoolBus/index.html
United Nations Human Development Report 2003:
http://hdr.undp.org/reports/global/2003/
World Hunger Notes: www.worldhunger.org/index.html

Notes

1 Joe Holland and Peter Henriot *Social Analysis: Linking Faith and Justice*, revised and enlarged edition, (Washington, DC: Orbis Books in association with The Center of Concern, 1983). See especially the 'Afterword' by Henriot, pp. 95-105, and also the whole of the first chapter.

2 Both *Social Analysis in the Light of the Gospel* (1983) and *Ireland Today: Reflecting in the Light of the Gospel* (1985) were published in Dublin and printed and bound by Folens. Healy and Reynolds published them on behalf of the Justice Office, Conference of Major Religious Superiors, as it was known then. It is now the Justice section of CORI (Conference of Religious of Ireland).
3 *Social Analysis: Linking Faith and Justice*, p. 10. Emphasis in original.
4 My description of the structures under the four headings draws heavily from *Social Analysis: Linking Faith and Justice*, chapter one and afterword, and *Social Analysis in the Light of the Gospel*, chapter three.
5 Syllabus, p. 61.
6 See for example, the criticisms by Moore McDowell of the US bishops' 1980s draft pastoral letter on the economy and, less stringently, of the Irish bishops' 1999 pastoral *Prosperity with a Purpose* in his contribution to a conference organised by the Irish Centre for Faith and Culture: Eoin G. Cassidy (ed.), *Prosperity with a Purpose: What Purpose?* (Dublin: Veritas, 2000), pp. 59-77.
7 S. Bruce, *Sociology: A Very Short Introduction* (Oxford, UK: Oxford University Press, 1999), p. 63, states that the most commonly accepted way of dividing society into classes is as follows: the working class (unskilled and skilled), the routine clerical class, the service or salaried class, small proprietors and self-employed, and farmers and agricultural workers. These are divided according to *the amount of control people have over their working lives*. This is a useful way of looking at class, but it leaves out certain groups of people, particularly those at the bottom and the top.
8 The book by Eoin Cassidy in this series (Veritas, 2004), on section A, *The Search for Meaning and Values*, has some material on Marx's philosophical position. The introductory books on politics by Minogue and Heywood have good sections on Marxism (see notes 11 and 12 below). A more detailed treatment of Marx is found in P. Singer, *Marx: A Very Short Introduction* (Oxford, UK: Oxford University Press, 2000). Also useful is R. Trigg, *Ideas of Human Nature: An Historical Introduction*, second edition (Oxford, UK; Blackwell Publishing Ltd., 1999), ch. nine, 'Marx'. Other chapters of Trigg's book deal with philosophers and philosophies directly relevant to issues in this course, such as Aristotle, Aquinas, Hobbes and Locke.
9 Part one of section E, *Religion and Gender*, deals with the issues mentioned in this paragraph; see the book by Sandra Cullen in this

series (Veritas, 2004). As there is a distinct section of the syllabus dedicated to the topic of gender, and a book in this series on the topic, I have not focussed on it in this book, although it is obviously a very important area of justice and peace in its own right.
10 Social analysis is not necessarily concerned only with problems – but it seems it is mainly focused on what is wrong. Certainly, the wording of this part of the section suggests a strong emphasis on problems, especially in 1.2: 'Social analysis in action'.
11 See K. Minogue, *Politics: A Very Short Introduction* (Oxford, UK: Oxford University Press, 1995), pp. 71-78, where the author discusses the duality of politics in terms of a divide between conservatism and liberalism, with socialism as a third approach somewhat complicating matters. Elsewhere, Minogue describes the basic political divide as one between realists and idealists, see ibid., pp. 59-60.
12 B. Ashley, *Living the Truth in Love: A Biblical Introduction to Moral Theology* (New York: Alba House, 1996), pp. 372-373, note omitted. See also A. Heywood, *Politics* (London: McMillan Press, 1997), chapter nine, where several types of capitalism and socialism are described, clearly showing the inaccuracy in seeing only one against the other.
13 news.bbc.co.uk/2/hi/programmes/this_world/3324089.stm and accompanying links.
14 See R. M Gula, *Ethics in Pastoral Ministry* (New York/Mahweh, New Jersey: Paulist Press, 1996), pp. 81-82 and 105-6. Gula is concerned with professional ethics for ministers, but the principle applies equally to the issues looked at here.
15 In addition to the books listed, there is material online. There is a useful summary of Lappé et al. *12 Myths about World Hunger* at the Food First website, following the 'Bookstore' and 'Backgrounders' links. Its specific web page address is www.foodfirst.org/pubs/backgrdrs/1998/s98v5n3.html. Legrain has his own web page, with some useful articles and information on his book at www.philippelegrain.com/ .
16 N. Ferguson, *Colossus: The Rise and Fall of the American Empire* (Penguin, 2004) p. 177 puts it like this: 'Part of the problem is that world trade is still far from being truly free. At least some of the blame for this can be laid at the door of the world's richest countries, which continue to pay subsidies to their farmers, equivalent to the entire gross domestic product of Africa. American producer support still amounts to around 20 per cent of gross farm receipts; the figure for the European Union is more than 30 per cent.'

17 See the excerpts from Church documents on social sin and structures of sin in *The Social Agenda* (2000), a publication of the Pontifical Council for Justice and Peace, article four, number 11, available online at www.thesocialagenda.com/article4.htm#11
18 See the CORI Justice Commission Policy Briefing on Poverty July 2004, p. 2. The complete document is available online at their site at www.cori.ie/justice/index.htm
19 CORI Policy Briefing, p. 4.
20 This quote is taken from one of the Combat Poverty fact sheets on poverty, 'The glossary of poverty and social inclusion terms' available at www.combatpoverty.ie/facts_jargon.html . At the end of the definition it refers to the following website for more information on this strategy: www.welfare.ie/publications /naps/index.html
21 Available at www.cori.ie/justice/soc_issues/index.htm .
22 Peadar Kirby, *The Celtic Tiger In Distress: Growth with Inequality in Ireland* (Basingstoke, Hampshire: Palgrave MacMillan, 2002) provides a detailed and highly critical analysis of the Celtic Tiger phenonemon. It is an excellent example of up-to-date social analysis. Dr Kirby is a senior lecturer in the DCU School of Law and Government.
23 Quotes taken from www.equality.ie/
24 The Golden Rule is treated below in chapter two part 1 under the heading of 'Justice as Fair Play'.

2

The Concept of Justice and Peace

Structure
Part 2 constitutes the heart of *Issues of Justice and Peace* and is divided into four as follows:

- (2.1) justice,
- (2.2) peace,
- (2.3) religious perspectives on justice and peace,
- (2.4) the challenge of violence.

Integrate religion
One of the problems with this structure is that the religious aspect appears confined to the third subsection. What then of the *other* subsections? Are 'justice' and 'peace' to be defined primarily in non-religious terms with a 'veneer' or 'gloss' of religion added later? Surely not in a *religious* education syllabus. The religious aspect is not peripheral but an integral part of the whole approach and so it ought to be integrated from the beginning. With this in mind, this chapter indicates some religious dimensions from the beginning, though taking a mainly philosophical angle at first, and then outlines a more comprehensive treatment of the religious details in subsection 2.3 below. The primary aim of the chapter as a whole is to clarify the central concepts: justice and peace.

2.1 VISIONS OF JUSTICE

COMPLEMENTARY WAYS OF UNDERSTANDING JUSTICE

This part looks at five ways to understand the concept of 'justice'. There is a singular moral principle or truth, namely justice, that we can look at and come to understand better from several points of view. Five of the most important of these points of view are indicated by the headings given in the syllabus (p. 63):

i   right relationship
ii retribution
iii fair play
iv the promotion of equality
v   the upholding of human rights.

These five points of view are not rivals or exclusive alternatives, but complimentary ways of coming to a richer understanding of the concept of justice. None of the five perspectives capture the whole of justice – we need to combine them into a coherent concept. If we look at justice from only one perspective, we will miss much of its richness as a moral principle to guide behaviour. One common approach today is to focus on human rights, for example, but this can be criticised as too narrow and too prone to a kind of selfish individualism that seriously neglects the social nature of the human person and the importance of relationships in human identity and life. To focus only on relationship, on the other hand, runs the risk of becoming vague about the requirements of justice, or becoming relativistic about their application. So it is very helpful to understand justice from a number of complimentary angles, so that the weaknesses of one approach are counteracted by the strengths of others. The specificity of the human rights approach, then, helps us to avoid the weakness of vagueness in the right relationship approach; the generality of the right relationship approach, in turn, puts the specifics of human rights into the proper context of the human person as essentially social and related.

(i) Justice: Right Relationship

As this is such an important perspective on justice, acting as a kind of overall context for correctly understanding the four further perspectives, it is necessary to make sure that the concept of *relationship* is clear, before looking at the full concept of *right relationship*.

Relationship and relationships

Though they seem simple, 'relationship' or 'relationships' can be understood too narrowly. They suggest friendships, particularly sexual ones. 'Relationship education' is commonly understood from this narrow perspective. In section F of the RE syllabus, a more accurate, wider definition is required. 'Relationship' refers to a connection between persons or things; it concerns how one thing exists in reference to another or others. One can appreciate the wide application of justice to every area of human life only when one clearly comprehends that there are many types of human relationship at many different levels. These include family connections such as husband/wife, mother/daughter, brother/sister, and other 'relations' (as the commonly used term describes them). Relationships also include various types of friendship, including, but not exclusively, girlfriend/boyfriend. Relationships are seen in many other spheres of social life and include neighbour/neighbour, customer-retailer, consumer-producer, employee/employer, and so on. At its most general, relationship refers to the connection between citizen and citizen and, more widely still, human and human.

In the spiritual sphere, relationship refers to the link between believer and believer – in the Christian tradition this will be seen as the relationship between sister and brother 'in

Christ' – and most importantly of all, the connection between God and the human person. This last relationship can be understood in various ways. The most important descriptions in the Christian tradition include Creator/creature, King/people, Father/son (daughter), Husband/wife, Saviour/saved/sinner, Shepherd/sheep, and others.

These are illustrative, not comprehensive, lists. Also, in each case given, one can read the pairing in the opposite direction, too, depending on which side of the relationship one wishes to emphasise. So, for example, employer/employee, wife/husband, and sinner/Saviour carry a different emphasis in working out the requirements of justice, than do employee/employer, husband/wife and Saviour/sinner.

It is also very important to mention that, even though relationships can most easily be imagined and discussed as one-to-one realities, there are other kinds too. We have one-to-many (the citizen to the state, for example), many-to-one (the state to the citizen, for example) and many-to-many (one state and its citizens to another state and its citizens, for example, or one religious group to another). An appreciation of this is highly relevant for a good understanding of justice as a directive principle for human society in varying ways.

We have looked at inter-personal relationships so far, but there are other types of relationship too. We are related to the earth, to the natural world. This is a relationship that features strongly in the third part of section F, which focuses on environmental concerns. It is a relationship that has always been acknowledged but its importance has received particular attention in recent years.

The wide scope of justice
There are many types and examples of relationships, or connections or links. We ought to avoid reducing our perspective on justice to only one or two types. This is a common reduction of the richness of justice, for example in

seeing it as exclusively individual to individual, or as state to citizen. It might be a good thing for the teacher to develop exercises to facilitate students getting a clearer idea of how many relationships characterise their lives and identities, and to see how justice is not confined to only one or two types.

'Right' relationship: the importance of ethical standards
The other key word in this first perspective on justice is 'right' – *right* relationship. It indicates that there can be a correct way to be in relationship, or a correct kind of connection – and therefore, as a corollary, an incorrect way to be related or an incorrect kind of relationship, too. The phrase 'right relationship' suggests that relationships can be judged by some standard. They do not simply exist: they can be evaluated. We can judge their rightness.

Different standards have been recognised down through the centuries in various places. The Judaeo-Christian tradition has placed great store on the Ten Commandments, the Covenant, the Beatitudes, the Golden Rule and other Biblical principles and norms. Christ is seen by Christians as the highest norm of right relationship. Other religions have their own ways of describing the standard of rightness for relationships in society, for example, the Varnas of Hinduism see it in terms of being faithful to one's place in an ordained scheme of social strata within the context of reincarnation and karma. Non-religious ways of understanding what the standard of rightness is have been developed too, and have sometimes been integrated with religious understandings. The other perspectives listed in this part of the syllabus are among the most commonly accepted: retribution, fair play (or impartiality), equality, and respect for specific human rights. Systems for legislation, judgement of law and law enforcement have been developed by organisations, states and the international community to establish standards for social relationships. (This would be a good place to make cross-reference to parts of section C on

Moral Decision Making that concern law and charters of human rights.)

One major moral implication of this first perspective on justice is that if relationships are not 'right', we ought to put them right, insofar as we can. A further implication is that we ought to avoid relationships being wrong in the first place.

Too general?
Still, even though we are a little more precise at this stage, we are still speaking at a rather general or abstract level of description. One advantage of this is to prevent us becoming too narrow in focus. It's worth noting that there is a valid general meaning of justice that sees it as 'moral rectitude', taking in all morality related to our treatment of others. An action that is 'just' is simply a good action, a right action; a 'just' person is a good person, and so on. This is worth noting, but it is very general. There is a more precise, more specific definition of 'justice': justice consists in giving to each person what is due to that person. (This is looked at in detail under the next heading, retribution.) How does the heading 'right relationship' enable us to understand this more specific definition?

The essential point: the social nature of the human person
'Right relationship' highlights the social nature of the human person. The fact is that we are all in relationship naturally, from the very beginning of our existence. The 'atomistic' view of the human person, which sees the person as an essentially detached unit (supposedly like an atom) is not adequate. A very *exclusive* 'individual rights' view of justice is incomplete and a distortion of reality. This first perspective on justice is particularly valuable in that it emphasises the social nature of justice based on the fact that we are essentially beings-in-relationship. This social nature of justice is reflected in the use of the term 'social justice'. 'Social' could be looked on here as a redundant adjective – isn't all justice social by

definition? It is, but the term 'social' is still necessary. An overly narrow understanding of justice became dominant over recent centuries, especially with the rise of rights language and its focus on individual immunities and entitlements, and also with the rise of capitalism and the free market and its emphasis on individual contract-keeping. These contributed to a concept of justice that neglected the wider social aspect, the common good aspect. This first perspective can remind us very usefully that justice is all about making sure that relationship-in-society is right.

Justice and Love – beginning to understand the difference
Justice is concerned with human persons as 'others'. It is primarily concerned with how we relate to others as, in a sense, strangers, or 'others', with a claim on us owing them something or who perhaps owe us something. To illustrate this consider, for example, married couples. They do not normally think of justice as a central norm for their relationships, but rather of 'love'. Usually a couple are too close to each other to think in terms of justice. It is only if they become estranged to some degree, that is become as 'others' or strangers to one another, that they think of the requirements of 'justice' *per se*. This is when they might consider bringing in impartial outsiders, such as lawyers or solicitors, to help them to clarify what is owed to whom and how their relationship is to be put 'right', at least to some degree. Of course, this is not to suggest that justice is unimportant for marriage; it is necessary as a minimum for any fair or peaceful relationship. But love goes beyond justice and is appropriate for normal intimate relationships and as the overall ideal for all relationships. Justice operates as *at least a minimum principle* of right relationship among 'others'. It specifies how people ought to relate to each other at the minimal level of person to person. More than a minimum is needed for true human fulfilment, however, and so justice as a minimum standard is not enough for all human

relationships or as the ideal overall principle of human interaction. Love is the highest moral principle.

Others are not completely 'other'
The notion of justice as adjudicating between 'strangers' is not an argument for seeing others only as strangers. The principle of justice points to the fact that others are never really complete 'strangers'; they are actually fellow human beings who share a common humanity. This common humanity binds us together as persons and is more basic than any other more specific relationship, such as family, neighbourhood, political party or religious organisation. We 'owe' others simply because they are human beings – this is the basis for justice as 'giving back what we owe' and 'rights language'. (Both of these perspectives are examined below.)

The importance of tolerance
Nevertheless, it is only realistic to acknowledge that we experience some others as strangers, and that we need to think out how to educate young people to respect others *as others*. In other words, we need to learn how to relate fairly and rightly to those we do not feel related to, those who are very different from us, those who seem strange or different. We also need to become more aware of the value of tolerance as a virtue and as a policy. By 'tolerance as a virtue' is meant the ability to put up with others' ideas or behaviour that we find difficult for some reason, even for good reason, because we wish to promote the common good of all. So, allowing for diverse religious beliefs is a kind of tolerance, for example, and it allows for freedom of conscience and worship and mutual dialogue and debate. Tolerance is especially needed as our society becomes less homogenous and more diverse in its makeup because of immigration, greater mobility, new communications technology, and so on. Tolerance is an aspect of justice as right relationship to others as (equal) others. Justice will play a

central role as a minimum ethical principle of fairness in guiding us in right relationships with those who differ from us in some respects, but who share the same human nature that relates us all.

Relationships are not all the same
That said, we should not focus exclusively on relationship with others as others. This could end up making justice the only ethical principle, which is wrong. We are in relationship with many people in deeply personal ways. These closer relationships are important and should not be neglected because of an undue emphasis on justice towards 'the other'. Such an undue emphasis could lead to an understanding of ethics as an impersonal, impartial treatment of all others as equals in a way that would seriously neglect the fact of one's relationships being structured, with some relationships having greater moral weight than other relationships. An emphasis on equality in relationships might actually lead to injustice. It is clear, for example, that parents ought not be so committed to a Third World development agency and its fund-raising activities that they fail to meet the needs of their own children fairly or adequately. If one focuses idealistically on the global equality of all, it can be easy to love 'mankind' in a somewhat vague manner, while loving the particular person in need near to you is difficult (and so they may become neglected)! We have special obligations towards those who are closely related to us, particularly by natural family bonds. A fear of becoming too parochial or narrow may lead some to argue over this point, but it would surely be foolish to treat one's family as simply equal members of the human species, with no appreciation of the special and particular relationship you have with them. Even if a commitment to particular relationships (to one's religious group or one's nation, to mention two prime examples) has contributed to some injustices in history, and this may make some people wary of allowing them their place in human life,

an emphasis on the importance of particular human connections, and their value for human fulfilment, is not necessarily a denial of wider obligations in justice to others who are related to us more generally as fellow human beings.

Some relationships are givens
Following on from the points in the preceding paragraph, it is worth noting that not all relationships are chosen relationships. Therefore, neither are the consequent obligations in justice a matter of choice. This is an area of much heated debate in ethics, and this book takes a particular side in this debate, one shaped by a Natural Law approach illuminated by Divine Revelation (as explained in the preface). Not all justice can be understood as 'social contract'. There are some relationships that are 'givens' and that require respect and attention, even if we have not chosen them. Morality does not reduce to free choice or total autonomy. This is highly pertinent to the issue of abortion, for example, particularly in the most extreme cases, but applies to many types of relationships. The abortion issue is the prime example, however, of a justice issue where some argue that a 'relationship' does not exist between the woman and the foetus (even describing them in this way implies a lack of relationship) unless the woman chooses. Looking at justice under the heading of 'right relationship' is a good way of highlighting the fact that relationship is essential to human identity and living, and that we are never detached isolated units who choose our relationships, and our consequent obligations, in complete freedom. A correct understanding of right relationship, in all its richness, can serve as a necessary balance to an overemphasis on (detached, free-floating) freedom as the central principle in ethics.

Relationships need to be ordered rightly
Right relationship requires some ordering of our various relationships, so that we will be able to meet the requirements of each connection in an appropriate and balanced way. This is

surely one of the most challenging aspects of living justly: treating each relationship with the appropriate kind and degree of attention that it merits and needs, and that we can practicably give it, without neglecting the requirements of other relationships. How often have you heard the primary challenge of ethical living expressed as 'trying to strike the right balance'? The basic Christian approach to this issue is to stress our obligations to God as the primary relationship, and one that permeates and shapes all other relationships. Our relationships with family, friends, neighbours and others are structured in a widening 'spiral', with the outer relationships normally getting progressively less attention than those closer to the centre. In accepting this kind of structuring of relationships, one wants to guard against being too insular, while appreciating that one simply cannot give all relationships equal attention without denying the specific quality of the closer relationships and the ethical requirements that flow from this.

Cross-reference
Cross-reference for Justice as Right Relationship could be made usefully to section C of the Senior RE Curriculum – *Moral Decision Making* – parts 2.2 (dealing with morality and the Christian tradition, with particular emphasis on Jesus' preaching and right relationship) and 3.2. (dealing with various moral theories including morality as right relationship).

(ii) Justice: Retribution

Though 'justice as retribution' may be read as a narrow focus on justice as punishment for crime, it has a broader meaning. First, this broader meaning will be examined and then a specific application to punishment for crime. One important point to be made clear from the start is that retribution is not the same as revenge or vengeance. Nor is it a concept that is outdated or inappropriate for our times.

The classic definition of justice

The classic definition comes from the mainstream Western tradition on justice, a tradition going back to Plato and even beyond. It defined justice as 'giving to each man what is his due'[1] (i.e. 'giving to each human person what is his or her due' – the tradition did not confine justice to males). It is a precise definition, but is open to many questions. What is this 'due'? How does anything become due to a person? What does this definition mean in concrete terms? Is it a reality for individuals only or is there a communal dimension? The other four perspectives on justice in part 2.1 help to answer such questions.

Justice and Love again

The very term 'retribution' echoes the classic Latin definition of justice: *ius suum cuique tribuere*[2] ('giving to each what is his due'). To render justice is to give to another what is due to him (or her). The word 'due' is important. It specifies a particular type of giving: a giving *back*. Justice is not about giving to another out of charity or love, as such. That type of giving is extremely valuable, of course, in fact, the highest moral principle. As we saw in the section above on right relationship, justice is distinct from love, though both are linked. Justice involves giving to another what he or she *already* owns or is owed.[3] In a sense, justice is merely restoring the original situation of equality between people, rather than giving to others out of our own generosity what we freely choose to give because we love them. Another way of putting this, is to say that justice specifies a minimal level of giving that pays back what we owe to others (and calls for others to pay back what they owe us), whereas love calls for going beyond this minimum to give more than we strictly have to out of generosity inspired by our unity with others.

Life and debt

Every time we do something, we 'disturb' the equilibrium of society. We become either a debtor or creditor, someone who is owed or who owes. Not only with regard to money matters (though we all know how much debt is built into our lives in this regard), but in every aspect of life, we are connected by relationships of debt to others. Again, note how a concept of the human person as disconnected (as atomistic unit) is inadequate. In reality, we are never disconnected. This perspective on justice focuses on this inevitable connectedness in terms of debt. A great deal of human life and human activity can be understood as the continual attempt to pay our debts (and/or demand payment of others) to restore the equality that characterises us as human beings. (This perspective on justice is therefore clearly connected to the fourth perspective in part 2.1, the promotion of equality.)

The eschatological aspect

The work of justice is never-ending in this earthly life as the natural equilibrium is never re-established completely or finally. This aspect of the unfinished nature of justice leads nicely to an appreciation of the religious perspective, in which a more-than-secular dimension of justice is given attention. An emphasis on a purely earthly justice can lead to evils, such as an acceptance of immoral means to achieve justice when moral means seem inefficient or weak. Violent revolutions have been inspired by the idea that complete justice must be achieved here and now, no matter what it takes. Ironically, the result has often been the death of many innocent people in the name of 'justice' or 'peace'. A religious perspective can support a clear acknowledgment of moral absolutes that prevent the cause of justice becoming an excuse to do evil to achieve good. Also, a religious perspective helps to remind us that complete justice is God's alone, not man's, and that there is a very important place for mercy as a quality that broadens justice and makes it more appropriate for fallen, sinful man.

Justice fulfils the one who pays back what is owed
St Thomas Aquinas, the hugely influential thirteenth century philosopher-theologian, says a very surprising thing about justice in the light of its retributive aspect. He claims that one who acts justly in giving to another what is his due is not doing the other good as such, but is merely refraining from doing him harm! The person who acts justly is actually doing himself good, by honouring his own humanity, which he shares equally with the other to whom he has given back what he owes, by acting virtuously as a good human being. Acting justly perfects us as human persons, fulfils us as moral agents and members of society, while protecting others from harm.[4]

This can be applied to the issue of helping the people of the developing world with regard to world hunger, for example. If our helping is 'justice' rather than 'charity' then it is so because the help we give is actually a 'giving back' – a retribution. In other words, our aid is actually owed to the needy people in question and is not a gift as such. How can this be? Surely we own our 'own' wealth! The issue of property and ownership is an interesting and challenging aspect of justice and peace. It deserves much thought and study.

Private property – three views
Broadly speaking, there are three approaches to private property:
(a) Private property is an absolute right
(b) Private property is not a right, and is unjust
(c) Private property is a qualified right with social obligations attached.

(a) The first approach makes private property an absolute right. This would mean that, as long as you have not gained your wealth by fraud or theft or some other unjust method, you own all your wealth and owe nothing strictly to anyone else (unless you enter into a contract or exchange). You can choose to give some money to help the developing world (or some needy people closer to home perhaps) but you are not obliged in justice to do so. It would be purely charity. This first approach is associated with liberal capitalism, and libertarianism in particular.

Its weakness is not hard to see: it is very individualistic and lacks a social conscience, especially in its extreme forms. As people are sinful and will be tempted to keep their wealth for themselves, it is naïve to expect charity alone to be sufficient to eradicate poverty and suffering. Another point to mention is that 'privately' gained wealth is something of an illusion: in fact, one gains wealth only as part of a society, its culture and history. There is no such thing as a totally independent individual. Each of us has gained from the community in many ways and so we owe it back. The honest acknowledgement of debt is at the heart of *retributive* justice.

(b) A second approach to property is one that rejects private property altogether and sees all wealth as common property. This approach is associated with socialism, and particularly its most extreme form, communism. It is difficult to see how a total 'social ownership' model can allow for retributive justice for individuals, because if no-one can own anything, no one can be owed anything – as an individual. Society can be owed, and so all 'private property' may be taken from individuals and given back to society. This would mean that the community would take all property and own it, distributing its use to individuals and groups according to criteria of justice. Such criteria might include need, contribution, and/or merit.

There are several criticisms of this approach. One major ethical criticism of this socialist position, especially in its more extreme forms, is that it immorally takes away justly gained wealth from people who have personally earned it. Another criticism, a more pragmatic one though it has ethical roots, is that socialism grants the state too much power and the state is not in a good position to distribute all the wealth wisely, so it would be an ineffective and inefficient system. It would produce serious disincentives to work and thus inhibit invention and wealth creation, and so all would suffer in the long run. Evil can flourish in any political system, but it could be argued that one that grants the state so much power will suffer from political corruption. Those who have the 'right' political status, or who unquestioningly support the status quo, may be rewarded above others, so that in fact there is not an equal distribution of wealth as ideally demanded by the socialist ideal.

(c) A third approach to property, based on insight into the social nature of the human person, is that one does not absolutely own anything, but one may own things in a qualified way. Owning private property can be moral as long as one's social obligations are met. Wealth is not evil or unjust in itself. The wealth of the world is created by God (or nature, in the secular version of this approach) and is meant for everyone. The wealth that one owns is rightly owned (but only if it is justly gained, which is not always the case) and should be used for one's own proper interests and those of one's family or dependents. What is 'surplus', however, is not one's own to dispose of totally as one pleases. If there are people in need, then one is obliged *in justice* to give them help out of one's surplus wealth. This surplus 'belongs' to them. This is the approach of the Christian tradition,[5] supported by faith and reason. Think of it like this: no wealth should be left idle or it becomes immoral waste. As all individuals are inescapably social, wealth should be used well, invested in projects and goods that will benefit the common good and not just the private good of rich individuals. Such an approach to wealth is just and healthy for all: everyone benefits from wealth creation and distribution that is fair and generous. No-one truly benefits from wealth hoarding or greedy indulgence, not even the one who hoards or indulges. This point is true even when looking at this earthly life only; it is fully appreciated, however, in the perspective of our eternal destiny, according to the Christian tradition.

In reality, we often find some mixture of the approaches one and two, of Right and Left, in the light of the insights mentioned in approach three. This is the situation in Ireland, where a centrist political approach is usually taken to social policy. Other nations of the world exhibit a variety of political approaches. Varying weights are given to the individual freedom/social equality balance, depending on context, political circumstances, social judgements, and so on. The two most interesting and difficult questions to be answered are how to work out what one's surplus wealth is and how each individual or group is to judge what a morally good choice of investment is. The answers to these questions will involve not only ethics and religious faith, but an understanding of economics and politics. The virtue of prudence shaped by experience and wisdom will be necessary to correctly evaluate, and continually reassess, the individual situations that arise in real life. (This echoes the first part of the section and its focus on social analysis.) The virtue of justice then makes the will ready to act on the prudent judgement of the intellect, giving to each what is due.

A specific application – crime and punishment
There is a more specific focus for justice as 'retribution'. This is the area of punishment for crime, which is what is often understood by the term 'retributive justice'. One focuses here on the idea of 'balancing' wrongs committed with punishments for these wrongs. If someone does an injustice, justice requires that the balance be put right. The famous phrase from the Bible, 'An eye for an eye, a tooth for a tooth,' (Ex 21:24) will often crop up in discussions of crime and punishment. This phrase expresses the retributive aspect of justice, though

somewhat harshly. Originally this kind of justice was probably an improvement on a more primitive type of 'justice' in which one murder was avenged by the killing of the original murderer's family or tribal group. Nevertheless, one must be very careful in an uncritical use of the well-known Bible phrase. The weakness of this understanding of justice is indicated by Christ's 'revision' of the Law of Moses in the Sermon on the Mount where he exhorts his followers to be people of peace (see Mt 5:38-48). This lets us know that, at least sometimes, it is right to be merciful and to forgo the *strict* requirements of justice, when there is a need to break the cycle of violence and patiently work for reconciliation.

What is punishment?
The retribution aspect of punishment is worth thinking about further, however, as it clarifies the nature of what we actually mean by 'punishment'. This is a delicate subject to talk about with a RE class, for several reasons, but worth doing nonetheless, especially as it is close to the experience of students in various ways, such as their experience of school discipline and sports discipline. More widely, it is a constant topic in the national and international news.

Many today see punishment of criminals mainly as a deterrent. The main point of imprisonment, for example, is often seen as the prevention of future crimes by the prisoner or other criminals. This understanding of the purpose of punishment is mistaken; it is not in fact punishment as such if it is purely for deterrence. Also, such 'punishment' is actually quite *un*just! Punishing a criminal (or a student, for that matter) purely to deter others is not justice. Or, at least, it is not by itself justice: another rationale is needed to make it punishment and to make it justice.

The rationale is this: The punishment must be merited. In other words, the punishment must be 'due' to the criminal for it to be (retributive) justice. The deterrent effect may be welcomed as a side-effect, but it can never be the main reason for punishment or else it will not be punishment. It is never morally right to punish an innocent person to achieve even a great good (such as reducing further serious crime). This is one reason why it is so important to make sure that accused persons are truly guilty before punishing them. This is why we have a justice system that can seem at times to favour the criminal, where criminals' guilt appears too difficult to prove beyond doubt, where there exist technical loopholes, and so the common assumption of many is that criminals often get away with their crimes. Though this may be sometimes true, it is the price we pay to have a truly just justice system. Even though there will always be room to improve our justice system to avoid criminals getting away with their crimes, it is safe to say that there will always be *some* room for them to 'get off', because society must guard above all against condemning the innocent. There can be no greater injustice than punishing an innocent person. (The death of Christ because of humanity's sins is the greatest symbol of this for Christians.)

Punishment as retribution
The true idea behind imprisonment as retributive justice is that the criminal has upset the balance of society by his crime, taking what is not his, failing to accept the rules that others live by, refusing to accept the limitations required by justice for healthy social existence. This upset balance needs to be set right. It is not acceptable to let things stay as they are; the wrong must be righted, at least in some way. This will involve the criminal being forced to give up something good of his own, to suffer some disadvantage that will make up for his previous taking unfair advantage (i.e. his crime). In the case of robbery, for example, mere restoration of the stolen goods will not do: these do not belong to the criminal and so he cannot give them to anyone, he can only give them back to their rightful owner. (Of course, in the case of murder, the life taken

can never be given back.) So justice demands that the criminal must be made to give up something, and in most cases it is his freedom or his money, through imprisonment or a fine/confiscation.

Capital punishment
The related issue of capital punishment (or 'the death penalty' – each term has its own connotations) is too complex to allow a complete treatment here. Only a few points can be made. There are a number of possible attitudes towards this topic, mainly the following:
- Against it in principle and in practice
- In favour of it in principle and in practice
- In favour of it in principle but not always in practice
- Not rejecting it in principle but mainly rejecting it in practice

(The final two attitudes are similar, but not the exact same: the last one is more negative towards capital punishment. It describes best the current position of the Catholic Church, though this is a position that may be developing towards the first position, that of total rejection of capital punishment.)

Some people are totally against the death penalty. There are various reasons for this but the main one is that human life is sacred, but capital punishment by definition involves deliberate killing of a human being and so must be wrong. Others, on the contrary, are very much in favour of capital punishment for serious crimes as an act of strict justice and a necessary defence of society and its laws. The position of the Catholic Church magisterium on the death penalty is neither of these, neither completely against nor completely for, though it could be said that it is veering more and more towards a rejection of the death penalty. As it is somewhat nuanced, it is worth looking a little more closely at the Church's teaching in this regard.

It can be argued that retributive justice does not strictly demand the death penalty in all serious cases if another appropriate punishment is available (such as life imprisonment). The current position of the Catholic Church is that the death penalty may be allowed for in principle as a punishment by the public authority, but in practice it is better to use 'nonlethal means'. The Church's position is neatly summarised in the *Catechism of the Catholic Church* in the paragraphs 2266 and 2267.[6] The Church does not accept the position that the death penalty is strictly necessary to punish serious crimes. It is strongly against the use of capital punishment in modern circumstances, while not insisting that it is obligatory to end its use everywhere. This is the position that Pope John Paul II has often expressed and one supported by many other bishops, clergy and lay people.

Why does the Church favour nonlethal means? To use nonlethal means instead of capital punishment is seen

- as a sign of respect for life (and a criminal's life is still human life),
- as an act of mercy (which is a reflection of God's attitude towards sinful man),
- as a way of calling for the conversion and repentance of criminals.

It is, in the words of the *Catechism*, 'more in conformity with the dignity of the human person' to punish a criminal with imprisonment rather than capital punishment.

Yet the Church is not totally against the death penalty in principle. Why not? Various kinds of argument can be put forward for the Church's position. When defence of society is seen as a primary aim of justice, then the following pragmatic argument in favour of the death penalty in principle could be suggested. In circumstances where imprisonment was not a practicable option (in a case of widespread anarchy, for example) or the continuing life of the imprisoned criminal was an extremely serious threat to social order and peace (as a symbol for some major terrorist organisation, for example), the use of the death penalty might be warranted morally to punish the criminal and protect society.[7] The death penalty is not to be rejected in principle because such extreme situations could occur and the death penalty could be needed. This is one reason why the Church does not reject capital punishment in principle.

The Church's position is neither a simple acceptance or approval of capital punishment nor a simple rejection of it. There is a certain tension in the Church's position, which has led some to hope and expect that its position is developing into a complete rejection, while others assume that this rejection has already occurred. Many cannot see how this teaching on the death penalty is coherent with teaching on other life issues. Being against abortion and for the death penalty is often seen as inconsistent. The Church, however, does not teach that killing criminals guilty of serious wrongdoing is wrong in principle, as abortion is. Capital punishment is the killing of criminals who are a deliberate threat to society, and it may be right in certain circumstances to remove that threat by capital punishment; whereas abortion is always the deliberate killing of innocent human life, which cannot be a deliberate threat to anyone, and so is always wrong in every circumstance. The Church clearly teaches that deliberate killing of the innocent is always a serious injustice, always gravely wrong.[8] Killing in defence may sometimes be morally right, though exactly why this is so is not clearly explained or taught definitively by the magisterium. This is an area of theological and philosophical reflection and debate. It has been proposed by some that those who attack society thereby forfeit their right to life; this could be used as an argument in favour of capital punishment in principle (though its acceptance or approval in practise is not decided by this argument).

An additional argument for the death penalty in principle, an argument based on religious faith, is that God has given the state the authority to take life as a punishment and as a defence of society, though only if strict conditions are met (such as clearly proven guilt and proper procedures of justice that guard against feelings of anger and revenge). This is the traditional argument in favour of the Church's position, one based on Biblical passages such as Genesis 9:6 and Romans 13: 1-4 and the tradition of the Church down through the ages. This faith-based argument, combined with the more pragmatic argument outlined above (concerning society's defence against the criminal), provides a basis for the Church's present position: not rejecting capital punishment in every possible circumstance, as it is not an absolutely wrong act, an intrinsically evil act, in contrast to abortions and all deliberate killing of innocent human life, which are intrinsically wrong.

It should be noted that the Church's teaching on the death penalty has been criticised by Catholic theologians, including some who are strongly faithful towards the Church's magisterium (teaching authority). Their argument is that the teaching is not infallible and is open to change based on biblical, theological and philosophical arguments. One basic philosophical argument is that killing in capital punishment is never a side-effect of justice or of defence, as it can be in a just war (which will be examined below in 2.4), but always a deliberate choice to destroy a human life, which is wrong in principle as well as in practice. The death penalty at its best is an evil means to a good end, according to this view, and so should be completely and always rejected.[9]

Other theologians accept the Church's teaching that the death penalty may be morally acceptable in certain circumstances, and the traditional religious argument for this, while firmly rejecting the death penalty in modern circumstances. Even if one accepts the traditional argument that God has given the state authority in principle to punish the guilty, even by death, it could be argued that there has been a radical change in how people view the state and its authority to punish. As modern society has lost its sense of the state's authority to govern and punish as coming from God, and sees it instead as merely a function of the people's democratic wishes, then the nature of capital punishment has changed accordingly. The infliction of the death penalty has become a kind of social anger or vengeance, rather than objective and transcendent justice. Thus, although capital punishment may have been acceptable, and even appropriate, in the past when people believed in a transcendent order of justice and the state's God-given right and responsibility to punish criminals, this is not so now when people no longer hold these views. Now, capital punishment is more likely to be seen as the people venting their anger and disgust through the instruments of the state justice system, rather than the state imposing objective justice to protect society by punishing the criminal and eliminating any threat. Capital punishment is the kind of punishment that, especially in modern conditions, can too easily appeal to our baser instincts and emotions and so become brute revenge rather than just retribution.[10]

The death penalty in practice has its own particular weaknesses as a method of punishment. One of the most obvious weaknesses is that execution of criminals is irreversible and so errors cannot be rectified and those wronged cannot be compensated in any way (and we know that there are miscarriages of justice in any justice system). Secondly, its methods are brutal and brutalising, which makes it always a difficult punishment to impose without in some way hardening oneself and society against the sanctity of human life. It 'offends' against the virtue that softens the harshness of strict justice, namely the virtue of mercy. Finally, it is a punishment that is seen to be imposed disproportionately on the poor and marginalised in society, and is thus an offence against the promotion of equality. It is not surprising that the Catholic Church is now taking an increasingly negative view of its appropriateness or necessity.

Retribution is not revenge
The distinction between revenge and retributive justice is important to clarify. Revenge is motivated by anger or bitterness; it is personal; it aims to harm another and to take pleasure in the infliction of harm. Justice as retribution, on the other hand, is motivated by a desire to set the balance of society right; it is impersonal; and it does not involve enjoyment of punishment in itself. This explains why our justice systems do not allow the victims to judge the criminal or to impose the sentence. This is why there is a time delay and why the system of justice is impersonal. (Of course, not all time delay is justifiable; nor is the impersonal nature of the justice system a good thing. Reform of the system is clearly necessary.) This is why justice must be 'imposed' by public officials not private individuals, as it is not normally the responsibility of private individuals to act on behalf of society in the enforcement of justice in relation to crime.

(iii) Justice: Fair Play

Play and fairness
Fair play is the most simple and direct understanding of justice, one that teachers and students will have no difficulty grasping. The phrase itself, fair *play*, suggests an exploration of this perspective using the student-friendly topic of sport. All realise what it is to suffer unfair treatment in many areas of life, but this is brought into focus easily by imagining playing a game. If the players are not willing to play fairly, this makes playing the game impossible. The rules, which should be known by all, set out what is required, at least in terms of what one is not allowed to do. Usually, there must also be an impartial and expert referee to interpret the application of the rules and to enforce obedience to them.

All this mirrors other situations of justice in other spheres of social life. Justice as 'fair play' is necessary for there to be any social 'game' at all. To interact socially in a healthy and fulfilling way, we need moral principles to guide and to unite us and to enable us to adjudicate between the conflicts that will inevitably occur.

A teaching example
Take teaching a class, for example. Unless there are agreed and known 'rules of play', then the 'game' of education cannot take place. One way to explain to a class that the rules of class are reasonable is to invite the students to place themselves imaginatively in the position of the teacher (or of another student, one who wants to learn). This is an example of getting students to understand justice as 'fair play'. Central to this is helping the students to see the situation impartially, to step out of their own biased perspectives and to see the situation from the perspective of the teacher or other students. Another aspect of the process is to get the students to see the purpose of class teaching and to note how certain kinds of behaviour contradict the purpose of education. As well as trying to get the students to see that they will benefit from an improvement in behaviour, one is also trying to get them to see the basic equality of all involved in the interaction. It is an attempt to get them to empathise, to realise that others have feelings and needs. More than this, one is trying to open their eyes to the fact that just as they have human feelings and needs, others have too, and all are equals. Others are bound by the rules too. The teacher is bound by rules as well, as all teachers are. The rules shape how one is to act within the particular 'game', in this case the education game. Without the rules, there would be no game and we would all be losers.

Further extension of the sport metaphor
Knowing the rules is not enough: they must be interpreted impartially and all must be willing to follow them. Parallel to the referee in sport, society needs judges and a justice system to

interpret the laws and to enforce them by imposing sanctions on those who break the rules. The sanctions help to create a kind of willingness, but it is not a particularly good thing to rely totally on the enforcement of the law and its sanctions to create justice, just as it is not good for a game for the referee to be needed at every second and for sanctions to be imposed frequently. There should be an internal acceptance of the rules by the players, and so there should be an internalisation of justice as fair play.

This points to an important aspect of justice, one highlighted by St Thomas Aquinas many centuries ago. Justice *as a virtue* involves a constant willingness to give others what is their due. Justice is not primarily a matter of the intellect, therefore, though it does have an intellectual aspect. Justice is primarily a moral virtue that shapes the will. In an important sense, justice is a habit learned by doing, rather than by studying or thinking. The habitual procedures and types of behaviour in a school and in a classroom will teach students a lot about 'justice'. Another virtue, prudence, is also important in carrying out just acts. Prudence is concerned with judging how to apply principles to actual situations. It relies heavily on knowledge gained by experience and maturity. It guides all the virtues. Justice education ought to concern itself with both the challenge of developing and understanding the 'willingness' aspect of justice (the moral dimension) and the 'judging' aspect (the intellectual dimension).

Impartiality is central

Impartiality is a central aspect of fairness. As noted, the referee must be impartial and be seen to be so, otherwise he will not be respected as a referee. The players must be treated as equals, in other words, and the rule of law must apply equally to them all. If the referee is partial to a player or to a side then there cannot be justice. This again is exactly how it is in the wider context. Justice demands in fairness that like be treated as like (and that different be treated as different). What makes any discrimination unjust is precisely the fact that it treats people who are alike or equal (in relevant respects) as unlike or unequal.

'Respect of persons', in the traditional phrase, is the great enemy of justice. In other words, to treat a person with partiality, when you should be treating him (and others) with impartiality, is a failure to be just or fair. The typical example of this is when someone is given a job purely because of his connections to those in positions of authority.

The Golden Rule

The most well-known rule for fair play is the 'Golden Rule' preached by Christ in the Sermon on the Mount (Matthew 7:12): 'In everything do to others as you would have them do to you; for this is the law and the prophets.' The Rule, known in many cultures, is based on equality (and so belongs with the next justice perspective too). You are enjoined to treat the other person as you treat yourself: this implies that the two of you are equal. You share an equal humanity and personality. This is why you should imagine what it feels like to be treated in a particular way, before you choose to act towards another human person in that way. The Golden Rule also implies the negative precept: do not treat others as you would not like to be treated. In some ways the negative formulation is a tighter moral principle, one never to be broken, whereas the positive formulation is looser, needing to be tailored to suit particular circumstances. One may never chose to do evil; one may choose sometimes not to do a non-obligatory good.

The Golden Rule is a powerful guide to what is truly just in any particular situation. It could have a profound effect on politicians, business people, government ministers, parents, traders, media people, and, indeed, all people in society. It can serve to overcome the selfishness that blinds and distracts each of us from the needs of the other person. Much immorality is lack of consideration of others, lack of empathy – in fact, a lack of moral imagination – rather than willing 'pure' evil as such. (This would be a good place to focus with students on the development of moral imagination. Role play or simulation games would be suitable strategies here.) It is not always difficult to determine what is 'fair', what is just. If you can put yourself into the position of other individuals, you can see how you should treat them. This suggests emphasising the development of imaginative empathy, rather than a narrowly cerebral approach to justice.[11]

The Golden Rule is not the whole of morality
Nevertheless, the Golden Rule is not sufficient in itself. First, one must want what is good for oneself. This might seem to be a trivial point – don't all people naturally want what is good for themselves? They do, but the full ethical value of the Golden Rule presupposes that one will desire the *true* good for oneself. It is important that one knows what is good for the self so that what one wants for others, following the Golden Rule, will be truly good for them too. Otherwise one may wish what is bad both for oneself and others and think all is fine because one is honest and consistent. A person may, for example, be willing to be manipulated by others as long as the manipulation is mutual and overt. The honest, no-strings-attached sexual relationship is the obvious example here, where people enter into a kind of mutual promiscuity in the understanding that all is fair and honest as long as no-one expects anything permanent from the relationship (and no-one gets pregnant or catches a deadly disease). Another example would be a reckless driver who enjoys taking serious risks and cannot see why others are not so 'brave' (and so drives in a dangerous manner). Another example would be a criminal who thinks little of himself and expects nothing from life and who commits crimes fully accepting that others have the right to do the same to him if they are able. It is not enough to be consistent; one needs to be honestly

searching and finding the true good for self and others. A commitment to the good is prior to justice as impartiality, justice as fairness. Justice as fair play fits into a wider context: morality as 'meeting the requirements for the search for human happiness or fulfilment'.

John Rawls

One of the most important, though intellectually demanding, examples of a secular, philosophical approach to justice as fairness is that of the twentieth century American philosopher John Rawls, who developed a system of justice centred on fairness.

To begin, Rawls imagines an 'original position' of total impartiality – all citizens begin behind 'a veil of ignorance' that prevents them from knowing what position in society they will have, what wealth they will have, even what ideas or beliefs they will have. All they know is that they will be members of a society where there will be relative scarcity of resources and so conflicts of interests. They must also have some minimal knowledge of social organisation, psychology, and economic theory. The question then is: what principles of institutional/social organisation would such impartial persons choose?

Rawls argues they would choose three principles, which would therefore be principles of justice as fairness. The first principle would be 'The Principle of Greatest Equal Liberty': everyone would rationally choose to have a system where the maximum freedoms were available to all. One's individual liberty would be subject only to allowing others their own maximum liberty.

The second principle is 'The Principle of Fair Equality of Opportunity', which would allow one to use one's freedom to work to better one's situation and maintain one's happiness.

The third principle is 'The Difference Principle'. This says that social inequalities are to be arranged in such a way that the least well-off in society benefit most. In other words, Rawls' system allows inequalities of wealth and power and status to exist, but only if they are to the benefit of the vulnerable and weak most of all. These inequalities could be to the benefit of others if such inequalities facilitated the creation of inventions, of technology, of jobs, of opportunities for all to avail of.

These principles are types of categorical imperatives, moral directives that one can happily choose to be universal, because they are chosen, or contracted, from a position of complete impartiality, in which all particular differences in real society are stripped away, and a kind of pure rationality is left to decide how social life is to be politically organised. In other words, they appear to be completely fair.

Strong points in Rawls' approach

Rawls' approach has much to recommend it, at least at first glance. Thinking similar to it is found in many liberal democracies, including Ireland, even if Rawls' name is not alluded to. It emphasises fairness and allows us to imagine it by means of the device of the hypothetical 'original position'. He also allows the least well-off a major place in the scheme – they are not to be disadvantaged, but rather privileged to a degree. This focus on the poor might seem highly compatible with the Christian vision of concern for the poor as central to justice. Rawls is arguably far better in this respect than is the utilitarian approach to justice, an approach that would allow the good of the few to be sacrificed for the 'greater good' of the many.[12] A utilitarian 'justice' might allow the sufferings of the least well-off, even though very bad and capable of practical improvement, to be accepted as the cost of a system that has a greater benefit for the majority. One could argue, for example, that a totally free capitalist system will lead to terrible poverty and suffering for some but that this is acceptable because the overall average income or overall economic progress is improving (or at least sufficient for the majority). Rawls rightly does not accept this way of looking at things and emphasises that the poor cannot be neglected if one is to be fair, and that they should be given a greater chance to have rights and benefits, subject to the Principle of Greatest Equal Liberty (which is the most important element in Rawls' system).

Some criticisms of Rawls
Rawls has been heavily criticised. His view of the human person is highly individualistic. In order to achieve complete impartiality, the individuals in the original position are shorn of all particular beliefs and relationships, yet it is these that constitute our identities. This is to miss the essentially social nature of the person and to neglect the particular relationships that shape the requirements of justice. (This is a point emphasised in the treatment of Right Relationship above.)

It could be that individuals in the original position would choose to take risks, hoping for a high position in society, rather than organise things to maximise the standard of living for the people at the bottom. Rawls assumes people will opt for safety over the chance to be wealthy. His system does not fully respect human nature.

Rawls does not really offer a reason for specifically wanting to help the poor, other than a kind of rational self-interest (in other words, you yourself might be poor, so it's better to arrange things to avoid this risk). This is not a sufficient foundation for justice, although there is a strong hint of the Golden Rule in it.

Also, most importantly, he focuses too much on liberty and neglects other aspects of morality and goodness. As noted above, the Golden Rule requires a prior commitment to the true good for oneself, so that one can wish true good for others. Rawls' system deliberately rejects any comprehensive understanding of the good life. He sees such comprehensive understandings as divisive and inescapably controversial in a pluralist liberal democracy. This creates a rather abstract, detached self who chooses the principles of justice, a self who does not hold any moral or religious beliefs as true. Their truth is not the issue; freedom is. This emphasis on freedom is questionable because it can lead to an approach to morality that sees freedom as the absolute principle, or even the only principle, such that all that matters regarding any moral position is that the person or group holds it freely. There is a serious neglect of the substantive issues concerning what is truly good for human beings and society, what it is that our freedom ought to be used to achieve. Justice, in other words, cannot be reduced to a bare, contentless liberty. What is due to persons is more substantial and complex than that.

We need to know why we are playing the game if we are to understand and willingly accept the rules as 'fair play'. Religious faith is a major guide in this regard, and it is no wonder that religion is often seen as a great support for morality and social peace and order.

(iv) Justice: The Promotion of Equality

The logic of justice

This perspective on justice is closely linked to the previous one. Why should we even *try* to put ourselves in the other's position, to see things fairly from his perspective, to work out what is due to him? The answer is that we are all equally human beings, each of us a person in our own right. This insight grounds understanding justice as 'the promotion of equality'. When we appreciate that the basic reason we have to respect our own personal needs and worth applies to every other person too, then we have come to understand the 'logic' of justice. Thus, when we fail to see the equal humanity of the other person, and act towards him as if he were basically inferior to us or our group (or perhaps even, in the most extreme cases, less than human), we act unjustly. Such failure lies behind much of the terrible injustices of the world. This is especially true of modern 'total war', in which the humanity of the enemy is ignored or denied and complete eradication is attempted, with the most horrible results.

Equality is not as simple as it seems.
Even though equality is clearly the basic principle of justice, and a matter that is not usually difficult to grasp or accept in general terms at least, it is not as simple as it first seems. Exploring its complexities can lead to an appreciation of the richness of the concept and reality of justice and an avoidance of naïve and simplistic notions of justice.

Equality versus freedom
One of the most persistent difficulties with equality as an essential aspect or grounding of justice is that it seems to conflict inevitably with freedom, another essential aspect of morality. We saw above that Rawls' system of justice allows for some social inequalities but aims to arrange them in such a way that the least well-off benefit ('The Difference Principle'). Why would anyone accept such a system of justice that includes inequalities?

An extended metaphor – dividing the pie
A possible answer can be explored by making use of an imaginary and somewhat simplified situation containing a pie and four persons (N, S, E and W). If they are all 'equal', this suggests they all are due a quarter of the pie. Such a division would be equal and so just. This is how many of us think of the problem of wealth and poverty at the local, national and international levels. We think of a set amount of national or world wealth, a set amount of people, and the undeniable fact of the unjust, unequal division of the wealth, where most get a little and the top few per cent get a lot. The number of people is commonly understood to be increasing and so the division is increasingly a problem, as it is commonly assumed that there is less and less to go to each individual.

Some problems with equality

There are problems with the original situation (mine, in this case, not Rawls'). Why should the equality of the four (N, S, E and W) entail that they each get a quarter of the pie? What if N made/bought the pie and so owns it?[13] Does he have to give away three quarters of it? Perhaps he does, we might reply, if S, E and W are in dire need and will starve if they do not get something to eat. A further question arises: Why don't they make their own pies? If they expect to be given a share of N's pie, or if they think they have a moral claim on an equal share of the pie, they might be tempted to do very little, or even nothing, themselves. The insistence on equality might create a strong disincentive for them to work and to better their situations.

Zero-sum thinking

Also, notice the assumption here of a limited, set amount of wealth – is it actually the case in reality that the amount of wealth to be distributed amongst a group of people is always set and unalterable? To assume so is called 'zero-sum' thinking and it is a common error in evaluating economic issues. It involves the assumption that there is a defined amount in the process or situation and that all exchanges or events will lead to the same amount at the end – all gains and losses add up to zero. 'If I lack something, it must be because you have it' sounds a bit daft. But that form of zero-sum thinking is similar to the more common idea, sometimes found in development education: 'They are poor [i.e. the third world] because we are rich [i.e. the West].' The idea here is that there is a set amount of wealth in the world and if we in the West have it, that is the cause of others not having it. Our riches are stolen from the poor. Thinking about world issues in the simple terms of our pie example is bound to lead to such inadequate assumptions and conclusions.[14] This is not to deny that the behaviour of those in the West has no effect on the well-being of those in the poorer parts of the world, nor that stealing has sometimes occurred (the slave trade is one infamous example).

Wealth creation versus wealth distribution
At present in our example there is only one pie. If N is bound in justice and law to share the pie, then the others may settle for doing nothing; if he does not share it, then even if only one or two of the others make their own pies, the net wealth will have risen. We now have a situation with, say, three pies, rather than only one, and it has happened because there was no sharing out of the original pie! (Or, at least, there was no assumption of, or carrying out of, a distribution according to only a strict equality principle.)[15] If the three now decide to share a quarter of their pies with the remaining pie-less member of the example (in this instance, S), then the overall situation is much better than the original sharing of one pie. The original situation left each with a quarter and the total wealth was only one pie; the situation now is that each has three quarters and the total wealth is three pies. Surely this situation is the one we would choose.

Dealing fairly with extreme vulnerability and need
However, what if the N, W, and E did not decide to share a quarter of their pies with S and subsequently S starved? Is this an injustice? One could reply that it depends on why S did not make his own pie. If it was because he was too lazy or too concerned with other seemingly more pleasant matters or because he is always fighting with E, then we might be distressed to see him starve, but describe it as a misfortune or a tragedy of his own making rather than an injustice. (Hopefully, even in this case, we would still support extending the hand of charity to help S.) If, on the other hand, S's lack of food was due to his bad luck or ill-health or, even more pertinently, E always picking on him or W's bad advice – then we might say that his lack of food was truly an injustice and that he deserves to be given a share in the others' pies.

Alternatively, we might decide that the mere fact of S starving is all we need to know about and that it alone renders his situation unjust, and none of the issues raised above should be worried about at all. The equality of N, S, E and W, in this perspective would mean that none of them ever 'deserves' to starve, no matter what his behaviour or situation, and that some wealth must therefore be distributed to him, at least insofar as it is necessary to prevent S (or any other person) falling below the level of basic well-being. This final alternative is the one most obviously in line with an understanding of justice as the promotion of equality and is a more humane response to serious hardship suffered by one's fellow man, one's related equal.

Applying the metaphor to real life
This extended example concerning the pie and N, S, E and W is not meant in any way to trivialise the issues it dramatises. The metaphor mirrors in a simple way many of the complex issues arising in the real world debates on justice and peace. It also serves to point out that simple reference to 'equality' may not solve all our problems. The metaphor is simplified (and imaginative extension of it in the classroom would be worth pursuing).

Problems of scale
In the real world we are faced with many more people than just the four in the example. The scale of numbers is one of the practical aspects that makes solutions to our justice problems so difficult, especially in regard to 'distributive justice' – justice concerned with the distribution of the wealth of the community amongst its members. It might seem obvious in a small-scale situation, such as a family or a classroom, that the wealth *should* be shared out equally; also, it might seem easy to work out *how* this is to be done. Neither is as obvious or easy in a large-scale economy.

Problems of incentives
One big issue is that of incentives. If we share out the wealth of the rich amongst everyone equally then we are reducing or eliminating one major incentive for all to work. In doing this, we may make the distribution more equal, but in the process make the overall wealth diminish. Thus, 'equality' can lead to trouble, perhaps even greater inequality in the long run. In Ireland, for example, we could demand that the tax rates be raised much higher to distribute the wealth of the rich to the poor. In one sense this is very Christian, respecting the 'Option for the Poor' that is central to much modern social teaching of the Church (and of Liberation Theology). It would also partially match liberalism's concern for the less well-off (following Rawls). The ideal of helping the poor is surely an appealing one when one realises they are equals. In spite of the attractive ideal, however, it can be argued that there are problems in reality with this vision. The net result of substantially raising taxes would not be good if it made Irish industry less competitive, foreign investment less attracted to Ireland, and working in their native land less appealing to the brightest and best of our youth. The ensuing fall in economic productivity, rise in unemployment and increase in emigration would lead to there being less wealth to distribute. And so the poor would be in a worse position than ever. Justice seems to demand more than mere equality. We want wealth, too, and productivity and progress, so that the equality will not be one of poverty.

Wealth takes varied forms
Another difference between the simple example and real life is that the example mentioned one form of wealth – a pie, or, more generally, food – whereas wealth comes in many forms and in different levels of scale. Think of the following things that form part of your 'wealth' – your health, your intelligence, your abilities, your good looks (admit it!), your education, your job, your family, your friends, your connections, your good

luck, your opportunities, your house and its location, your history, your previous success, your moral virtue, your faith. That's quite a long and diverse list; it is not comprehensive. Is it unjust if you have more of these overall than someone else? Is it unjust if you have even one of these more than someone else? Can we even measure how such diverse forms of wealth are 'distributed'? Is it to be expected that these forms of wealth should be distributed equally? Who would be the distributor? What would be the criteria for distribution?

The 'problem' of free will
Another important issue is that of free will. Suppose that we found a way to distribute the various forms of wealth mentioned above in an equal way. What would be required by justice *after* that, if any person should squander some of the wealth distributed? Should there be another distribution later to offset the effects of people using their free will to waste their wealth? Should there be regular distributions to do this into the future? Individual free choice is often neglected in discussions of justice, especially with regard to equality. This is very much the case when the perspective taken follows the social science approach. This approach tends to see things in terms of causes and effects rather than in terms of individuals' choices and the consequences of these choices. The analysis is often at the level of society or social structures rather than at the individual level. (This was already mentioned in the chapter on social analysis.) Putting it roughly for this particular perspective on justice: How can we ensure that all people are equal when they have the freedom to mess things up? Put another way: Does an emphasis on equality lead inevitably to coercion to prevent people using their free will to mess things up for themselves and/or others?

Types of equality
As has been demonstrated in this section so far, the perspective on justice as the promotion of equality is not as simple as it

might seem. There are several complexities in it. One way of coping with these complexities is to become more precise about 'equality'. We will examine four different concepts of equality:

(a) equality of condition (radical egalitarianism)
(b) equality of opportunity (liberal egalitarianism)
(c) basic equality (equality of needs)
(d) a combination of b and c.

(a) One type of 'equality' is the concept of *equality of condition*. This is the equality that many of the more radical thinkers on justice and peace have in mind. It looks for equality of results. So, to give a few examples, equality of condition would expect and demand that an equal proportion of males and females would be in government, that students in school would achieve equally good grades, that all citizens would be equally influential in running the country or locality, that all would have the same amount of monetary wealth, that all philosophies and ways of life would be seen as equally valid, and so on. If these situations did not occur, at least approximately, then radical egalitarians (as those who espouse this kind of position are often called) would see this as injustice. They would argue that because we are all equal, our situations should be roughly equal. All inequality is a result of injustice in this view. Social structures need to be radically changed to effect this equality. Until they are, social structures cannot and should not be seen as morally acceptable.

This is a very strong view. It lies behind some of the most idealistic writing on justice and peace issues. It might seem to be the normative Christian view, because it emphasises the equality of all people as Christianity does and it criticises the injustices that deny or contradict this equality. It has its problems, however, which some of the examples mentioned above hint at. Is it really unjust that people differ in their grades in exams? Is it wrong that there is a smaller proportion of females to males in government? Is it really true that all points of view and all lifestyles should be seen as equally valid? People can differ in their judgements on these issues, even while agreeing that justice is the ideal. Radical egalitarianism also leaves out of the picture the place of free will mentioned above. Even if we got to a situation where people had equal everything, how could we prevent inequalities from developing when individuals began to use their (originally) equal talents, for example, to achieve unequal degrees of effectiveness and success? Would it be just to level down people's achievements, so that none get ahead of others?

(b) A less radical approach to equality is found in the concept of *equality of opportunity*. This is an approach associated with Rawls, other supporters of liberalism and anyone who values giving all people an equal chance to compete for jobs, benefits, and so on. To return to the sporting metaphor of the previous section ('Fair Play'), we could see this approach as expecting and demanding that all are allowed to compete 'on a level playing field', a phrase often heard in justice-issue discussions. Once everyone is guaranteed an equal chance to succeed, then the fact that some might do better than others is not seen as an injustice, but as a piece of bad luck or just the way things are. The fact that some proportions might not turn out equally, such as the ratio of male to female in government, would be seen as the result of leaving it to individuals to freely choose what way they wish to develop their abilities and use their opportunities. The opportunities would have to be equal; the results or conditions not so.

Proponents of the previous view (equality of condition) argue that merely giving people 'equal' opportunity is not sufficient because they do not all start off equal. This means that some people will make better use of opportunities than others who start off at a disadvantage. Think about students in school. They are given equal teaching and equal exams, but some will do better than others because they have better home situations or better health or better prospects, and so on. Equality of opportunity will not get rid of the inequity in education, radical egalitarians argue, but will merely preserve the unjust status quo. The problem with this diagnosis, though it has some truth in it, is that the disparity in exam results is not fully explained in the terms the radicals use. Perhaps some bad results are the result of freely taken poor decisions of individual students or their ignoring the best efforts of others to help them. Maybe some students are naturally brighter than others and will always do better, unless something is done to depress their chances of success in order to raise the chances of those less able students. Also, it is not always clear *how* we are to radically eradicate inequalities. It is easy to write rhetorically about how imperative it is to create equal results or conditions, but it is not as easy to describe how this can realistically be done without massive coercion, and/or discrimination against some for the sake of others, or a miraculous transformation of human nature and society to make utopia possible.

(c) A more modest concept of 'equality', which might be called *basic equality*, suggests itself as the most realistic and ethically sound. It is focused on the basic needs of all and guarantees a bottom line below which no-one ought to be let fall. Justice demands that this basic level of equality is always to be guarded and maintained. There are basic goods essential to human well-being that all should have reasonable access to. There is a threshold below which no-one should be allowed to fall. This basic level would include things such as food, drink, shelter, education and other rights that we will look at in the next section.

(d) There is a fourth possibility. Combining (b) and (c) gives us a concept of equality that includes a basic guarantee of necessary goods for all with freedom of opportunity for all to improve their lot further. Thus basic equality combined with a guaranteed equality of opportunity for all would help to ensure that no-one is prevented from making use of their opportunities because of a lack of the basic goods or rights, while ensuring that no-one would be denied the chance to excel or move above the average by an ideological insistence on a levelling 'equality'. We should not expect or demand that there will always be an equal outcome in every case; nor should we look on every inequality as necessarily unjust or evil.

A hotly debated area
How one thinks about the issues around justice as equality will depend on one's views on such matters as how much is 'naturally given' and how free are our choices. This author's views are shaped by a belief that promoting freedom of opportunity while guaranteeing basic goods for all will be the most effective way to promote equality both in the long run and for most people. Radical egalitarian schemes to make all equal are too vague or unrealistic to be truly helpful. Human nature tends to make utopian plans either mere dreams or real nightmares (think of the communist revolutions that went so sour). We are all equal in basic human dignity and worth, and so the inequalities that exist in terms of wealth and success, though they are not always necessarily the result of injustice, always challenge the better off to help those worse off.[16]

(v) Justice: The Upholding of Human Rights

A popular approach
This is a common way today of expressing the obligatory nature of 'justice' and of specifying its requirements. Many teachers teach about justice (and peace) with a strong or dominant human rights emphasis. This will make this section appealing, but it may also mask a problem. Familiarity with

the area may prevent sufficient engagement with its complexities.

A common approach to teaching about human rights consists of looking at vivid examples of rights abuses, listing the various rights, explaining the meaning of them and insisting on their importance. This relies heavily on the Universal Declaration of Human Rights of the United Nations (1948).[17] This section of the chapter suggests some ideas on rights that might take the teaching a little further into the richness of the topic (as will combining it with the other four perspectives on justice and the religious perspectives in 2.3).

Definitions of rights
The keywords for understanding rights are:
- Entitlements
- Liberties
- Immunities
- Claims

The most useful definition to begin with is: A 'right' is *an entitlement*. It is 'something due' to a person. This is a direct link back to the classic definition of justice mentioned regarding retribution: justice is giving a person his due. Put another way: justice is giving a person his right or rights.

Other related ways of defining a right include seeing it as something one can rightly *claim* from others (for example, from the state), or a *liberty* or *immunity* that one is entitled to. These keywords (entitlement, due, claim, liberty, immunity) suggest a certain complexity in this area. Using one rather than another will depend on the context and the particular right in question. There can be controversy about whether a particular right is an immunity or liberty or an entitlement, as will be discussed below in relation to the debates around social and economic rights. Sometimes more than one term will be suitable for a right. For example, religious freedom is a liberty right, but is best understood as an immunity from state or other coercion in matters of religion. In some cases, to take another example, one's right to life can ground a claim made against an aggressor who wishes to attack your life – but one's right to life, one's entitlement to be allowed live, does not depend on one's being able or willing to make a claim (think of the position of the unborn foetus who cannot make any claim but who has a right to life that ought to be respected always).

Also, one should note that a right is not the exact same thing as a 'privilege' or an 'interest'. A right is something one has to be given whereas a privilege is more optional, something one might have to earn or merit. An interest refers to something one has a desire or preference for, but it does not necessarily mean that one is entitled to it in strict justice, which is what a 'right' suggests.

Not all rights are 'human rights'

Another distinction that must be made here is between 'human rights' and other rights such as 'civil' and 'legal' or 'special' rights. Human rights are the specific focus in this part of the syllabus. These refer to entitlements or liberties/immunities that are based purely on our being human. They are what used to be termed 'natural rights'. They are not created by the government or others; they are not conferred on us by any external authority. They are recognised, not created; inherent, not earned. When we speak of them as 'inalienable' we refer to another very important aspect of human rights: they belong to us essentially and cannot rightly be separated from us (that is, made 'alien' from us). There is a strong connection here with natural law thinking. Moreover, it is easy to see how this way of thinking can lead to thoughts of a creator God – how else can we offer any rationale for human rights that are 'inherent'? The other categories of rights (civil/legal) refer to rights that are specified by positive law, sometimes referred to as 'justiciable rights'. Some of the more specific legal rights may not be inherent at all, but are created by human authority and may depend for their justice entirely on the legal process that specifies them and the civil authority that judges and enforces them.

The UN Universal Declaration of Human Rights

Having looked briefly at the definition of 'human rights', it is time to look at some specific rights. The UN Universal Declaration of Human Rights is one primary resource in this respect. Mary Ann Glendon has written a very useful book on the process of drawing up and negotiating the Declaration, which analyses its articles in detail.[18] Behind the shaping of the Declaration lay a very interesting and complex process. It was both a product of its time and a document for all time. The Second World War had just finished and the UN established. There was a strong desire to assert the unity of humankind and the rule of law. It was clear that the laws of countries as discrete, sovereign units were not sufficient, Nazi Germany having used corrupt legal means to establish its totalitarian regime, and so the idea of a Bill of Rights for all humanity was formulated and a commission set up, with members from diverse states, to discuss and draft such a document. Eleanor Roosevelt was appointed chairwoman of the commission, which included members from several cultures. Although they were unable to agree on a foundation for human rights, they were able to agree on a general list of rights that were based on a thorough examination of the many examples of bills of rights, constitutions and other such sources from around the world and from several periods of history. After a number of drafts, a final 'Universal Declaration of Human Rights' was agreed and published. It was not a binding covenant – covenants came quite a bit later (published in 1966 and ratified in 1976). The Declaration was a document that outlined aspirations and aims; it was a call on the world's conscience, rather than a legal document that could be used to call governments and international bodies to strict account. Maybe this is why so many countries could sign it, countries as diverse as the US, the USSR, the UK, France, China, and so on. (The USSR and its satellite countries, however, did not vote for or against the Declaration in the deciding debates. Communism was especially fearful of those rights that stressed the freedom of the individual and the Declaration was emphatic on these.)

Two classes of rights: political/civil and social/economic/cultural
One problem the commission faced was the 'division' between the political and civil rights on the one hand and the economic, social and cultural rights on the other. This problem is embodied in the fact that two separate Covenants were later deemed necessary to make the Universal Declaration more binding – one for each 'class' or 'set' of rights.

The first set of rights concerned such things as freedoms of speech, movement, religion, conscience, and rights to vote and to protection of the law. You could see these rights as 'negative' – they set out what government or others must not do to interfere in the individual's freedoms. They were very much supported by the US and other liberal democracies.

The other set of rights were (and are) more controversial. Economic, social and cultural rights concern such things as the right to food, shelter, healthcare, education, work, social insurance. These rights are more 'positive' in nature – they ask for a commitment to do something tangible about basic necessities of life. Just who is being asked (or told) to do something is a thorny question; so, too, is just what is to be done. What does a 'right to work' entail, for example? Does it mean that the state is bound to give me, and all its citizens, a job? Does it mean that an employer has to employ me? Does it mean that I ought to expect a job to be provided for me by someone else? Does it mean that if I am not employed, this is in itself an injustice and, as such, I should be compensated? The socialist states were very supportive of this set of economic, social and cultural rights; the liberal capitalist states were not, seeing major difficulties in upholding them effectively. Some states in the developing world saw difficulties, too: how could they be expected to provide substantial benefits for their citizens when they had so little in resources or wealth?

Cassin's Portico – the unified whole
The 'clash' between the two sets of rights is an interesting area to explore with students, perhaps combining it with what some students may have done in history and economics regarding the political and economic differences between socialism and liberal capitalism. The Declaration includes both sets of rights as parts of a unified whole, an aspect worth studying. A diagram in Glendon's book, based on an image used for the Declaration by one of its most important drafters, R. Cassin, is helpful here. It views the Declaration as a Temple-like building ('Cassin's Portico').[19]

The Preamble of the Declaration and the first two articles set out its presuppositions, the basic values on which the Declaration is founded: Dignity, Liberty, Equality, Brotherhood. Like a set of steps on a firm foundation, these lead us into the building, which is supported on four pillars.

The first Pillar concerns articles 3-11, rights to do with the individual's life, liberty and personal security. These outlaw homicide, slavery, torture and arbitrary arrest; they assert one's right to a fair trial and to presumption of innocence, and so on.

The second Pillar concerns articles 12-17, rights in civil and political society. These rights have to do with such things as one's privacy not being interfered with, freedom of movement, and rights regarding marriage and family. It also includes reference to 'the right to own property alone as well as in association with others' (article 17, [1]). The phrase 'private property' was deliberately not used so that all the nations could accept the Declaration, including those such as the Soviets who were against private property! This exemplifies an important point – the list of rights is not 'automatic'. It is not obvious what is or is not a 'right'. One may have to talk at a very general level to get acceptance by all of a list of rights. What each one means in concrete situations and in particular political and social settings may vary. However, even a general agreement, including some elements of compromise (such as this exclusion of the word 'private' from article 17), can be useful in guarding against gross violations of rights and in perhaps ensuring that a specific area of rights is at least promoted to some degree.

The third Pillar in 'Cassin's Portico' concerns articles 18-21, rights to do with the 'polity' or governance. These refer to freedom of religion, opinion, assembly and the right to participate in government. These rights were 'a group of rights in which representatives of liberal democracies took special pride', but which the Soviets labelled as 'hollow words'.[20]

Again, we see the need to understand the controversial nature of human rights and the need for some political compromise in agreement and promotion of rights in the real world.

The fourth Pillar concerns the Economic, Social and Cultural rights mentioned above. In the Declaration they are listed in articles 22-27. If articles 3-20 refer primarily to what must not be done *to* people, these articles refer to what must be done *for* people.[21] Eleanor Roosevelt was very sorry that these two sets of rights were later separated into two Covenants. This separation 'undercut the Declaration's message that one set of values could not long endure without the other. It suggested a retreat from the proposition that a better standard of living cannot be accomplished without larger freedom, and freedom is threatened by dehumanizing living conditions.'[22]

The final part of the Portico image for the Declaration (and its understanding of human rights) is most important – it's the roof, or the pediment. This refers to the final three articles, 28-30, which round off the document. These are articles that might be neglected by a teacher or class, coming at the end of the list, but they are essential for understanding the Declaration and for avoiding a narrowly individualistic concept of rights. In fact, in the preceding articles regarding social rights, the Declaration itself may be criticised as encouraging an individualistic misunderstanding of rights. Instead of presenting these articles as rights of the individual ('Everyone has the right to…') in order to keep consistency of style throughout the document, the framers of the Declaration would have been better advised, according to Glendon, to adopt:

> the obligation model. To couch the social security and welfare principles in terms of a common responsibility might have resonated better than rights in most of the world's cultures and would still have left room for experiments with different mixes of private and public approaches.[23]

The final three articles are an important reminder that rights must be seen in a wider context than merely personal or individual claims or demands or freedoms. Article 28 was originally going to be article 3, to set the scene at the beginning with the foundational articles 1 and 2, but it was kept till the end because it was thought better that it be mentioned after the specific rights had been listed. This article mentions that 'everyone is entitled to a social and international order in which the rights and freedoms set forth in this Declaration can be fully realized.' This is a nice link back for us to the social analysis section of this RE module, where we saw the importance of economic, political, social and cultural structures. 'Man is a social and political animal', as Aquinas said, following Aristotle, and this means that one's individual rights cannot be upheld unless the structures of society *at every level* are right and just.

Article 29 is also highly important. It refers to duties. Two of the most frequently mentioned weaknesses of rights language are that it is selfish and individualistic. Think of the problems in understanding morality in terms of what I am due, rather than what I owe others. Anyway, as well as being morally weak, an exclusively rights-based approach will not work: if no-one has duties, who will promote and vindicate rights? If everyone is claiming from others, who will give to others?

Another dimension of this issue is briefly developed in article 29(2), namely the area of respect for others' rights as the necessary limit for claiming or demanding one's own rights. It is worth noting the exact wording of this article. It mentions the importance of 'securing due recognition and respect for the rights and freedoms of others' but it also adds 'and of meeting the just requirements of morality, public order and the general welfare in a democratic society.' This reminds us that it is not only a bare freedom for all that limits one's claims to individual rights or justice, but a wider understanding of society and morality that notes the importance of other dimensions of morality, especially its public dimension. This is most important as a warning to the teacher not to reduce morality to rights alone.[24] Not even the more specific area of justice, as part of morality, should be reduced to rights, as is indicated clearly by the fact that the area of human rights is only one of five perspectives on justice in this syllabus.

The final article of the Universal Declaration states that no-one may destroy any of the rights or freedoms set out in the document. This is a reminder of the 'bottom line' of morality. None of us is entitled to destroy what is necessary for the flourishing of individuals in society. Another way to understand the definition of human rights, therefore, is that they specify particular, obligatory conditions for human fulfilment and development as social individuals. Human rights are the minimum conditions necessary for our flourishing.

Pacem in Terris

Another primary source of information about human rights, and another list of them, is Pope John XXIII's encyclical, *Pacem in Terris* (1963), in which understanding human rights as conditions for human flourishing is emphasised. So, too, is the social dimension of rights, including the international and global levels. It is interesting to compare and contrast the two documents (of the UN and of the Pope).

One thing that stands out in the papal encyclical, not surprisingly, is the religious dimension of human rights. Pope John stresses that human rights are based on human nature, which is created and shaped by God. There is a moral order that comes from God, therefore, and it must be respected if we are to be at peace. The implications of this moral order are specified in the various rights shared by all human beings.

Religious freedom and the purpose of rights

The pope lists rights much as the Universal Declaration did but there is a greater integration of the social with the political from the start. There is more of a clear impression that rights exist for a purpose. Take religious freedom, for instance. (This right is more fully treated in 'The Declaration on Religious Liberty' of Vatican II, promulgated in 1965). Why do we have such a right? One answer is that we simply are free to believe whatever we like just because no-one knows what is really the case in religion and it is all a matter of personal guesswork. Instead of this rather 'thin' understanding of religions liberty, one based on scepticism, the Pope and the Catholic tradition sees religious liberty as something that should be promoted by individuals, groups and states to enable us to search for the truth and, finding it, to shape our lives by it. In other words, this human right, which forbids the state or anyone from interfering with the individual's or group's religious belief or practice, is a necessary condition for participation in the search for truth and wisdom.

Participation

Here we meet another useful keyword in the area of rights: 'participation'. Rights enable us to participate in our own development as individuals in society, and to contribute to the integral development of our society and world too. This is a far cry from a selfish, individualistic concept of rights, which can be seen as the major potential weakness in this perspective on justice.

Other Definitions of Justice

Having looked at the five perspectives listed in the syllabus, it is worth noting briefly some other definitions of justice or types of justice. These are useful in making our concept of justice more specific and more adaptable to all situations.

Commutative justice concerns equality and balance in private exchanges between individuals. Buying or selling a bike is an example; signing a contract to do a job is another.

Distributive justice concerns how the social whole distributes its benefits (and burdens) amongst its members according to merit and/or need. This justice is less strictly 'equal' and more proportional in its assessment of what and how much is to be distributed. Social welfare is an example of this kind of justice.

Legal or *General* justice is mentioned by Aquinas, not as a particular kind of justice, but as any just act that is chosen with the common good in mind. It is a reminder that justice is not a private matter but a social matter: it concerns our living in society in harmony and balance. We should always choose and act with a view to the common good of the community.

More recent terminology includes *Contributive* justice, which is similar to General justice, in that it concerns the contribution made to the social whole by the individual (or groups). Paying one's taxes is an example of this.

Lastly, *Social* justice concerns how society provides 'the conditions that allow associations or individuals to obtain what is their due, according to their nature and their vocation' (*Catechism*, par. 1928). There is a strong connection between a concern for reforming social structures (as seen in chapter one above) and working for social justice.

Systems of justice are essential

Once one has defined an intellectual understanding of justice and its principles, there is another dimension that must be appreciated: the practical dimension. In this respect, it is worth looking at the details of the various systems of justice that exist at many levels of society. Think of all the people, resources, energy, time, discussion and debate that are dedicated to working out the details of justice at all the various levels of social existence. In schools, for example, there is a lot of attention given to deciding justice matters. The same is true at the various levels of politics. Systems of justice are an essential aspect of justice. The important thing to note here is how an effective and good justice system is a combination of principle and procedure. The principles are the moral and practical truths we have just been examining above under the five headings concerning justice. The procedures are ways of promoting and protecting these principles and following them in a concrete manner to find what justice means in particular cases. So, for example, strict impartiality is a feature of any good justice system. No good justice system will countenance a judge or member of the jury being related to the accused. Notice, too, the great care and effort made to ascertain the relevant facts about what the relationships in question really are, or what is owed to whom and how much, or what actually happened and who did this or that, and so on. Witnesses are called and cross-examined, their claims tested for consistency and accurate detail. It is remarkable, also, how the accused is always seen as meriting a defence – justice must be assessed and enforced in a balanced and fair manner. As already noted, justice is not revenge: it is balanced, impartial retribution.

Complex justice systems, and laws to guide them, are needed to clarify when things are equal or unequal, so that it can be seen whether like is being treated as like, as justice demands, or whether compensation is due. Working out whether something is truly a 'right' is a difficult task and can be very controversial – witness the debates over privacy, same-sex marriage, free speech and citizenship, for instance.

Attention to all this is necessary to help make justice less abstract. Also, it is good to avoid giving the idea that justice is always a matter of private judgement, when in fact it is usually a social activity. Students will be guarded against scepticism if they keep in mind that much can be, and is, actually agreed and worked out regarding specifics of justice, even though the task is an on-going and very challenging one, full of controversy, conflict and dramatic interest. Finally, it is important to keep reminding students that quick judgements of cases of conflict or dispute over justice issues are to be avoided. We live in an age of 'trial by media', where often we are expected to make up our minds about difficult and highly complex issues or cases after an hour or less of television documentary or press coverage. It is worth teaching students the difficulty of judging well and the requirements necessary to achieve this. It demands personal virtues of justice (willingness to give what is due) and prudence (wisdom and knowledge) as well as social systems and procedures.

2.2 VISIONS OF PEACE

Peace is not defined in the syllabus, nor are any perspectives specified or headings given. We are told to give two definitions of peace and to explain and illustrate the links between justice and peace. The mention of 'two types' of peace suggests an inadequate concept of peace be compared and contrasted with an adequate concept, a false peace contrasted with a true peace.

Types of Peace

An inadequate notion of peace
One inadequate way of defining peace is that it denotes an absence of overt discord or dissension. This rightly points to a kind of harmony or feeling of security that is characteristic of 'peace', but this can ignore hidden or unacknowledged injustices that prevent real harmony or lasting security. A marriage can seem peaceful, for example, if there are no arguments or overt unpleasantness, though beneath the surface there is a lack of respect or affection, or even a kind of violence or fear suppressing any observable conflict. Such a marriage is not a 'right relationship' based on fair play and respect for equal rights and responsibilities, not to mention mutual give and take motivated by love. The same can be said about a country or international scene that seems to be one of peace in that there is no war, but where there are injustices such as an arms 'race' or dictatorship. It too is merely an illusion of peace if there is not true justice.

True peace
The *Catechism of the Catholic Church* defines true peace in contrast to an inadequate notion:

> Peace is not merely the absence of war, and it is not limited to maintaining a balance of powers between adversaries. Peace cannot be attained on earth without safeguarding the goods of persons, free communication among men, respect for the dignity of persons and peoples, and the assiduous practice of fraternity. Peace is 'the tranquillity of order' [quoting from St Augustine's *City of God*]. Peace is the work of justice and the effect of charity [referring to Isaiah 32:17 and *Gaudium et Spes* 78]. (Paragraph 2304).

Charity, or love, is needed for there to be a full harmony of affections and thoughts, for there to be fullness of unity. But justice is necessary, too, if the obstacles to peace are to be removed for charity to do its work. This is why Aquinas, in the *Summa Theologiae,* dealt with 'peace' under the heading of the virtue of Charity rather than Justice:

> Peace is the 'work of justice' indirectly, in so far as justice removes the obstacles to peace: but it is the work of charity directly, since charity, according to its very nature, causes peace. For love is 'a unitive force' ... and peace is the union of the appetite's inclinations. (II-II, q.29, art.3, reply 3.)

In other words, if there are injustices, or a lack of willingness to give to others what is due them, then this will prevent there being peace. So justice, this willingness to give what is due, is necessary for peace. But what is meant by 'the union of the appetite's inclinations'? Aquinas realised that peace is rooted primarily in the hearts of people, rather than in the politics of nations or the mere external states of affairs of society.

Peace begins within the person
One's inner desires can be at war; they need to be focused on a source of unity, namely what is truly 'good'. Also, one's choices need to be in harmony with one's judgements of what is good, which constitutes the peace of a good conscience. This 'individual' peace is necessary for 'social' peace. Individuals whose desires are disordered and in conflict, and whose consciences are bad, will never be people of social peace. Aquinas seems to have grasped what lies at the heart of our difficulties in achieving peace in our world: people do not desire the truly good and they do not follow their consciences. Such people can only create or enjoy an illusion of peace. True peace comes when you love God with all your heart and so your

desires are united in their focus on God's will, and you love your neighbour as yourself, and so your neighbour's desires (for the good) are your desires too, and you are living in harmony. So, Aquinas realised that peace is linked with goodness (See *Summa Theologiae* II-II, q.29, art.2, reply 4).

The religious perspective
Thus, the religious perspective considers true peace to be possible only when our inner personal desires and choices and our outer inter-personal relationships are ordered rightly in harmony with the Divine will, which desires our well-being and peace.

Secular peace and religious peace
This leads us to consider a contrast between another two 'types of peace': secular or 'this-worldly' peace and religious or spiritual peace. Both are truly 'peace', but the latter is peace at its fullest. This was explored by Aquinas when he saw that the fullness of peace is found only in 'the perfect enjoyment of the sovereign good, and unites all one's desires by giving them rest in one object'. Here, Aquinas is referring to the complete peace that God wishes us to enjoy as the end of our earthly life. This is what we pray for when we wish those who have died to 'Rest in peace', the ultimate wish. It is the enjoyment of the Good (that is, God) without any hindrance or distraction in heaven. It is the fulfilment of all our desires. Here on earth, our enjoyment of peace is never this perfect as there is always some element of distraction or disturbance.[25] We can only enjoy God's peace now as an anticipation of the full peace to come in his kingdom. As Catholics pray in Mass, 'Lord Jesus Christ, you said to your apostles…'. Or, as the famous prayer of St Augustine goes, 'God, you have made us for yourself, and our hearts are restless until they rest in you.'

An integral understanding of peace

A focus on heaven, however, should not lead us to neglect earth; emphasis on God should not distract us from the needs of man; examining the inner dynamics of peace should not prevent us from recognising that the internal and external worlds are mutually interactive. An integral Christian understanding of peace is well expressed in the following quote from the 1968 Medellín Church document by the Latin American bishops, who were interested in justice and peace in both earthly and heavenly dimensions:

> Peace is, above all, a work of justice... It presupposes and requires the establishment of a just order... in which men can fulfil themselves as men, where their dignity is respected, their legitimate aspirations satisfied, their access to truth recognized, their personal freedom guaranteed; an order where man is not an object but an agent of his own history...Secondly, peace is a permanent task... A community becomes a reality in time and is subject to a movement that implies constant change in structures, transformation of attitudes, and conversion of hearts... Finally, peace is the fruit of love... It is the expression of true fraternity among men, a fraternity given by Christ, Prince of Peace, in reconciling all men with the Father. Human solidarity cannot truly take effect unless it is done in Christ, who gives Peace that the world cannot give... Love is the soul of justice. The Christian who works for social justice should always cultivate peace and love in his heart.
>
> Peace with God is the basic foundation of internal and social peace. Therefore, where this social peace does not exist there will we find social, political, economic and cultural inequalities, there will we find the rejection of the peace of the Lord, and a rejection of the Lord Himself.[26]

Non-violence as lifestyle and as form of protest

The distinction
One way to understand the distinction mentioned under (and within) this heading in the syllabus is as follows. *Lifestyle* implies a deep integration of 'non-violence' into one's philosophy of living, whereas 'as form of protest' suggests engaging in non-violent protest as a strategy to achieve a particular aim, or as a specific way to 'fight' against violent methods of achieving aims. Someone following a non-violent *lifestyle* or philosophy might have little interest in trying to affect others in the wider society or trying to effect social change. Instead, the focus would be on personal or group purity or holiness, living distinct from the 'world' or even apart from it. The Amish sect are a good example of this, and so too, to an extent, are the Mennonites and Quakers (or the Society of Friends). The Jain religion is a prominent non-Christian example. Non-violence as *protest* may be combined with non-violence as lifestyle, for example in the life of Gandhi (see below), but it may also be a distinct form of non-violence. A person or group who accepts some legitimacy for violence (for self-defence, for example) might nevertheless be a strong supporter of non-violence as the most morally appropriate form of protest or social action for change.[27] There is quite a lot of material on the web about non-violence as a form of protest or as a strategy for social change.[28] Techniques such as sit-ins, marches, strikes, boycotts, and others are explained and sophisticated teaching strategies for nonviolent action are developed and made available.[29]

Gandhi and King
Looking at the lives and writings of two famous people, MD Gandhi and Martin Luther King, Jr, could be a very concrete way of engaging with this section, though avoiding a superficial treatment of what are rather clichéd examples. An excerpt from the well-known film *Gandhi* is one practical

possibility. The web has other material on this renowned icon of non-violence.[30] With regard to Martin Luther King Jr, his 'Letter from Birmingham Jail' is well worth studying.[31] The online King Center has plenty of material that could be used in the classroom. Six principles of non-violence, based on King's work, have been outlined as follows:[32]

1 Non-violence is a way of life for courageous people.
2 Non-violence seeks to win friendship and understanding.
3 Non-violence seeks to defeat injustice not people.
4 Non-violence holds that suffering can educate and transform.
5 Non-violence chooses love instead of hate.
6 Non-violence believes that the universe is on the side of justice.

Further, six steps of non-violence, based on the Birmingham Letter, have been outlined:[33]

1 Information gathering
2 Education
3 Personal commitment
4 Negotiations
5 Direct action
6 Reconciliation

Details can be found on the website: they show how a commitment to non-violence is not necessarily a 'cop-out' or an easy option, but a challenging and inspiring way of being committed to justice and peace. This section on 'non-violence' is very closely related to the next on 'conflict resolution' and part 2.4 below on 'Violence'. Role-play as a teaching strategy would be particularly appropriate for these topics, as we are very much in the area of developing attitudes and skills rather than learning facts and figures.

It almost goes without saying that a commitment to non-violence can be deeply religious, supported strongly, for example, by the Judaeo-Christian tradition. Pope John Paul II, for example, is well known for his prayers for peace and warnings against war and violence. In *Centesimus Annus* (1991), the Pope wrote:

> I myself, on the occasion of the recent tragic war in the Persian Gulf, repeated the cry: 'Never again war!'. No, never again war, which destroys the lives of innocent people, teaches how to kill, throws into upheaval even the lives of those who do the killing and leaves behind a trail of resentment and hatred, thus making it all the more difficult to find a just solution of the very problems which provoked the war. Just as the time has finally come when in individual states a system of private vendetta and reprisal has given way to the rule of law, so too a similar step forward is now urgently needed in the international community. (Par. 52)

The Pope links the move away from violent attempts to find solutions to problems to development of the rule of law at the international level. Only a deep respect for law, and justice which is the foundation of law, can enable society to live non-violently and to solve its problems effectively and morally.

Conflict resolution

There has been a great deal of interest lately in peaceful 'conflict resolution'. One reason for this is that our world is so full of conflicts, most of which concern issues of justice. Look at a newspaper or teletext news page and notice how many of the stories are about matters of justice or injustice, and how to judge between the two in particular instances. Issues of justice are at the heart of human life. This is the 'drama' of humanity, and conflict is the driving force of all drama – as all English teachers will tell you. Dealing with conflict takes up a great deal of human time, energy, and resources – as *all* teachers will tell you! How to do this well is a very important challenge. It could even be claimed that justice is an enemy of peace, the numerous claims and counter-claims of justice being seen as a kind of threat to peace. Take industrial relations, for example. Strikes and industrial disputes are sometimes portrayed as a threat to the public image of a company or a nation's competitiveness and prosperity. Perhaps it would be much better if we could all just go about our business in peace and contentment. This is simplistic and it fails to distinguish between the false and true peace (as described above). A superficial 'peace' is not real peace and disturbing an illusory 'peace' in the cause of genuine justice can actually promote genuine peace. The means by which one pursues the cause of justice, of conflict resolution, should be good means.

Definitions and models
Conflict resolution is all about dealing with conflicts at various levels – from family through business through national and international spheres – in a way that achieves the good end of resolution by means that are truly good. It involves a focus on means of resolution that allow or enable both (or all) parties to 'win' – instead of the usual 'win/lose' outcome of adversarial methods of dealing with conflict. Different 'models' of conflict resolution have been developed and applied to conflicts both small and large. The University of Colorado has a very good site about conflict resolution with a huge amount of detail and a thorough online training programme.[34] Here are some central concept definitions from its glossary page:[35]

> *Conciliation* involves efforts by a third party to improve the relationship between two or more disputants. It may be done as a part of mediation, or independently. Generally, the third party will work with the disputants to correct misunderstandings, reduce fear and distrust, and generally improve communication between the

parties in conflict. Sometimes this alone will result in dispute settlement; at other times, it paves the way for a later mediation process.

Conflict resolution: This term (along with dispute resolution) usually refers to the process of resolving a dispute or a conflict permanently, by providing each sides' needs, and adequately addressing their interests so that they are satisfied with the outcome.

Dialogue is a process for sharing and learning about another group's beliefs, feelings, interests, and/or needs in a non-adversarial, open way, usually with the help of a third party facilitator. Unlike mediation, in which the goal is usually reaching a resolution or settlement of a dispute, the goal of dialogue is usually simply improving interpersonal understanding and trust. [Note how this site distinguishes the aims of resolution proper and dialogue: this may meet the syllabus's 'Outcomes' requirement of defining dialogue; see syllabus, p. 63]

Mediation is a method of conflict resolution that is carried out by an intermediary who works with the disputing parties to help them improve their communication and their analysis of the conflict situation, so that the parties can themselves identify and choose an option for resolving the conflict that meets the interests or needs of all of the disputants. Unlike arbitration, where the intermediary listens to the arguments of both sides and makes a decision for the disputants, a mediator will help the disputants design a solution themselves.

Examples and applications
The work of George Mitchell in the Northern Ireland peace process is a good example of a mediator in action. It remains to

be seen how successful the process will be.[36] Non-violent methods of conflict resolution are relevant to many countries and the international situation. *Centesimus Annus* emphasises as an example the amazing non-violent revolutions that occurred in Eastern Europe in 1989. More recently, on 1 May 2004, ten new countries, mainly from Eastern Europe, joined the European Union, a living witness to the possibilities of peaceful and lasting change through non-violent means. It is inspiring to note how the European Union has developed so much that it is now unthinkable that members would attempt to resolve differences or conflicts of interest by violent means.

2.3 RELIGIOUS PERSPECTIVES ON JUSTICE AND PEACE

Knowing the wider context
The main religious traditions' understandings of justice and peace are treated in this part. Teachers should be familiar with the wider context in which the justice and peace dimensions of these religions find their fullest meaning. If, as seems likely, teachers in Catholic schools choose to teach section B of the overall RE syllabus (on Christianity), then they will have to choose between teaching section C (World Religions) *or* D (Moral Decision Making). It would be most helpful if all three sections were taught, but this is neither practical nor required. In any case, the teacher who knows all sections (especially B, C and D) can incorporate any extra material and comment necessary to make the specific focus of this section an intelligible and fair presentation of the different religious traditions.

A common misunderstanding of religion and morality
There is a commonly held conception of the link between religion and morality or justice often called the 'Divine Command' theory of morality. This sees religion as essentially an

added extra to morality, an extrinsic addition of divine authority to moral rules and duties. 'We should be moral purely because God commands it' is the basic idea in this way of (mis)understanding morality. This idea is true but incomplete, and so quite narrow and distorting. For religions such as Christianity, Judaism and Islam the commands of God are of the highest importance and form an essential aspect of morality, its very foundation in fact. There is more to morality than this, however, and this 'more' is very important. The problem with the 'Divine Command' theory is that it can become a view of God as a kind of Big Boss in the sky who issues commands somewhat arbitrarily about what is good and ought to be done and what is bad and ought to be avoided. Also, there is often a strong emphasis on the power of God to punish anyone who disobeys his commands. Sometimes this punishment is so emphasised that we end up with an image of a very angry or vengeful God, only dying to catch us out and punish us, whereas God is 'dying' to save us, not punish us. (In the Eucharist, Christians celebrate the fact that God died on the cross to save us.)

In this narrow understanding of religion's relationship with morality, religion is appreciated as a powerful motivator for justice, a strong social and historical support for social morality and peace, but no more than that. In fact, sometimes theistic religion is not thus appreciated, but rejected as somehow less than moral, presuming that a focus on achieving a reward for one's good deeds (and avoiding punishment for evil deeds) makes being moral seem a narrow spiritual self-interest, a kind of religious selfishness. Religion can also appear as a paternalistic imposition of morals on people who are able to choose maturely to do good for the sake of goodness, rather than to placate an angry Divine Boss.

A better understanding of the relationship
God is more correctly seen as the Creator of all, infinite and utterly mysterious in Himself, pure goodness and love and

therefore the foundation of all morality. His commands are never arbitrary, therefore, but always an expression of his own nature, which is love. This is understood in different ways by the various religions, but it must be emphasised that all see God's will as a powerful exercise of concern and love, and never a mere exercise of power. All the major religions (except Buddhism) share the idea that man ought to live in a way that is compatible with God's way of acting, with God's will. God is the foundation of justice; his will is our peace. So, religious faith is seen as giving us a deep conviction of the reasonableness of being just and loving in all circumstances, even when it is not to our immediate or selfish advantage, as well as giving us specific directions on how to be just and loving and offering us the necessary aid to enable us to live good lives.

The four religious topics
The syllabus requires any two of four religious traditions to be studied. All four are treated here, and several references are indicated for further study of each of the four. There is a particularly detailed treatment of the dominant tradition in Ireland, the Judaeo-Christian tradition. The four topics are:

i   The Judaeo-Christian tradition
ii The Zakat of Islam
iii The four Varnas of Hinduism
iv The Eightfold Path of Buddhism.

(i) The Judaeo-Christian vision of justice and peace
Judaism and Christianity share a lot in common regarding justice and peace, but they are each distinctive traditions. Even within each of the traditions, particularly Christianity, there are varying perspectives, and it is practically impossible to do full justice to them all. This book speaks mainly from within the

Catholic tradition in treating of Christianity, a tradition that has the advantage of a certain unity, clarity and authority.

Natural Law and Revelation
The Judaeo-Christian tradition generally accepts what has been said about justice and peace above in 2.1 and 2.2. Some elements of the tradition would stress the religiously revealed aspect and downplay the humanly reasoned aspects, but all would basically agree with a vision of justice as right relationship, retribution, fair play, the promotion of equality, and the upholding of human rights. They would also agree that peace is to be valued very highly, but not in a superficial way, or to the detriment of justice. The Catholic tradition emphasises the natural law, and so it sees all morality as rational and thereby accessible to human thinking. This allows the Catholic tradition to accept much of the classical thought on justice (from the ancient Greeks and Romans mainly); insofar as it is truly reasonable, it is always compatible with God's revealed will. Secular traditions in Western history have been influenced by the Biblical traditions and religious ways of thinking have been influenced by the secular. The degree and nature of these influences, and their appropriateness and correctness, and the possibilities of combining and integrating the religious and the secular, are matters of controversy and continuing debate, debate which this syllabus invites teachers and students to join.

A narrative approach
This section of the chapter takes a mainly narrative approach, as distinct from the thematic approach taken so far. This is distinctive of the Judaeo-Christian tradition: it understands justice and peace through story. This story is seen as is our story, the human story. It is a true story, *the* true story. It is a single unfolding story – a strong sense of linear time ('history') is emphasised by the Judaeo-Christian, in contrast to the more circular sense of time found in Eastern religions. The

foundational chapters of this singular story are in the Old and New Testaments of the Bible.[37]

Justice: faithfulness to a relationship

The understanding of justice conveyed by this story is that of 'faithfulness to the requirements of a relationship'.[38] 'Right relationship' is the perspective on justice most obviously related to the Biblical perspective.

Creation

'Right relationship' is seen first of all in terms of creation. The opening chapters of the Bible form a kind of prologue to the whole story. God creates an ordered and good universe including human beings who are created in God's image (see Genesis 1). The basic equality of all human beings is strongly supported by the creation accounts. There is another strong message too: human beings are creatures with inherent value living in a world that is valuable. We are 'meant-to-be', personally made by the infinite supreme Being, not mere accidental products of an aimless and mindless process, such as Darwinian evolution would understand us to be. The human person is given a task by God. In the first chapter of Genesis this is expressed by the command to 'fill the earth and subdue it' (Gen 1:28); the second chapter sees it in terms of cultivating and caring for the garden (see Gen 2:15). It is worth emphasising the fact that the human person is described in essentially social terms in these chapters (see Gen 1:27 and 2:18). It is also clear that the human person can know the basic rules for living and is expected to abide by these rules. In Genesis 2 this is expressed in terms of God telling Adam and Eve to eat of any tree in the Garden but not the tree of knowledge of good and evil, whose fruit will kill them (Gen 1:17).

Original sin

The human person lives within a context that is a 'given', created by the infinite, wise God, a context that ought to be respected. Unfortunately, the original human parents did not respect this given. They sinned. We should not think of this 'original sin' in flippant terms, such as robbing an orchard or eating an apple (the bible does not say the fruit was an apple); nor should we think of it in terms of a bossy God laying down an arbitrary law in order to catch out the humans who are inevitably going to sin anyway. This kind of interpretation is a misreading of the whole story and does not make sense of how it fits into the rest of Scripture and its message. It also fails to reflect accurately the Judaeo-Christian's understanding of God. The imagery of the story is meant to convey a nuanced reality in a vivid story-form – we are creatures living in a social context, in an ecological context, who have the gift and responsibility of conscience and free will, and whose moral judgements and choices shape us and our world. The first sin was an extremely serious matter, involving a failure to trust and obey God, by accepting the words of a creature (the 'serpent', who traditionally is seen as Satan) above the Word of God, and by attempting to make ourselves 'like gods'. The story sees the original sin as our proud attempt to (re)write the moral rules independently of God the Creator. All sin shares this characteristic.

Original sin is a profound act of injustice, understood as unfaithfulness to the requirements of the relationship of creature to Creator. It can be seen as a refusal to give God what he is due as God; it treats God disrespectfully as our equal though we are not equal to God. It is a decision not to give God his 'rights', so to speak, by proper obedience and trust in his guidance.[39] The original right relationship (referred to as 'original justice' in the Catholic tradition) is ruined by this original sin. And this original sin spoils what we might call the 'original peace' that God willed for his creation. Relationships shaped by sin are characterised by distrust or hostility or lack of harmony. (Notice how the man blames the woman and she blames the serpent – sinfulness causes a strong tendency towards passing the blame.)

The effects of sin

The rest of the human story is affected by this beginning as all humankind is wounded by the original sin of the first parents of the human race, which has broken the right relationship that God willed to exist between him and us.[40] This damaging of the right relationship between 'man' and 'Maker' affects religious faith (the man and woman hide from God and lie to him); it also affects the social reality of life (Adam and Eve are ashamed of their nakedness); it affects even the relationship between man and the environment (childbirth and work on the land will be painful and difficult from then on; the serpent and the humans are enemies).[41] Death is 'installed' into God's creation by this abuse of our freedom. Henceforth, the realties of disharmony and distrust, and death and suffering, will affect our thinking and acting as individuals in society. Our minds will be darkened and our wills weakened, as Catholic tradition puts it. Injustice and lack of peace are thereby made more prevalent and dominant.

The spread of sin and the Covenants

Sin soon spreads, as is seen in the story of the first fratricide, Cain's murder of Abel (Gen 4), and the following stories of humanity becoming more and more sinful, so much so that God sends a flood, and begins again with Noah, his family, and the animals. Even after this new beginning, sin still continues to spread, symbolised in the Tower of Babel story and its focus on the continuing quest of mankind to reject its rightful relationship with the Creator God and to attempt to become gods in our own right. All that results is a 'Babel' of different languages, symbolising difficulties in communication, difficulties that continue to make achieving justice and resolving conflicts peacefully such endless challenges. It is into this context of injustice and disharmony that God enters with his Covenants.

Noah

With Noah and his descendents (and the whole world), God makes a covenant (see Genesis 8:15–9:17). This is a covenant of peace. It is a simple covenant, with little relation to justice as such in detail, (although it does seem to require the death penalty for murder in 9:6). It shows that peace is God's will for his creation, symbolised by the rainbow.[42]

Abraham

In Genesis 12 we enter a new phase of the story. This is where God's covenant with Abraham and his descendents is begun. Here, the focus is on a particular people, who are chosen by God from all the nations to be his people. At first, the requirements of the covenant are simple, based mainly on belief in the one God, and circumcision as the sign of belonging to God's chosen people. Also, the people travel to the promised land and live there. After a time, however, the people become enslaved in Egypt and a more developed phase of the covenant begins.

Moses

God liberates the Israelite slaves from Egypt, working through Moses. This is a famous story and it has much to say about justice. The Exodus has become a symbol of God's desire for people to be free from all slavery. It has been seen by both Jews and Christians as the pivotal story of the Old Testament. For Jews, it is especially associated with their identity as God's chosen people, which they celebrate each year in the Passover. Christians see it in a more general light, as a sign of God's will for everyone and for all society. The Catholic magisterium (the pope and bishops' teaching authority) has recently cautioned against reducing the Exodus story into a political manifesto. It is not about a merely political liberation: it is essentially about freedom with a religious purpose, bound up with the establishment and strengthening of the religious identity of God's people, and it includes the Law or Torah which God gives his people to guide them in the paths of righteousness.[43] It has social consequences *because* it is religious.

The Ten Commandments
An integral part of this liberation from slavery is the giving of the Law, in particular the Ten Commandments (see Exodus 20 and Deuteronomy 5). One might be tempted to see these as essentially concerned with personal morality, or religious morality (especially the first three Commandments), and opt instead for a focus on the later prophets' sayings on 'social justice' issues. This would be a mistake, however, as the Commandments are the centre of the Torah and the Covenant, and it was the prophets' role essentially to call the people back to the Torah and the Covenant. The Commandments summarise the requirements of the Covenant, especially the requirements that are universal and permanent.

There were many other laws in the original Covenant, (as can be seen by a browse through Exodus, Leviticus and Deuteronomy), most of which are not accepted as law for Christians, who view them as particular rules or customs creating an identity for the chosen people of the Old Testament time. Some of these particular laws, such as those to do with sacrifices, are no longer laws even for Jews, circumstances having changed radically. Jews differ amongst themselves over how to interpret the application of the Torah. Traditionally, the Torah is the subject of much debate. Both Jews and Christians, nonetheless, accept the particular importance of the Decalogue, or Ten Commandments, and they have served as an outline of morality for centuries in Western civilisation as a whole, influencing our laws, institutions, moral codes and assumptions, education systems and content, and more.

The Commandments are a specification of justice's requirements
The Ten Commandments are an outline of how to live as a community, and living as a community is the primary focus of

justice as a virtue. They point out the basic rules, mainly in negative precepts, and so are specifications of justice and its requirements for good social relations and peaceful existence. (Perhaps an historical focus on the Commandments has led the Christian tradition to see morality as primarily a matter of justice or law rather than a matter of love, which includes and supports the basic requirements of justice and law but seeks to go further.) We are required to respect religion and its call to acknowledge the Creator with reverence. We are to respect family, and especially parents, and all social authority. Marriage is not to be threatened by lust or adultery. Life is to be held as sacred; murder is a sin. The right to own property is assumed, theft being strictly forbidden. Honesty in a court of law is a strict obligation, and honesty in general is a mark of a good community, God's community. Jealousy and envy are to be avoided, which shows an awareness of how these 'inner' realities can have destructive 'outer' effects on how we live together as individuals in community.

The Commandments are a school of freedom
These Commandments are not mere arbitrary commands from the Boss, as the 'Divine Command' theory of morality would have it. George Weigel puts this well, making an interesting connection between law, justice and virtue on the one hand, and freedom and happiness on the other:

> The Ten Commandments are an elementary school of freedom – freedom lived for goodness and happiness, freedom lived according to laws that liberate. These are the basics. Without them, neither the moral life nor any sort of genuine freedom is possible. The Ten Commandments are not a capricious set of injunctions, but basic moral rules that emerge from taking the human thirst for goodness and the human desire for happiness seriously. [...] To live freely means to rid

ourselves of the habits of slaves, just as the people of Israel were called to do at Mt Sinai. To worship rightly, to honor parents and the sanctity of life, to deal honestly and justly with others – these are the virtues of freedom, the habits of free men and women. That is why God enjoined them in the Ten Commandments – to bind us in order to liberate us for goodness and for love.[44]

The Jewish tradition: some comments
The Torah, including a strong emphasis on practical living out of the Divinely given law, was the basis for community life and remains so for Jews now. Here is how one encyclopaedia describes the ethical side of Judaism specifically, in which duties of justice are integrated into a more general concern for communal well-being and peace:

> A passage in the traditional [Jewish] Prayer Book enumerates a series of virtuous acts – honouring parents, deeds of steadfast love, attendance twice daily at worship, hospitality to wayfarers, visiting the sick, dowering brides, accompanying the dead to the grave, devotion in prayer, peacemaking in the community and in family-life – and concludes by setting study of Torah as the premier virtue. Here is exhibited the complex variety of ethical behaviour called for within the Jewish tradition. To parental respect and family tranquility are added, in other contexts, the responsibility of parents for children, the duties of husband and wife in the establishment and maintenance of a family, and ethical obligations that extend from the conjugal rights of each to the protection of the wife if the marriage is dissolved. The biblical description of God as upholding the cause of the fatherless and the widow and befriending the stranger, providing him with food and clothing (Deut 10:18), remained a motivating factor in the structure of

the community. Ethical requirements in economic life are expressed concretely in such a passage as Lev 19:35-36: 'You shall do no wrong in judgment, in measures of length or weight or quantity. You shall have just balances, just weights, a just ephah, and a just hin'; and in Amos' bitter condemnation of those who 'sell the righteous for silver, and the needy for a pair of shoes' (Amos 2:6).[45]

Notice the injunction to look after the orphan, the widow *and the alien or stranger*. This aspect of the Torah is much emphasised in modern theological writings on social justice because one can apply the principle involved to an issue of justice that is very much a challenge today, as it was then: how to treat fairly and equally those who are most vulnerable, those who are weak and defenceless, and those who are not a part of the community, those who are different. For much of its history since the first century, Judaism has been the religion of people who *themselves* have been the outsiders, the aliens, the strangers – relying on the justice and compassion of others, including Christians, who often did not treat Jews with justice and compassion. There is always a danger for any religion, or any close-knit community, that it turn its attention in upon itself and its own need for security, justice and identity and so fail to see the needs of the wider community and the need for communities to reach out to each other across cultural boundaries. There is also the related danger that any religion with power will treat outsiders, or 'aliens', as threats to be minimised or even eliminated, rather than fellow human beings who have been created by God in his image. This has not been much of a possibility for Jews for much of their history as they were vulnerable minorities in sometimes hostile surroundings; it has long been a possibility and temptation for Christians and continues to be so for many religious and non-religious groups with power today.

Due to their historical experiences, Jews have emphasised the importance of developing strong community and have developed a deeply felt concern for their own needs as a people and tradition. In the shadow of the Holocaust, for example, there has grown a strong Jewish emphasis on civil liberties and rights for minorities within the context of political liberalism.[46] A concern for the world in general has not been lacking, however, amongst Jews. There has been a belief amongst Jews that by their faithfulness to the Covenant and its requirements, as God's Chosen, they can witness to the world that God is both great and good and so invite the world to obey the God who has made us all in his image and who calls all to goodness through the covenant with Noah. This universal side of Judaism is emphasised in recent writings by UK Chief Rabbi Jonathan Sacks.[47]

There is a strong Jewish emphasis on the human person as *imagio Dei*, created in God's image, and therefore both able to know some wisdom and to merit justice and respect, even though there are differences within and between communities. This doctrine is shared with Christianity and is at the heart of the Judaeo-Christian vision of justice and peace.

The prophets
Moving back to the narrative of the Bible, we now look at the prophets who were a major element of the religious and political life of the Jewish people in the centuries before Christ. A strong concern for community and its requirements is central to the prophetic books of the Bible, which call the People of God back to the Covenant that gives them their identity. (The prophets are especially concerned to challenge the leaders, the kings, to rule with justice, as the leaders of a nation have a particular responsiblity for the quality of justice and peace in a nation and between nations.)

Religious concerns are integrated constantly into concerns with ethics, and in particular justice. Hosea writes:

> Hear the word of the Lord, O people of Israel; for the Lord has an indictment against the inhabitants of the

land. There is no faithfulness or loyalty, and no knowledge of God in the land.

Swearing, lying, and murder, and stealing and adultery break out; bloodshed follows bloodshed.

Therefore the land mourns, and all who live in it languish; together with the wild animals and the birds of the air, even the fish of the sea are perishing. (Hos 4:1-3).

Knowledge of God is linked with behaving ethically. When there is a lack of faithfulness and justice, there is 'no knowledge of God in the land'. Why is this? Here we come upon another central concept in the Biblical way of understanding morality, including justice and peace. *God is a God of justice.* As stated in Deuteronomy 32: 3-4 says: 'For I will proclaim the name of the Lord; ascribe greatness to our God! The Rock, his work is perfect, and all his ways are just. A faithful God, without deceit, just and upright is he'. We are called to imitate God: because he is loving and just, we are to be loving and just. As Moses says to the congregation in Leviticus 19:2: 'Speak to all the congregation of the people of Israel and say to them: You shall be holy, for I the Lord your God am holy.' The rest of Leviticus 19 specifies how this is to be done and it includes many justice norms, such as respecting the alien among them as a citizen, because they themselves were aliens in Egypt (and, it is assumed, God treated them with justice and mercy by setting them free). This is how we come to know God in a real way: by *our* action matching *his* action.

So, without love and justice even the most rigorous 'religious' practices will be of no avail, and will even be a kind of evil in God's eyes. This is famously expressed in Amos 5: 21-24:

I hate, I despise your festivals, and I take no delight in your solemn assemblies. Even though you offer me your burnt offerings and grain offerings,
  I will not accept them;

and the offerings of well-being of your fatted animals
  I will not look upon.
Take away from me the noise of your songs;
I will not listen to the melody of your harps.

But let justice roll down like waters,
and righteousness like an ever flowing stream.

(See also Jeremiah 7: 5-10.)

We find a close correlation between idolatry and injustice in the prophetic literature. When man loses sight of the reality of God as God, and puts his trust in earthly things, and even dedicates his life to mere worldly people, things or causes, he easily falls into selfish, greedy, manipulative or violent behaviour. Only faithfulness to the real God of Israel can protect the person and the community from such foolishness and such immorality. This is why the first Commandment (and the second and third too) is not irrelevant in studying justice and peace. There is a strong lesson in the Bible that man loses his sense of perspective when he loses sight of God's place as Creator and Lord, and with this loss of perspective comes injustice, dishonesty and greed.

Judaism, following the Old Testament emphasis on ethics, and developing it through rabbinic, medieval and modern writings, places more importance on behaviour than doctrine.[48] The most important thing is to obey the Torah, to be faithful to it. A lot of writing on justice issues has a strong emphasis on activism and action, sometimes to the neglect of doctrine, thus echoing the Jewish approach. What of the Christian approach?

The Christian tradition
One way to answer this question is to see *Jesus* as another prophet with a number of wonderfully inspiring teachings about love and justice, and a model life to match and imitate.

Sometimes this prophetic Jesus is seen as a universal preacher, in contrast to an alleged narrow Judaism; sometimes he is seen as a Jewish teacher, following in the footsteps of Isaiah and Amos. Both approaches are inadequate for various reasons. The one point to stress here is that Christ is a teacher and model, but more than just that.

Jesus' teachings
Jesus' *teaching and example* are certainly important, and the teacher ought to be familiar with the details of these. To mention some examples:
- Christ's 'mission statement' (Lk 4:18-21)
- The incredibly rich Sermon on the Mount/Plain (Mt 5-7 and Lk 6:17-49)
- The parable of the Good Samaritan (Lk 10)
- The parable of the Prodigal Son (Lk 15)
- The parable of the Rich Fool (Lk 12: 16ff)
- The parable of the Rich man and Lazarus (Lk 16: 19ff)
- The saying about giving to Caesar what is Caesar's and to God what is God's (Mk 12: 17)
- The teaching on true greatness in the Kingdom (Mt 18:1ff)
- The insistence on the necessity of constant forgiveness (Mt 18:21ff)
- The answer to the rich man seeking the way to salvation and perfection (Mt 19:16ff).

In all his teachings, Jesus echoes the call of Lev 19:2, which we have already alluded to as central to Judaism, to imitate the God of justice. In Matthew, Christ says: 'Be perfect, therefore, as your heavenly Father is perfect' (Mt 5:48). In Luke, Christ says 'Be merciful just as your heavenly Father is merciful' (Lk 6:36). The parallel suggests that the perfection of God that we are to imitate is not one of power or strength but one of justice and mercy.

Jesus' example

Jesus embodied justice and mercy in his deeds too. Examples include:

- Christ calling a tax-collector to be an apostle (Mt 10)
- Christ meeting with the tax collector Zacchaeus (Lk 19)
- His many healings of lepers and sick people, even on the Sabbath (e.g. Mk 2)
- The miraculous feedings of the crowd (e.g. Jn 6)
- His table fellowship with outcasts and sinners and his attitudes towards the socially despised (e.g. Lk 7: 36ff)
- The washing of the apostles' feet (Jn 13)
- Christ forgiving those who crucified him (Lk 23: 34)
- His promise of salvation to the repentant thief (Lk 23: 40-43)

The Incarnation

What more is needed? We need to mention further who Christ was and is: God. The doctrine of the Incarnation is central to Christianity. God became man in Jesus Christ and lived among us (see John 1: 14). What might the Incarnation say about justice and peace? Amongst many possible answers, the following can be suggested:

- All things human are sanctified because God shared and shares our life.
- The mystery of the Incarnation emphasises the humility of Christ, who though he was God, emptied himself of his status and power to come and save us by sharing our life and our death (see Phil 2: 5-11), and so argues against any reliance on human pride or mere strength. Might is not right.
- It strongly reinforces the value of empathy and entering into the situations of others in order to be with them in compassion and to help them effectively.
- As Christ became one of us in a real way, not just pretending to have a body but actually being born bodily, (as both the

Bible and early Church Councils insist), Christianity sees the importance of the bodily dimension of human living and the necessity of providing for the bodily needs of humanity, such as in health care and social security.

Providing for the ordinary earthly needs of people is inspired also by Christ's concern with the bodily needs of others in his ministry (as mentioned above). We can see this continued through history in the Church's involvement in education and health care and in charity work in so many parts of the world. We also see it in the lives of the saints, worth studying in this context.[49]

The Redemption

One important doctrine that may be easily overlooked when dealing with justice and peace from a Christian perspective is the Redemption, a doctrine that is sadly neglected. This doctrine finds little space in religious education about justice issues, except insofar as Jesus' death is an example of injustice and oppression and martyrdom for a good cause. The Redemption is much more than that.

- Christ's death is the example of complete selflessness, of perfect sacrifice for the sake of others.
- This perfect sacrifice is perpetuated in the Mass, according to Catholic faith, and this is one of the reasons why the Eucharist is so central to Catholicism.
- By his perfect love, courage, obedience, faithfulness, humility and perseverance, Christ makes up for our failure in these and other areas of virtue and goodness. He makes possible for us a right relationship with God (and with each other and all creation) by getting rid of the dead weight of our failures and all the 'negativity' that drags us down as individuals and fragments us as community.
- He reconciles the world to God and makes peace by his Cross, as St Paul says so wonderfully in Ephesians 1 and 2.

- Christ demonstrates the depth of God's love for us and so makes our love all the greater: 'We love because he first loved us' (1 John 4:19, and see the whole chapter).

The New Commandment
Christ goes further than the commandment 'Love your neighbour as yourself' and the commandment to love God with all your heart, which summarised the whole of the Law and Prophets (see Mt 22:36-41). The 'new' Commandment is: 'love one another as I have loved you' (John 15:12) Christ's love, which is God's love made flesh, is the inspiration and source of our love, and this will of course include justice, though go beyond it. The more Christians can immerse themselves in the true story of Christ's love for us, made especially clear by his Passion and Cross, the more they are challenged and enabled to become like Christ and to love as he did. We enter into this story by word and sacrament, by song and drama, by prayer and meditation, by the example of the saints and by our own experience of faith (especially by our own suffering accepted with faith and hope).

The Resurrection
Thus, the central religious and moral principle of imitating the just and merciful God of the Old Testament is fulfilled by imitating Christ of the New. His life and death become a pattern of life for Christians and for all. His Resurrection is strongly emphasised today, and rightly so. It is central to Christian faith and should inform Christian thinking on justice and peace. It continues the theme of the Incarnation, highlighting the sacredness of bodily life and bodily reality (Christ rose *bodily* from the dead). It also focuses our attention on life after death.

Justice and life after death
This area of life after death can be seen as a 'rival' to justice and peace issues, a distraction from concern for this world's good.

We are either going to emphasise saving our souls, as the 'old' Catholicism allegedly did, or we are going to be modern and focus on this world and its improvement (or its complete political and social transformation) instead of eternal salvation. This is actually a false dilemma. A properly integrated approach will acknowledge the close link between salvation and justice, between eternal life and earthly life. Christ's Resurrection is our guide here. His body is raised, glorified and transformed (the Transfiguration was the anticipation of this during his ministry), and so is somehow different and unrecognised at times in the post-Resurrection appearances such as the Road to Emmaus in Luke 24. However, the same Jesus who died is raised, with the wounds of his crucifixion still visible to touch (as the apostle Thomas experienced in John 20). This suggests that our worldly justice and love will be glorified in heaven. Our good works are done with the help of the Father's grace, in communion with Christ, led by the Spirit. We do not save ourselves, but are saved 'in Christ'. Nevertheless, we are personally involved in our salvation by our co-operation in Christ's redemptive work of justice and mercy as members of his body on earth, the Church. In other words, what we do here on earth is not lost but transformed and fulfilled in the eternal fullness of life in communion with God and the saints in heaven.

Eschatology is an important area of Christian doctrine, one that may be neglected in teaching on justice and peace, which can too often focus exclusively on this-worldly concerns. A concern with the life to come is not necessarily exclusively individualistic or selfish. It is worth noting how the Bible speaks of heaven and eternal life in *social* terms rather than exclusively individualistic terms. Of course, it is as individuals that we make our decisions – no one else can make our free choices for us – and so the individual matters for Christianity, and for the Judaeo-Christian 'vision' more generally. But heaven is seen in the Bible in strongly communal terms, for example in the image of the new Jerusalem in Revelation 21-22, the final chapters of the Bible story, the ultimate fulfilment of the whole drama of our existence. Heaven is seen there as a city, which is a social reality, and so the virtues that enable us to live in the Church, in society, in the civil world, namely the virtues of justice and social charity, are the virtues of heaven too. (Or, at least, they prepare us for fulfilment in heaven.)[50]

The Kingdom of God

The 'Kingdom of God' (or 'reign of God' as it is often translated now) is one of the most important concepts in the Synoptic Gospel accounts of Christ's ministry, and one of the most widely mentioned in modern Christian theological writing about social justice. Christian tradition, as acknowledged clearly in the *Gaudium et Spes* passage referred to above, distinguishes the Kingdom (in its fullness) from earthly progress. Christianity does not consider that we human beings can achieve the Kingdom by our individual efforts, nor by political schemes or economic plans or structural adjustments or social revolutions. It is God's work, his gift and grace. This means that all human work for justice and peace is 'relativised', put into proper perspective and protected from fanaticism and extremism by a focus on the Kingdom of God. Concern for justice can sometimes lead to awful things being done in the name of progress and even for the cause of peace. To counteract this, God, and his strict concern for the dignity of the human person and the common good of all, must rule in our hearts and minds and actions. We can, however, participate in the growth of the Kingdom by our response to God's call to us to live 'in Christ' a life of holiness and justice (or 'righteousness' to use the Biblical term synonymous with justice). Starting with grace-inspired conversion, we are justified by God and sanctified by the Spirit. We are established in a right relationship with God, and so can act justly towards others with increasing ease. With God's rule established in our hearts through conversion (renewed each Ash Wednesday and Lent), we can see differently. Our vision improves. We see our neighbour as our equal, created in God's image and called like us to belong to God's people and God's Kingdom. We all share the same origin and potential destiny and so, the same dignity and worth.

The Church and Christian tradition
Such has been the message preached and (at its best) embodied by the community of disciples of Christ, the Church established by him and guided by the Spirit. It is in and through this Church that Christ's gospel lives on and is spread to the whole world. As a constitutive element of this, various aspects of justice and peace have been explored and put into practice over the past twenty centuries.[51] One development was the work done on natural law and the virtue of justice by St Thomas Aquinas in the thirteenth century. Thomas, based on his acceptance in faith of the Biblical doctrine of man created in God's image, was able to see that the human person can participate in God's providential care for his creation (including man himself) by using his reason. Thus, we can naturally grasp the basic moral principles that enable us to live well as individuals in society, called to happiness and perfection. This 'participation' is the 'natural law' and it is just the kind of thing explored earlier in this chapter when the meaning of 'justice' was examined by the light of reason under the five headings of right relationship, retribution, and so on. (The treatment there of 'retribution' in particular was heavily indebted to Aquinas' approach.) Aquinas also devoted a large amount of effort to explicating the virtue of justice in some detail.[52]

Modern approaches (i): Christ and Culture (Richard Niebuhr)
Three distinctive modern Christian approaches to justice and peace issues will be outlined now. One is the Christ and Culture Typology[53] developed by Richard Niebuhr, an influential

twentieth-century Protestant theologian.[54] It provides a way of analysing possible approaches to 'culture' based on the Gospel. It can be applied to several aspects of Christian life and thought, but is particularly interesting with regard to justice issues. There are five possible 'ideal types' of relationship of Christ to culture, (or of Christian discipleship or Church attitude to the dominant non-Christian culture), according to this way of analysing Christianity.

1 *Christ against culture*: this would be expressed in a Church that saw the wider world or society as basically unjust and unreachable or 'unsavable' because it is totally corrupted by sin. It would lead to a sect-like, insular focus on the Church community itself and its own identity and holiness. The Church would be siege-like in its mentality, concerned mainly with its own affairs and the salvation of its own members, and would not seek to influence public policy. It would result in an otherworldly piety and a downplaying or even rejection of 'justice and peace' issues.

2 *Christ with culture* (or Christ *of* culture): this would be expressed by a Church that accepts and celebrates the status quo as basically good – just and peaceful. The emphasis would be on how Christians already fit into the society and culture. Patriotism might be strongly emphasised. There would be a strong temptation for the Gospel to be assimilated into the wider culture and its concerns and assumptions, such as an uncritical acceptance of liberalism, capitalism, or socialism (depending on the context).

3 *Christ in paradox with culture*: this would be expressed by a Church that is 'in the world but not of it'. It is seen in a Christianity that works with the best in politics and other social institutions, but never in a totally 'accepting' way because it is conscious that God's Kingdom is 'already, but not yet' realised. So this is Christian work for justice that is always in tension with the world, though not in a way that rejects the world.

4 *Christ above culture*: put positively, this is a Church that accepts the good in culture (human rights language, for example) but seeks to enlighten it, or purify it, by the higher wisdom and grace of God's revelation, a revelation that is always superior to any merely human or natural culture. More negatively, this could be expressed by a strongly judgemental and even 'triumphalist' Church seeking a great degree of direct control over public life (civil law, public institutions, etc.).

5 *Christ transforming culture*: this would be expressed by a Church that sees itself as 'a leaven in the lump of personal and public life which allows for a legitimate autonomy of secular disciplines and seeks to influence but not necessarily to control institutions.'[55] It is seen in an emphasis on working from within secular institutions to bring the values of Christ to the wider world. It is less religiously direct and less focused on faith issues than the 'Christ above culture' type, and more at home with the world than the paradox type.

These five types are not necessarily found separately in distinct people or churches – they are more like tendencies than defined qualities, and could be found in various combinations in the same person or organisation. Though Niebuhr's typology can be read as a list of options, one of which is judged best, in fact, they could be all appropriate responses to different situations or different realities. Not everyone accepts this typology, and it is best viewed as heuristic rather than historical, a way of explaining patterns and provoking discussion rather than a description of actual persons or groups. It provides an interesting way to look at the various ways Christians down through the centuries and in our own time have interpreted the New Testament material in such varied ways.

The 'transforming culture' type is the one that many modern writers on justice and peace think is the best (although many

Christian evangelical writers opt for the 'paradox' type and the Christ 'over culture' is seen by many as the official Catholic position). The Catholic Church sees some aspects of culture as totally unacceptable (for example, abortion and torture) and so the 'against culture' type seems to apply; some aspects of culture are fully acceptable, (such as fundraising to aid the developing world) and so fit the 'with culture' type; some are a mixture of good and bad (such as 'separation of church and state', which can be understood in various ways) and so might fit the 'paradox' or 'against culture' – or perhaps the 'transforming culture' type. The typology is not always easy to apply; but trying to apply it can open up perspectives and insights. One major issue is how direct, or explicitly religious, should the influence of the Church be on public life and justice issues associated with public life. Some would say the Church should be indirect and implicit, downplaying the faith dimension and the controversial aspects of the Gospel in favour of a co-operation with the culture in order to transform it (type five); others see this as a kind of assimilation of the faith to the secular (or unjust) culture and an ineffective method of working for justice.

Modern approaches (ii): Catholic Social Teaching
'Catholic Social Teaching' (or 'Catholic Social Doctrine' as it is sometimes called) is something all Catholic RE teachers ought to be very familiar with, as should all Catholics, though it has been called 'Our best kept secret' because it is not as widely known as it should be. It refers to a body of teaching and moral principles taught mainly through a series of Church documents, beginning with Pope Leo XIII's *Rerum Novarum* in 1891. These documents (mainly papal) address the social issues of the day. For example, *Rerum Novarum* focused on the worker problem of the late nineteenth century in the wake of the Industrial Revolution. The documents also uncover principles relevant to other issues and future problems. This was shown in Pope John Paul II's development of Leo's teaching in his own

encyclical *Centesimus Annus*, on the hundredth anniversary of the foundation document of the 'tradition' of CST – i.e. Catholic Social Teaching. The documents are available online in full.

CST basic principles: the US bishops' list
Catholic Social Teaching's basic principles have been variously listed. The US bishops, having outlined the scriptural and sacramental heritage, put forward the following list of CST principles in their pastoral letter on issues of crime and punishment (Nov 2000):[56]

1 *Human Life and Dignity:* This means that any social policy or programme or any personal action must respect the worth of every human person affected. It outlaws all degrading, destructive, cruel, or unjustly discriminatory treatment of others. As all people are created in God's image, the basic necessities of life must be available to all. One must always treat others in a way that acknowledges their conscience and freedom (though this does not forbid imprisoning criminals whose freedom may be rightly limited as punishment for them and as protection for society). Directly destroying the life of any innocent human being is always unjust.
2 *Human Rights and Responsibilities:* This is a direct link back to the fifth perspective on justice seen above in 2.1. 'Rights', however, are clearly correlated here with 'responsibilities'. Catholic morality does not accept an extreme individualism that focuses on individual freedoms and desires, but rather on the individual-within-community, with both entitlements and duties.
3 *Family, Community and Participation:* This is characteristic of the Catholic tradition (and also of the Jewish tradition). Again, we see a rejection of any purely individualistic philosophy that views the person as essentially a detached unit free from all ties and neutral between all connections.

Instead, CST sees the person as essentially related. This is a direct link back to the first of the perspectives on justice we looked at in 2.1 – 'right relationship'. The protection and strengthening of family based on marriage is central to the Catholic vision of justice and peace, and the Judaeo-Christian tradition as a whole. This is a point of some controversy in that other 'visions' may see this as an unjust restriction of individuals' freedom to create their own versions of relationship and reproduction. (There is a need here for the teacher to be familiar with Catholic Sexual Ethics and its relationship with CST.) The principle of 'participation' is a very useful way of assessing much that goes on in society at the political and cultural levels. CST emphasises that all individuals should be invited to, and facilitated in, being involved in the government and organisation of society at its various levels. This is a principle that outlaws unjust exclusion or marginalisation of persons or groups.

4 *The Common Good:* This is a principle that draws our attention to the goods that we share as social beings. Again, the emphasis is on the essentially social nature of the human person and the importance of taking into account the wider effects of all policies, choices, actions. We are part of a web of relationships and should not see life in narrowly individualistic terms as a matter of 'looking after number one'. The common good is not a good that 'number one' can achieve by himself or enjoy by himself. Our fulfilment as human beings is not a purely private affair. This principle alerts us to the dangers of any philosophy of life that is indifferent to public life and social issues.

5 *The Option for the Poor and Vulnerable:* This is more widely known to many RE teachers by the first half of the phrase, but the inclusion of 'and Vulnerable' is helpful in that it highlights the fact that the 'poor' are not just the economically badly off, but all persons who are in danger or in serious need or 'fragile' in some way. The word 'option'

refers to the idea that individuals and society should make choices in a way that deliberately takes special care for the effects of our actions, programmes and policies on those who are less able to fend for themselves or deal with adversity on their own. The 'poverty proofing' aspect of Irish political policy-making is an example of this.

6 *Subsidiarity and Solidarity:* These are rather technical terms, but very useful. *Subsidiarity,* in the words of the bishops, 'calls for problem-solving initially at the community level: family, neighborhood, city, and state. It is only when problems become too large or the common good is clearly threatened that larger institutions are required to help.' This principle protects against an intrusive and paternalistic welfare state, or a 'statist' philosophy, that takes away people's initiative and personal sense of responsibility and ability. It prevents the local being swallowed up by 'big business', or 'Big Brother'. 'Small is beautiful' (in Schumacher's famous phrase) sums it up. 'Big when necessary' is one way to explain *solidarity,* which is a kind of balancing community principle. This principle highlights the social charity binding us together as fellow human beings. It insists that we care for all people, not just for personal, local and parochial concerns.

7 *Respect for the Integrity of Creation:* This is not mentioned by the US bishops in their letter on crime (as it does not directly apply there) but it is seen as a constituent principle of CST generally. It is looked at it in chapter three below.

These principles taught by the Catholic magisterium are inspired by Biblical sources and by Sacred Tradition, as well as by the best in social philosophy and experience.

Latkovic's interpretation
Another similar, though distinctive, list of CST principles is provided by American Catholic theologian Mark Latkovic, (influenced greatly by Germain Grisez):

1. Human dignity
2. Distributive equality of common goods
3. Division of labour
4. Authority
5. Participation
6. Subsidiarity
7. The common good
8. Christian love[57]

Here, it is worth noting that numbers 1-4 include the basic equality of all human beings, while they allow for a functional inequality that is not essentially unjust. CST takes a more moderate view of inequality than a strict radical egalitarianism that would reject all inequalities as unjust in principle. Though there is an irreducible basic equality of all human beings that must never be violated or neglected or oppressed, there exist some inequalities of wealth and status and talent that are not necessarily a result of injustice, nor always matters to be deplored and tackled by radical actions (such as, for example, wide-sweeping quotas or affirmative action policies, or severe government confiscations of the property of the wealthy). Also, authority is not only morally acceptable, as some views only reluctantly admit, but morally *required* for a just community to be possible. Of course, it must always be a responsible authority guided by moral truths and shaped by the virtues of prudence and justice and not a brute assertion of strength or an opportunistic seeking of status and control.

Archbishop Martin's outline of CST
Most succinctly, Archbishop of Dublin, Diarmuid Martin, recently summarised CST under three headings at a recent lecture.[58] The three principles are:
- The dignity of the human person
- The unity of the human family
- The integrity of creation

Archbishop Martin's main point on CST was that 'the primary principle that should drive international development is charity'. By this he highlighted the priority of 'love' – treating the other with generosity *as a person* – over a reluctant 'justice' that fails to respect the poor as active subjects in their own development rather than passive objects to be treated or pitied. This love, or 'solidarity', goes well beyond the narrow concerns of the now dominant rational utilitarianism that relies on the principles of self-interest, comparative advantage, national interest and security. The poor need to have a voice in the creation of a new world order. They need democratic institutions and opportunities, and increased respect for their rights, especially their freedoms. However, they also need their 'capacity' to be improved, not just a bare freedom – otherwise they will not benefit from globalisation and the free market. By 'capacity' the Archbishop refers to the various types of wealth necessary for living and developing as individuals and society. Education will play a vital role in this development of capacity (including perhaps internet-facilitated links between educational institutions in developed and developing countries). Archbishop Martin also emphasised that rules are necessary to protect the poor in trade. Again, mere freedoms are not enough in the real situations of developing countries in a demanding world. It can be seen from all this that Catholic Social Teaching is not a specific political programme or ideology or party – but it will have concrete effects if taken seriously. It is an approach to justice and peace that incorporates much of the insight from the five perspectives on justice seen in 2.1 above, especially right relationship, equality, and human rights, seen in the light of the Gospel embodied and proclaimed by Jesus Christ.

Modern approaches (iii): Liberation Theology
The third modern movement of Christen thought on justice issues is Liberation Theology, which is found in both Catholic

and Protestant forms, although it has been associated mainly with Catholic theologians. A central feature of this approach to doing theology was mentioned above in comments on how the Exodus story can be read in a very political way. Political reading of the Bible is found in much modern study and teaching of Scripture, and has become part of mainstream Christianity in a moderated form. Read Mary's Magnificat (Lk 1), for example, with the image of the poor of the developing world in your mind and heart – and see how different it, and Mary, appear. In much Liberation Theology, the political tendency is strong and the focus is very much on this-worldly concerns.

The perspective taken is that of the poor and oppressed. Their experience and concerns are primary. This kind of theology typically starts with injustices, and usually gross injustices such as heavy political oppression or mass hunger or wide-spread poverty in developing countries. It began in Latin America in the late 1950s and grew in the 60s and 70s. It insists that theology is to be focused on the needs of the poor, not on abstract academic debates or controversies.

The authority of the hierarchy is somewhat suspect, as are all hierarchical structures, especially in some forms of Liberation Theology. (It should be said that this theology appears in various forms, some more extreme than others. I am painting in broad brush-strokes here.)

The world tends to be seen in vivid black and white terms – good and evil, oppressed and oppressor. The rulers, the rich, the capitalist, the white man, the 'establishment', even the Church hierarchy – all may be judged to be oppressive and perhaps corrupt.

From being mainly a concern for economic justice and political participation for the poor of Latin America, Liberation Theology has come to influence various types of social analysis and social interpretation. It can be seen in the structure and wording of this very syllabus itself, in my opinion, especially in part one. It influences various political theologies, such as feminist theologies.

Behind it is an analysis of society and/or the Church in terms of class war or deeply entrenched social conflict, in which revolution or radical change, rather than gradual reform as such, is promoted to replace the unjust structures and systems with completely new ways of thinking, feeling, acting and 'structuring'. Its Christian vision of justice has been influenced to some degree by Marxism, though to what extent is highly debated. So, typically, it claims that the whole capitalist system must go and be replaced by a new system of co-operation and care, some kind of socialism usually (though the details are generally not specific, nor the method or strategy to achieve this utopia). Or, to apply it to the perspective of 'justice as equality' in a religious context, it's not just that women must be ordained, for example, but the whole hierarchical structure of the Catholic Church must be replaced by a radically egalitarian community that avoids the oppressive rule and teaching of the old unjust Catholicism.

This is a powerfully rhetorical kind of justice language, hugely inspired by the Exodus story and a focus on the historical Jesus emphasising his conflict with the religious and political establishment of his day. It can be criticised as too utopian and too unrealistic, especially in the light of the fall of communism in 1989 and the apparent triumph of liberal capitalism since, but it remains a potent challenge, nonetheless, to any approach to theology (or RE) that fails to take seriously the realities of poverty and injustice and exclusion and powerlessness suffered by too many people. It challenges us to imagine new ways of organising society and not to be complacent with the status quo.

Although the Catholic magisterium has criticised it for its tendencies towards a reductionistic reading of the Bible, its materialism, and its suspicion of, and even rejection of, Church hierarchy and authority in the name of radical egalitarianism, a 'liberationist' perspective has been integrated into the Church's own justice language and rhetoric. This is evident in the 1986 document on Christian Liberation issued by the Congregation for the Doctrine of the Faith, and in the Pope's criticisms of extreme capitalism in *Centesimus Annus* in 1991 and his support for third world debt reduction or cancellation in the years surrounding the Millennium Jubilee year.

Liberation Theology has had an effect on many approaches to justice and peace. For example on human rights:

> The specific contribution which liberation theology has made to the Catholic theory of human rights is that it has insisted that the interests of the marginalised should be at the heart of the Christian vision and that political work for justice is a requirement of the gospel. The preferential option for the poor and the denunciation of all forms of economic and social privilege are regarded as the ways in which the Christian should work for the establishment of the kingdom on earth.... [Its] analysis transformed the traditional approaches and gave them new vigour. In addition it led to the reconceptualising of the Christian understanding of mission, replaced the work of charity with justice and developed the kind of vision which was the basis for a new style of Catholic development agency.[59]

Two neglected issues: judgement and mercy
To finish this overview of the Judaeo-Christian vision of justice and peace, I want to mention two aspects that might be in need of development in theological reflection and religious education: judgement and mercy.

Judgement
The first, judgement, and in particular divine judgement, is an aspect of faith that is, in my opinion, sadly downplayed in

recent times. Yet, it is central in the Biblical vision of the just God. The OT prophets are highly judgemental – the reader cannot miss it! Constantly we are reminded, 'Thus says the Lord...' and what follows is often a warning of dire consequences if the people do not mend their ways immediately and do penance for their sins, notably sins of idolatry and injustice. In the NT, Christ's teaching is also very much focused on God's coming judgement. His famous parable of the Last Judgement (Mt 25), for example, is bound to be central in any presentation of the Christian vision of justice. It clearly states that our treatment of others, especially the least among us, shapes how God will judge us and our final destiny on the last day. We must look after others in practical ways or else we will face an eternity of punishment, separate from God and the community of heaven. Our neglect or rejection of others in their need is in fact a neglect or rejection of Christ himself – 'you did it to me' – and so our failure to be just or loving is our separating ourselves from God and salvation. Unless we sincerely repent our sins in this life, we shape ourselves as persons-separated-from-God in the next. This is a well-known dogma of the Christian religion. It would surely be a powerful force for good, a strong motivation for just and loving behaviour, especially in the face of the temptation to be selfish, greedy, violent, negligent, or careless, yet it is doctrine that is no longer emphasised. It needs to be rediscovered and presented anew.

Mercy
If it is to be a healthy worldview, however, and not a distorted kind of 'fear-based' religion, Christianity must integrate this doctrine of divine judgement or justice with the doctrine of divine mercy. In both the OT and the NT, God is presented as a God of justice *and mercy*. (It is important that one does not fall into the mistake of seeing the OT as portraying a God of wrath and justice and the NT as portraying a God of mercy and love.

This is inaccurate and particularly unfair to Judaism.) This part of the new RE syllabus is focused on justice, but it will be radically incomplete if it neglects the mercy aspect. 'Pure' justice is not necessarily a good thing. As Psalm 129/130 (the *De Profundis*) says, 'If you, O Lord, should mark iniquities, Lord, who could stand?' In other words, if God was totally just, we would all be justly doomed. But God is merciful. 'God's mercy is his steadfast love, by which he continues to love his creatures despite their sins and does everything necessary to save fallen humankind.'[60] God continually calls his unfaithful people back to the Covenant (see the prophet Hosea on this theme).

Justice alone is not enough to deal with a sinful and evil world; mercy is needed to conquer evil. Mercy goes beyond justice to give to others gratuitously in order to overcome the effects of evil. Mercy tempers any enforcement of justice that would be overly harsh, though it does not cancel out the objective requirements of justice that ought to be respected to facilitate the healing of divisions and building up community. As God has been merciful towards us, so we too ought to show mercy. By doing this, we open ourselves to the reality of God's mercy: 'Blessed are the merciful, for they shall obtain mercy' (The Beatitudes, Mt 5); 'Forgive us our trespasses, as we forgive those who trespass against us' (*The Our Father*, traditional wording).

The new commandment (John 15) is that we love one another as Christ has loved us. How has Christ loved us? The short answer is: with boundless mercy. It is not surprising then that mercy is a central theme of many parables. How else can we understand, for example, the fact that the vineyard owner pays all the workers equally a day's wage, even though some have worked only a few hours, and some who only responded at the last hour (see Mt 20)? The answer is that the vineyard owner symbolises God, whose love goes beyond strict justice in its reaching out to all to offer salvation to any who will repent and believe in the Gospel. While justice is idealistic, mercy is more practical: it deals with people as they are. It takes weakness and the effects of evil seriously. Mercy is embodied in Christ's death on the cross 'while we were still sinners' (see Romans 5). Mercy is central to the Gospel and to the mission of the Church. It promotes reconciliation which is essential to the establishment of peace.

Sometimes, mercy will ask that we even forgo our strict rights, so that others will be helped, so that the common good will be served. It prevents an emphasis on justice from tying us up in knots. If our Christian judgement and action for justice is too calculating or rigid, we will lose proper perspective, which should be God's perspective, the perspective of merciful love. Mercy is not mere pity; nor is it condescension.

The Catholic tradition has listed classic examples of works of mercy. Echoing the parable of the Last Judgement (Mt 25), the *corporal works of mercy* are:

- Feeding the hungry
- Giving drink to the thirsty
- Clothing the naked
- Sheltering the homeless
- Visiting the sick
- Ransoming the captive
- Burying the dead

The *spiritual works of mercy* are:
- Instructing the ignorant
- Counselling the doubtful
- Admonishing sinners
- Bearing wrongs patiently
- Forgiving offences
- Comforting the sorrowing
- Praying for the living and the dead (See the *Catechism* 2447.)

Examples like these shape our thinking in highly specific ways and form a useful way to examine conscience. Mercy completes justice, moderating it and contextualising it. Life, with all its richness and its challenges, cannot be adequately measured on a scales.

(ii) The Zakat of Islam

The wider context
This, one of the five pillars of the Islamic faith, offers a very focused topic to study, and along with the Varnas of Hinduism section, it is narrower in scope than the other religious topics studied in this part of the syllabus. The wider issues of Islam and justice and peace are not specified, but it would hardly be possible for a teacher to completely ignore further issues. There will be some opportunity in this regard under other headings in section F, such as 2.1 on 'Equality' and 2.4 on 'Violence', especially 'Just war'. This book does not deal with the wider issues of Islam and justice – the topic is too complex to deal with adequately in the space available. Here, all that will be said is that Islam has an obvious extremist element that has engaged in horrendous acts of terrorism, but that these extreme elements are not necessarily characteristic of Islam as a whole, though they may be partially inspired by Islamic beliefs. (A fuller picture of Islam will be found in section C of the course, which should be well-known before teaching this section.)[61] Though there are some who argue otherwise, this book takes the position that Islam at its best is a religion of peace. Like any seriously held belief system, including Christianity, it can lend itself to fanaticism, it can be distorted to 'justify' violence and injustice. The focus on Zakat in this part of the course offers a chance for the teacher to show a clearly positive side to Islam: its concern with donating from one's wealth to aid others in need.

Basic meaning: purification
Often known to beginners studying Islam as a kind of almsgiving, or charity, Zakat is actually more correctly translated as 'purification':

The third pillar is the obligatory tax called Zakat ('purification,' indicating that such a payment makes the rest of one's wealth religiously and legally pure). This is the only permanent tax levied by the Qur'an and is payable annually on food grains, cattle, and cash after one year's possession. The amount varies for different categories. Thus, on grains and fruits it is 10 per cent if land is watered by rain, 5 per cent if land is watered artificially. On cash and precious metals it is 2 per cent. Zakat is collectable by the state and is to be used primarily for the poor, but the Qur'an mentions other purposes: ransoming Muslim war captives, redeeming chronic debts, paying tax collectors' fees, jihad (and by extension, according to Qur'an commentators, education and health), and creating facilities for travelers. After the breakup of Muslim religio-political power, payment of Zakat has become a matter of voluntary charity dependent on individual choice.[62]

References in the Qur'an
Zakat is mentioned in The Qur'an in 'The Cow' 2: 177:

>...virtue means to believe in God [Alone], the Last Day, the angels, the Book and the prophets; and to give one's wealth away, no matter how one loves it, to near relatives, orphans, the needy, the wayfarer and beggars, and towards freeing captives; and to keep up prayer and pay the welfare due ('Zakat'); and those who keep their word whenever they promise anything, and are patient under suffering and hardship and in time of violence.[63]

Another reference is in 'Repentance' 9: 60:

>Charity [Zakat] is (meant) only for the poor, the needy, those working at (collecting and distributing) it, those

(possible converts) whose hearts are being reconciled (to yours), for (freeing) captives and debtors, and (in fighting) in god's way, and for the wayfarer, as a duty imposed by God. God is Aware, Wise.[64]

The literal meaning of 'Zakat' is 'growth' or 'purification' and it strictly refers to an obligatory monetary contribution. Another term, 'sadaqat' also occurs in the Qur'an, and refers to 'any kind of charity which is given for the sake of God'.[65]

Overall meaning
J. Jomier calls it a kind of 'social taxation' that has become quasi-official and has been regulated by all kinds of laws. In Islam the *Zakat* has been a factor of solidarity and unity.[66] (However, 'taxation' may be the wrong term as it connotes a payment that one must pay or be punished, whereas Zakat is more like charity, paid out of love of God, voluntary payment of an obligatory gift to the poor.) It supplements private almsgiving. The 'Qur'an recalls the rights of the most disadvantaged and [...] the *Zakat* was a way of gaining these rights for them.' Only the almsgiving of Ramadan can go to non-Muslims; the rest goes only to Muslims, as Muslims have paid it.[67]

Purification
One excellent website to study the Zakat and Islam in general is the 'Zakat Information Centre' at Islamicity.com.[68] The piece there on Zakat by Jamal Badawi emphasises that Zakat is motivated by love of God, by one's faithfulness to the Covenant with God. Also, Zakat purifies both the individual and society from greed and injustice. God owns everything, so no human being owns anything absolutely. All we have we have in trust only and we must use it well and morally. Property is the domain of God, and Islam accepts the legitimacy of private ownership but only when one acts knowingly, justly and

generously as a 'trustee' of God's property. Zakat is not paid on one's basic needs or one's principle residence, or one's tools of profession.

The 'Glossary' page at Islamicity says this about 'Zakah' (which is another way to write Zakat in English):

> It is to be used in eight categories for welfare of the society that are mentioned in the Qur'an, namely: the poor, the needy, the sympathizers, the captives, the debtors, the cause of Allah, the wayfarers, and for those who are to collect it. The amount to be collected is 2.5%, 5%, or 10%, depending on the assets and the method used to produce it. For example, it is 2.5% of the assets that have been owned over a year, 5% of the wheat when irrigated by the farmer, and 10% of the wheat that is irrigated by the rain.

There are diverse Islamic understandings of the role of Zakat in the contemporary world.[69] Some have seen it as akin to socialism. For example, al-Nasser, the president of Egypt from 1957-1970, declared Islam and socialism compatible. Others have been reluctant to do this as socialism can be connected with atheistic communism. One modern problem is how to integrate the low level of Zakat with the relatively high level of taxation needed to fund a modern state. One solution, seen in Pakistan and Saudi Arabia, is to levy Zakat on companies, not just individuals as has been done traditionally, and sometimes the categories to be included in the Zakat are extended. The integration (or non-integration) of Islam with modernity is an ongoing area of debate and controversy, as it is for other world religions; how Zakat is to be applied is one admittedly minor element of this.

(iii) The Four Varnas of Hinduism

Basic meaning
This is a complex topic, associated with India and its social structure based on traditional Hinduism. The view of justice seems to be that it requires fitting in to that social structure, faithful to family and society traditions, so as to progress spiritually. The central idea is to live in harmony with the cosmic or natural order (the 'Rita'), which is respected according to the duties of your state in life, your Varna being a prime determinant of this state and your duties.

The challenge of understanding Hinduism
Hinduism is an enormously complicated religion and it is very difficult to understand fully this way of viewing justice. It cannot but seem to many Westerners that Hinduism neglects the equality of all people and the moral superiority of a meritocratic society over one that allows people to be assigned their place in the social hierarchy according to their birth. Still, even if RE teachers might be put off by the foreign nature of this part of the course, (or worried about misunderstanding it), it is worth trying to engage with another way of thinking about justice.

In some ways actually, it is not totally unlike the traditional Irish emphasis on accepting the will of God and playing one's proper role in society according to where one found oneself, presumably by God's will – 'blossoming where you are planted'. It could be said that all societies try to justify their structure and give it a security and permanence to make life peaceful. This is perhaps what the Varna doctrine aims to do for Indian society.

Varna and caste
What is a 'Varna'? The term is often thought to refer to the caste system, though 'Varna' is not strictly synonymous with 'caste'.

Varna: 'Varna is a larger group comprising smaller caste groups doing different jobs and maintaining different family traditions.'[70]

There are four Varnas:

1   Brahmans (religious leadership)
2   Ksatriyas (government and law)
3   Vaishyas (agriculture, industry and commerce)
4   Shudras (skilled labour).

The nature of the caste groups varies throughout India, but the four overall groupings, the 'Varnas', are constant. (The caste groups, the subsections, are known as 'jatis'.) Living your life according to the Varna you belong to, and to a lesser extent being faithful to the smaller caste within that Varna, is central to Hinduism. One encyclopaedia explains its importance thus:

> The caste system, which has organized Indian society for many millennia, is thoroughly legitimated by and intertwined with Hindu religious doctrine and practice. Four social classes, or Varnas – Brahmans, Ksatriyas, Vaishyas, and Shudras – provide the simplified structure for the enormously complicated system of thousands of castes and subcastes within Indian society. Although it is not certain whether a society limited to four classes was ever more than a theoretical ideal, there is a sense in which they map out socioreligious reality. Such is evident from the Purusa hymn (Rigveda 10.90), in which the statement that the Brahman was the Purusa's mouth, the nobleman (Ksatriya) his arms, the Vaishya his thighs, and the Shudra his feet, gives an idea of their functions and mutual relations.[71]

Another writer comments on the duties of life (dharma) associated with being a member of a Varna:

Varna dharma: (Sanskrit) 'The way of one's kind.' [...] Within Varna dharma are the many religious and moral codes which define human virtue. Varna dharma is social duty, in keeping with the principles of good conduct, according to one's community, which is generally based on the craft or occupation of the family. Strictly speaking it encompasses two interrelated social hierarchies: 1) Varna, which refers to the four classes: brahmin, kshatriya,[72] vaishya and shudra; and 2) jati, the myriad occupational subgroups, or guilds, which in India number over 3,000. Hence this dharma is sometimes called jati dharma. The class-caste system is still very much a part of Indian life today. [However,] many modern Hindus propose that social status is now (and was originally) more properly determined by a person's skills and accomplishments than by birth. Mobility between jatis, or castes, within Hindu communities worldwide is limited but not impossible, and is accomplished through marrying into a new jati, or changing professions through persistence, skill and education. Shastris say that once a person breaks out of his Varna or jati of birth and changes 'caste,' it takes three generations for his family to become fully established in that new strata of society, provided the continuity is unbroken. [73]

Particular duties of each Varna
To be just is to respect and live by the duties attached to the particular Varna one belongs to by birth. These duties are:

- The 'Brahmin' Varna has the responsibility of religious leadership, including teaching and priestly duties.
- The 'Ksatriya' Varna has the responsibility of governing and enforcing the law.

- The 'Vaishya' Varna has the responsibility to engage in business, commerce, industry and agriculture. It includes landowners and merchants.
- The 'Shruda' Varna has the responsibility to do the skilled work, and it includes skilled artisans and labourers. This Varna is very much seen as below the other three: Shruda do not receive the sacred thread, nor can they study the *Vedas* (Hindu Scriptures).

The various duties of each Varna are based on what is assumed to be the inherent nature of the persons born into that Varna. Duties are outlined in the *Bhagavad-Gita*, chapter 19, verses 41-44. More specific duties are assigned to one based on the caste one belongs to (i.e. one's 'jati'). A hierarchy of castes has developed and a strong tradition of following the footsteps of one's father and family. Brahmins today can be found in occupations associated with the other Varnas, but the Shudras are always at the bottom (or near it).

The issue of discrimination
Difficulties arise because of the hierarchical nature of Varnas and castes and the social fragmentation, unjust discrimination and inequality that results and is exacerbated by this. It seems as though Hinduism provides a religious rationale for a strict class system. Members of the upper castes consider those of the lower to be unclean. Because of this emphasis on ritual purity, social interaction between castes is largely prohibited. Intermarriage is frowned upon, though legal; even dining together is avoided. Touching those in Varnas below one's own Varna is polluting.

This notion of touching those in lower Varnas as polluting brings to mind a particularly unattractive feature of Indian social history and life, the 'untouchables'. There is a large group, ranked below the fourth Varna and so outside the Varna structure itself and lower than the lowest Varna, called the 'untouchables' (more formally and correctly called 'Dallit', meaning 'oppressed, crushed').[74] This group does jobs such as dealing with corpses and working with leather. In 1949, untouchability was abolished by Indian law, (it is in article 17 of the Indian constitution of 1949) but it has not disappeared, and caste loyalty is still a feature of marriage, employment and politics. Gandhi gave the untouchables the name of 'harijan' (children of God).

Justification by Hindus
Though it can seem to outsiders very unjust, the Varna system is seen as good by many Hindus. One Hindu website praises it in this way:

> The Varna dharma system – despite its widespread discrimination against harijans, and the abuse of social status by higher castes – ensures a high standard of craftsmanship, a sense of community belonging, family integrity and religio-cultural continuity. Caste is not unique to Hinduism and India. By other names it is found in every society. The four Varnas, or classes, and myriad jatis, occupational castes, or guilds, form the basic elements of human interaction.[75]

So it would seem that Hinduism sees the four Varnas as basic groupings of all human beings in all societies. Going still further, one Hindu scripture, the *Mahabharata*, sees the division into four as a result of sin:

> There is really no distinction between the different orders. The whole world at first consisted of Brahmanas. Created equal by the Creator, men have in consequence of their acts, become distributed into different orders. They that became fond of indulging in desire and enjoying pleasures, possessed of the attributes of severity

and wrath, endued with courage, and unmindful of the duties of piety and worship.[76]

This same scripture makes this informative statement, which directs our attention to the importance of the wider context within which Hindus accept Varnas:

> All men are equal in respect of their physical organism. All of them, again, are possessed of souls that are equal in respect of their nature. When dissolution comes, all else dissolve[s] away. What remains is the inceptive will to achieve Righteousness. That, indeed, reappears (in the next life) of itself. When such is the result (that is when the enjoyments and endurance of this life are due to the acts of a past life), the inequality of lot discernible among human beings cannot be regarded in any way [as] anomalous.[77]

Past lives and Varnas
This scripture seems to clearly blame what we in the West might call 'present injustice of social position' on one's past sins (in previous lives) and to see the possibilities of gaining 'equality of condition' as depending on acting rightly and so gaining a better position in the next life. One is able by one's conduct to raise one's position, with a view to becoming a Brahmin finally and so being able to achieve spiritual salvation.

A more sociological interpretation
However, another way to justify this doctrine is to say that any society will need to have division of occupation if it is to function well, and so people will automatically find themselves in occupations that suit their natural talents and dispositions – and this is basically what Varnas are, social positions based on natural qualities, which ought to be evident in the way one acts. What makes the Varna doctrine distinctive is the lack of

freedom of movement in this life between social positions and the fact that one's birth is taken as determinative of one's social position, a view that is anathema to modern liberal societies, which value freedom and equality highly and look negatively on privilege based on birth, especially if it is wide-spread in a society. It should be noted that not all Hindus accept a completely birth-determined Varna system – in this as in all areas, Hinduism is complex!

Part of a religious world-view
Hindus who accept the doctrine of the Varnas mainly do so as a 'revelation', and one linked to other religious beliefs. The belief in reincarnation is important, because it claims a multitude of lives are lived by each person on his or her way to salvation, or 'moksha', which is release from this illusory material world and an escape from the wheel of existence with its endless cycles of birth, death and rebirth. Therefore, our Western idea that you live only one life is foreign to the Hindu culture, and our emphasis on equality in this one life is not as obvious to them perhaps, as they can see equality as a reality achieved over a vast number of lives. Whether or not reincarnation is a true doctrine is therefore a most important question to answer in coming to a judgement on whether the Varnas express an adequate notion of justice.

(iv) Buddhism: The Eightfold Path

The Eightfold Path is central to Buddhism.[78] It is constituted by:

1 Right views
2 Right intention
3 Right speech
4 Right action
5 Right livelihood
6 Right effort

7   Right mindfulness
8   Right meditational attainment

(The terms can be translated in different ways.) These aim to free one from the illusions of egoism, an aim that is central to Buddhism, which is more like a philosophy than a religion in that it leaves out any reference to God (in its Theravada form).[79] However, Buddhism can be seen as a system of beliefs and practices concerned with transcending the ego, and if one accepts this as a central characteristic of religion, then Buddhism is a religion. The Eightfold Path specifies how one is to transcend the ego. We will look at only some of the Paths here, the ones most clearly connected with concerns of justice.

Right intention
Here is a description of the second of the paths:

> While right view refers to the cognitive aspect of wisdom, right intention refers to the volitional aspect, i.e. the kind of mental energy that controls our actions. Right intention can be described best as commitment to ethical and mental self-improvement. Buddha distinguishes three types of right intentions: 1. the intention of renunciation, which means resistance to the pull of desire, 2. the intention of good will, meaning resistance to feelings of anger and aversion, and 3. the intention of harmlessness, meaning not to think or act cruelly, violently, or aggressively, and to develop compassion.

It is clear that this path has much to contribute to a life of justice and peace by promoting self-control or self-mastery. Much as the classic 'Western' virtues of moderation and courage do, right intention prepares the moral agent to act well and selflessly for the good of his fellow man in a spirit of brotherhood. In other words, it enables one to act justly by dealing with the obstacles to acting justly: selfish desires, anger, hatred and fear. It is interesting to note how, in Buddhism, developing both the mind and the will are important aspects of developing wisdom – it is not enough to merely know about justice and peace, one needs to be willing to act justly for peace. This acknowledgement of the importance of having a right will is an echo of the Western tradition on justice looked at under the heading of 'Retribution' above in part 2.1. (at the beginning of the section), where justice is defined in terms of having a willingness to give to others what one owes them.

Right action
The fourth path in Buddhism is described thus:

> Unwholesome actions lead to unsound states of mind, while wholesome actions lead to sound states of mind. Again, the principle is explained in terms of abstinence: right action means 1. to abstain from harming sentient beings, especially to abstain from taking life (including suicide) and doing harm intentionally or delinquently, 2. to abstain from taking what is not given, which includes stealing, robbery, fraud, deceitfulness, and dishonesty, and 3. to abstain from sexual misconduct. Positively formulated, right action means to act kindly and compassionately, to be honest, to respect the belongings of others, and to keep sexual relationships harmless to others. Further details regarding the concrete meaning of right action can be found in the Precepts.

There is a clear connection between this section on the Eightfold Path and the section on the Five Precepts in part 3.2 below. Both should be read together. The precepts specify the meaning of right action.

A system of self-development

Humphries states that this path – right action – is 'the keynote of the Eightfold Path, for Buddhism is a religion of action, not belief.'[80] Buddhism claims that 'the motives of wrongdoing are always one of four: desire, hatred, delusion, or fear, and the practice of the Eightfold Path removes the power of these four. Hence the pilgrim lives the loftiest of ethics every hour because he has lost, by the unification of his consciousness with life, the very power to do otherwise' The Eightfold Path 'is a system of self-development according to law, a graded process of moral evolution within the law of Karma. It is the Middle Way between the two extremes of unnatural asceticism and self-indulgence.'[81]

Karma and justice

By Karma, Buddhism refers to its own understanding of 'natural law', a law of cause and effect – every action has its cause and one reaps the rewards of one's actions. This is a kind of universal retributive 'justice', one not of God, but of nature, a justice that repays everyone according to how he has acted. Buddhists believe this repayment may be in a future life, in a further reincarnation on the road to enlightenment. The Eightfold Path is a way of learning about and accepting this law of life, and of coming to see that one is part of a unified whole life, rather than a separate self. 'If life be one, compassion is the rule of it, a "feeling with" all forms of it by the littlest part... Each must perfect himself, his own brief vortex in the flow of life; each is responsible for the changing complex of attributes called Self which grows only as the craving 'ego' dies.'[82]

The Buddha's summary of his doctrine

'Work out your own salvation,' said the Buddha, 'with diligence.'[83] Acting justly or rightly is seen as a way of purifying yourself of egoism that keeps you from enlightenment, from the truth about the oneness of reality. The Buddha summed up the ethics with this saying, 'Cease to do evil; learn to do good, and purify your heart.'[84]

Mindfulness, Loving Kindness, Compassion and Wisdom

Meditation is central to Buddhism – training the mind to become Mindful of the present moment and the consequences of our deeds, speech and thought. Meditation practices enable the heart and mind to show Loving Kindness and Compassion to all beings. Finally, they aid one in finding Wisdom, when one is freed from the grasping deluded Ego to become an enlightened one, a 'buddha'. 'In this way we arrive at a moral code which is decided by each person for themselves literally in every moment of their lives. And so the Noble Eightfold Path itself has been reduced to two main principles regarding Right Mindfulness and Right Action – First we become increasingly aware of our inherent goodness, our true nature, and this happens through mindfully observing the mind itself in the present moment. Then we employ the stability of that good heart to inform how we behave in the world.'[85]

Explicitly social aspects of Buddhism: Boddhisatvas and Engaged Buddhism

Mahayana Buddhism adds an interesting element that is linked to the idea of caring for others: this is the concept of Boddhisatvas, 'spiritualised beings who delayed their own enlightenment, choosing to remain on earth, until all beings are freed from suffering.'[86] Another interesting recent development is 'Engaged Buddhism'. 'Traditionally, Buddhism was concerned with the removal of the causes of suffering through the individual. Today, some Buddhists are concerned with working to bring about changes in society, improving the welfare of those who suffer. They see their work as the engagement of compassion in the suffering world...'[87] Further material on Buddhist ethics can be found online.[88]

2.4 VIOLENCE

Legitimising violence
One way people have tried to 'resolve' conflict over rights' claims, or over justice disputes, is through violent means. Hence, the protection of personal rights or national rights (to security, for example) are reasons some have given to attempt to legitimise violence. But a good end does not justify an evil means, as the classic ethical principle puts it. Such an attitude leads to people treating other people as objects rather than subjects, as things rather than persons. We should never treat others as mere means to our own ends, as Kantian philosophy, Christian ethics and common morality have all realised. Any view of the human individual as merely a cog in a machine, or a unit in a collectivity, must be rejected as unworthy of the dignity of the human person correctly understood. Violence cannot be justly legitimised by claiming it is necessary to deliberately harm the few for the benefit of the many. Perhaps you do have to 'break a few eggs to make an omelette', but people are not eggs.

Types of violence: personal and structural
But what is meant by 'violence' anyway? The syllabus requires us to define two types: personal and structural. 'Personal' violence refers to people harming other people, abusing them or injuring them, especially in a physical way. What is 'structural' violence? The mention of 'structures' brings us back to part 1.1 above and its focus on various social structures. These structures can harm people, sometimes greatly harm them. The power embodied in social structures can abuse the people whom the structures should be helping to flourish. The harm done by unjust laws is a classic example. Aquinas referred to unjust laws as 'a kind of violence' back in the thirteenth century.[89] And so they still are today. One does not have a moral duty to obey such laws, but what one should do about them

will be a matter of prudent judgement in the particular circumstances. One might have to endure injustice perhaps, if immediate resistance was to lead to greater suffering or harsher injustice. One might work gradually for reform of the law. Or, in some circumstances, one might have to revolt against violent, unjust laws (and the despot or tyrant enforcing them). Again, note the link between this part of the course and the sections above on conflict resolution and non-violence.

Structural 'violence' may be predicated on all unfair and seriously harmful political, legal or social procedures or systems, especially when deliberately used to subjugate innocent or vulnerable people. The violent putting down of peaceful protest is another obvious example; routine so-called 'legal' torture still another. Poverty, caused or exacerbated by unbalanced and unfair economic policies or wicked political decisions, particularly when this poverty is extreme, even to the point of causing widespread death, could be termed a kind of violence. 'Institutionalised violence' is how the 1968 Medellín conference described it:

> As the Christian believes in the productiveness of peace in order to achieve justice, he also believes that justice is a prerequisite for peace. He recognizes that in many instances Latin America finds itself faced with a situation of injustice that can be called institutionalized violence, when, because of a structural deficiency of industry and agriculture, of national and international economy, of cultural and political life, 'whole towns lack necessities, live in such dependence as hinders all initiative and responsibility as well as every possibility for cultural promotion and participation in social and political life,'...thus violating fundamental rights.[90]

This applies not only to Latin America. Dealing with institutionalised violence is a very big challenge, and has evoked or provoked various different ideas on how to meet this challenge, some revolutionary in character, some even violent in character. The Catholic Church has been cautious about supporting revolutionary violence as it is so extreme and risky, although warranted and just. Speaking of a kind of 'violence' seems the correct type of language to describe the awful levels of poverty and marginalisation of peoples in many of the least developed countries and even in some of the developing countries. Is it appropriate to use this strong language for poverty and other injustices in Ireland? Such language could inspire action for justice, but might it not inspire bitterness or even violence? It could be seen as subversive of society to some extent, or at least as somewhat hostile and alienated. Would a reformist or gradual approach be more appropriate here? Would they be appropriate even in extreme situations abroad? Or is it too timid and casual to speak of gradual 'reform' in the face of seriously unjust situations?

It should be emphasised that one can always *do something* to help improve matters of human rights violations and political violence. Amnesty International, for example, can be contacted to provide the teacher with specific, up-to-date information. In fact, setting up an Amnesty group in the school would be a practical way to extend the teaching of this section of the RE curriculum (though it should be noted that Amnesty is not a religious organisation). Prayer for peace would be an appropriate regular part of Catholic school practice and ethos.

Just War Theory
War is the most extreme example of violence, especially in modern times. 'Just war theory' claims it can be justified, though only under strict conditions. This section of 2.4 will be quite a popular area as it is (unfortunately) very topical and dramatic. It is controversial both in its principles and, more so, in its application to concrete situations. A RE teacher should 'teach the controversy' rather that presenting a bland or

simplistic interpretation of the material. One way of 'opening up' the topic imaginatively might be through some powerful war poetry (the students may already be studying such poetry as part of the English curriculum) or some newspaper or video images of war and its effects.

Pacifism

Pacifists reject in principle all use of violent means to deal with conflicts. Pacifism finds adherents in many religious traditions, particularly forms of Buddhism and other Eastern faiths. Christianity has pacifists too, but it is not an obligatory part of mainstream Catholicism. This might seem strange in the light of Christ's Sermon on the Mount (Matthew 5-7), with its familiar phrases 'blessed are the peacemakers', 'turn the other cheek' and 'love your enemies'. In addition, the example of Christ in his acceptance of death is strikingly non-violent. The pacifist theme has been central to the writings of several Christian theologians in recent years, notably Stanley Hauerwas.[91] In the Catholic tradition, a pacifist stance has been developed by Michael Baxter,[92] and writers associated with the Christian Workers movement in the States.

The paradox of living in an imperfect world

Even though there is a strong theme of non-violence in the Gospel, however, the Christian tradition has grappled with a paradox since early times: how can we love both our enemies *and* ourselves, family, friends, neighbour, country, and church if we stand by passively and let our enemies attack and harm us? Would it even be 'love of enemy', to let him take over our land and lives, to kill and injure our loved ones and damage or destroy our way of life? Faced with the reality of sinful man and our proclivity to violent, greedy and threatening behaviour, the Christian faith tradition has allowed for the state to protect the innocent from unjust aggressors, even to the extent of using lethal force to do so. In fact, this has been seen as a serious duty of the state, though one hedged with many temptations and dangers.

Development of the just war tradition
In earlier times, the Christian tradition (developed especially by Augustine and Aquinas, amongst others) allowed for war to punish the evildoer and to get back what had been taken unjustly, as well as for defence of society against aggressive attack. Now, however, only self-defence (of the nation or group) is accepted as a *'just cause'*. It is thought that modern political and military conditions make it more moral to deal with injustice and punishment by political and judicial means (e.g. international trials concerning 'crimes against humanity'). There is some serious debate, however, about the justice of military humanitarian intervention in situations such as Rwanda (where no intervention took place, to dire effect), Bosnia and Kosovo. These situations seem to call for an extension of just war thinking to allow for strong nations to intervene to stop genocide and such evils in other countries, even if these countries are not a direct threat. Just war theory continues to shape international law; this Christian tradition has become part of the way people think and talk about war issues now.

Just war: some issues in teaching about it
'Just Cause' is only one of a number of conditions for just war, according to the general theory (there are variations). These conditions are so strict that some think they strongly counsel pacifism in practice, if not in principle. Many reject war in the modern world because its methods are so powerfully destructive and risky, even though in principle the theory of just war is considered valid. This poses a challenge to the teacher: to help students to learn about the principles of the theory but also to apply them accurately and fairly to real situations. There is, however, a practical problem in this respect, especially

evident in recent experience of trying to judge the morality of recent wars (against terrorism). How can teachers and students judge accurately and fairly when it is so difficult for anyone to find out the facts? This difficulty is a combination of the natural complexity of war situations and the deliberate withholding of information from civilians (which is often understandable and acceptable) and their deliberate deception by propaganda too (which is not). There is no easy answer to this difficulty, except to remind ourselves that in any moral issue the main practical thing is to do one's best to inform one's conscience as well as one can. The just war theory is primarily directed in the first place at those who make the decisions to go to war and who decide how it will be waged. It is a matter that concerns the citizen too, and this is an important point, but those who have the fullest information and the responsibility for the community are the ones for whom the theory is most useful and most directly pertinent. Justice and prudence are very much necessary virtues for leaders.

Conditions for a just war
So what are the conditions for a just war?[93] The *'jus ad bellum'* conditions deal with why and when recourse to war is permissible: just cause, competent authority, right intention, last resort, probability of success, and proportionality. The *'jus in bello'* conditions deal with the conduct of war: proportionality (the harms done must be worth the damages) and discrimination (which prohibits direct attacks on non-combatants and non-military targets). Whether a particular war fulfils these conditions or not is a matter of interpreting and evaluating empirical facts, and is not something that can be determined by moral principles in the abstract. Below is a list of the conditions, with a brief description of what each one means. Then some questions relating to the recent war against Iraq (in the light of the particular condition) are mentioned. The treatment here is limited and suggestive rather than a final

word on the topic. It should be noted that one need not confine one's analysis to the Iraq war. Other situations to look at include Afghanistan (2001-2002), Kosovo (1999), Bosnia (1995), Vietnam and the Second World War. One's understanding of the principles of just war will be somewhat distorted if one looks only at one war, especially one as questionable as that in Iraq in 2003. It is also useful to look at situations where there was no just war but one might have been warranted, such as in Rwanda in 1994, and where one was delayed to ill effect, such as in the appeasement of Hitler in the 1930s.

The conditions for just war can be listed as follows:

Jus ad bellum
- Just cause
- Competent authority
- Right intention
- Last resort
- Probability of success
- Proportionality

Jus in bello
- Proportionality
- Discrimination

Just Cause: This means that the war must be aiming for justice, which is presently understood to mean defence against an unjust aggressor. It is a developing area of international debate, however, whether 'just cause' goes further than self-defence of a nation or group. Does it not also include the responsibility of nations not under any threat to intervene in the situation of a country facing extreme civil war or genocide (think of Rwanda or Kosovo in the 90s). It would seem reasonable to say that a powerful country or coalition of countries ought to intervene militarily as a humanitarian measure to save a country from severe violence and chaos, even if this intervention is not any kind of self-defence for those who are intervening.

Questions under this heading about the recent Iraq war include such issues as whether the war was actually a defensive war, whether it was a response to an unjust aggressor, whether it was a humanitarian intervention to liberate a people from tyranny and oppression, whether it was an opportunistic war for America's economic gain in the Middle East, whether it was to make Saddam disarm, whether it was really about the threat of weapons of mass destruction or not (the failure to find them raised serious questions here), whether it was mainly about regime change, whether it was an appropriate response to the threat of terrorism, whether there was any real link between Iraq and Al-Quaeda, and so on.

Competent Authority: This refers to the requirement that a war be declared only by a nation state or other internationally recognised authority.

The main debate in relation to this and Iraq is the question of whether the US (and its allies) had the rightful authority to declare and wage war or whether this ought to be the prerogative of only the UN (or at least sanctioned by the UN). This is a particularly difficult issue to resolve, especially as there is not yet a real consensus on what exact authority the UN has or ought to have. There is also ongoing debate on the relationship between sovereignty of individual states and international authority of multi-state organisations or alliances.

Right Intention: This refers to the requirement that the just cause must be the honest reason for the war, and not merely a pretext for a selfish, malicious or vengeful action.

In relation to Iraq, the question is whether the reasons given for it, in particular the threatening behaviour of Saddam and his lack of co-operation with the international community over several years, are the real reasons for the war. Only those who made the decision can answer this question completely; others can only make an educated guess, in the midst of claims, propaganda and sometimes shrill debate. This condition is a reminder that morality is essentially about having the right intention in everything you choose to do – you need to be both completely sincere and well informed.

Last Resort: This requirement is very important and easy to understand. As war is so destructive and risky, it should only be declared if all other reasonable efforts have been made to resolve the conflict first. It should be noted, however, that it will always be possible to say that something extra can be done in the way of negotiations, meetings, etc. There comes a time when those with responsibility must judge if non-violent methods are no longer useful (or even dangerous – remember the inadequate appeasement of Hitler in the 30s).

Regarding Iraq, it could be argued that Saddam had had plenty of time to comply with disarmament requirements and had failed to do so, such that waiting any longer was futile or dangerous. On the other hand, others argued that the weapons inspectors should be given more time to do their job comprehensively. We now know that if they *had* been given more time, they would have concluded correctly that there were no weapons of mass destruction in Iraq, and one major reason for war would not have seen the light of day.

Probability of Success: This forbids any reckless use of violent methods or any foolish throwing away of human lives, even though the cause be just. Obviously, this will be a judgement call by the authorities, and never totally known for certain.

Winning the immediate war seems to have been a correct application of this condition regarding Iraq; winning the ongoing battle seems so far to be another story. Success is an interesting term. Stopping an actual attack on one's country can be practically assessed to be a complete success; how are we to judge a pre-emptive war to fight terror?

Proportionality: This condition can be understood in two contrasting ways. For some it means that we must weigh up the deaths and destruction and weigh up the benefits of the war and judge which is the more weighty. Such calculations, however, are characteristic of utilitarian approaches to morality, which have been judged both philosophically weak and theologically wrong, especially if they constitue the exclusive method of making moral judgements.[94] What the 'proportionality' condition actually entails, according to an alternative view, is that the lethal force planned must be only what is required to achieve the just cause: war as a means must be 'proportionate' to its end or objective. This forbids the just side from imposing unfair or extreme conditions on the enemy, such as unconditional surrender; it also forbids policies of killing or abusing prisoners. This condition applies both before the war in its planning and during the war in its execution.

Some have argued that the war in Iraq was proportionate in that civilian casualties were kept to a minimum, but it is difficult to agree on what an acceptable minimum is with regard to civilian deaths. Even one dead innocent person seems too much to accept. Nevertheless, just war is impossible unless some level of unintended civilian casualties are morally acceptable, though only as a side-effect. This is one reason why some people reject the notion of a modern just war: inevitably, many innocent people will be killed in a modern war. Weaponry has become more accurate and more 'discriminate' to some degree, but the level of destruction and death caused by modern warfare is still very high. In addition, the recent example of the torture of prisoners in Abu Ghraib shows clearly how war conditions can bring out the very worst in soldiers. It is extemely difficult to keep war proportionate. Perhaps it is impossible. It can be morally acceptable to go to war, therefore, only if the evils risked by not doing so are so terrible that the awful side-effects of war are to be preferred, albeit reluctantly. Even if it is not possible to rationally weigh and compare evils with total accuracy, it seems necessary to do *some* kind of calculation of side-effects of different choices (to go to war or not) in order to judge whether a particular war might be just. In addition, once it is judged that there is a proportionate reason for just war, it must be planned and carried out only with the degree of force necessary to defend the innocent and repel aggression. Such seems to be the full significance of the *proportionality* criterion.

Discrimination: This is an interesting example of a positive use of the term 'discrimination'. It means there should never be any deliberate attack on non-combatants. This was noted above in dealing with Proportionality, and it should be noted that these conditions overlap considerably.

Is just war truly just or is it a necessary evil?
One way of understanding these conditions is to see them as marking out a way of making sure that a war really is a 'just war'. Only if all these conditions are met can one be truly said to be engaging in an act of justice, which is what a just war is. Of course, not everyone agrees with this. Many consider just war to be an evil, though a necessary evil. Though this is a popular opinion, it presents serious ethical problems. Such an acceptance of just war as a necessary evil makes it seem morally acceptable to do some evil acts (a) if the end is good enough, or (b) if the good outweighs the evil, or (c) if you simply *have* to do it. These three types of rationale are really rationalisations, mere excuses, and are philosophically and theologically unsound. They can be used to rationalise any manner of evil acts. Even though just war theory does limit the use of such rationales by its rigorous conditions, (and this is in its favour), seeing it as a necessary evil remains highly problematic.

A better approach towards justification of just war: forfeiting right to life

Another way to justify killing in just war is to see it as killing people who have forfeited their right to life by engaging in unjust aggression and refusing to respond to peaceful attempts to resolve the conflict. Therefore, only combatants may be rightfully killed or targeted and only by those who act on behalf of the common good of the unjustly attacked state or people. This view sees direct killing of the unjust aggressor as morally justified once one follows the strict conditions specified above.

A more nuanced justification of just war: killing accepted only as a side-effect

Still another way of explaining why just war can be a good act, even an ethically required act, is to emphasise that the acts in a just war are acts of defence, with the killing accepted only as a side-effect of this defence. This explains why the action must be only what is required to stop the attack and no more (this is the 'proportionality' condition mentioned above), and why only combatants may be targeted (the 'discrimination' condition). It explains why one must threaten first, if this will serve to stop the attack, and then inflict a minimal level of injury if this will successfully achieve the aim of defence, and, finally, accept killing only if all else fails. In other words, if the attack is stopped and no-one is killed, this would be seen as a successful just war; whereas in a war of vengeance or anger, killing and injuring many is seen as essential to the success of the war. These are two very different types of war, two very different uses of violence.

Church documents and other sources

Church documents relevant to the just war theory include:
- Vatican II, *Gaudium et Spes*, (1965), nn. 77-82.
- US Bishops, *The Challenge of Peace*, (1983), esp. nn. 80-110.

- John Paul II, *Centesimus Annus*, (1991), nn. 17-19.
- *Catechism of the Catholic Church*, (1994), nn. 2302-2317.

There is plenty online regarding the principles and application of just war theory. For example, the *First Things* journal (www.firstthings.com) is a good source for arguments in favour of the Iraq war and just war theory in general; the Sojourners website (www.sojo.net) offers opposing arguments. Other resources are listed below.[95]

Further Reading

Abrams, E. 'Review of *A World Made New* by Mary Ann Glendon', *First Things* (June/July 2001) online at:www.firstthings.com/ftissues/ft0106/reviews/abrams.html

Aquinas, St Thomas, *Summa Theologica (Summa Theologiae)*: www.newadvent.org/summa/

Aquinas, St Thomas, *Summa Theologiae: A Concise Translation*, translated and edited by T. McDermott (Allen, Texas: Christian Classics, 1989).

Arneson, R.J. 'Equality' in R.L. Simon (ed.), *The Blackwell Guide to Social and Political Philosophy* (Oxford, UK: Blackwell, 2002).

Baker, J. 'Equality' in S. Healy and B. Reynolds (eds.), *Social Policy in Ireland: Principles, Practice and Problems* (Dublin: Oak Tree Press, 1998).

Barnes, P. *World Religions*, 'Into the Classroom' series (Dublin: Veritas, 2003).

Baxter, M. 'Just war and pacifism: A 'pacifist' perspective in seven points', *Houston Catholic Worker*, Vol. XXIV, No. 3, May-June 2004, online at: www.cjd.org/paper/baxpacif.html

Beauchamp, L. *Philosophical Ethics: An Introduction to Moral Philosophy* (Boston: McGraw Hill, third edition 2001).

Bergman, S. *A Cloud of Witnesses: 20th Century Martyrs* (London:

Font paperbacks, 1998).

Berke, M. 'A Jewish appreciation of Catholic Social Teaching' in K. Grasso, G. Bradley and R.P. Hunt, *Catholicism, Liberalism and Communitarianism* (Maryland: Rowman and Littlefield, 1995).

Britannica CD©2000 Deluxe Edition 1994-1998, Encyclopaedia Britannica Inc.

Brugger, E.C. *Capital Punishment and Catholic Moral Tradition* (Notre Dame, Ind.: University of Notre Dame Press, 2003).

Brugger, E.C. 'Catholic Moral Teaching and the Problem of Capital Punishment' in *The Thomist* 68 (2004).

Catechism of the Catholic Church, 1997 edition (the Vatican archive): www.vatican.va/archive/catechism/ccc_toc.htm

Charles, R. *Christian Social Witness and Teaching: The Catholic Tradition from Genesis to Centesimus Annus*. Vols. 1 and 2 (Herefordshire: Gracewing, 1998.)

Charles, R. *An Introduction to Catholic Social Teaching* (San Francisco: Ignatius, 1999).

Congregation for the Doctrine of the Faith, 1984 'Instruction on Certain Aspects of Liberation Theology' (*Liberatatis Nuntius*)

Congregation for the Doctrine of the Faith, 1986 'Instruction on Christian Freedom and Liberation' (*Liberatis Conscientia*), [both CDF documents can be accessed in full from the Congregation's doctrinal documents page at: www.vatican.va/roman_curia/congregations/cfaith/doc_doc_index.htm]

Cullen, S. *Religion and Gender*, 'Into the Classroom' series (Dublin: Veritas, 2004).

Department of Theological Questions/Irish Inter Church Meeting, *Freedom, Justice and Responsibility in Ireland Today* (Dublin: Veritas, 1997).

Donohue, J. 'Biblical Perspectives on Justice' in J.C. Haughey (ed.), *The Faith that does Justice*, Woodstock Studies, vol. 2 (New York: Paulist, 1977).

Dulles, A. 'Catholicism and Capital Punishment', *First Things* 112, April 2001.
Farrell, W. *A Companion to the Summa*: www.op.org/Farrell/companion/
Forrester, D.B. *On Human Worth: A Christian Vindication of Equality* (London: SCM, 2001).
Geisler, N. *Options in Contemporary Christian Ethics* (Grand Rapids, Mich.: Baker House, 1991).
Gill, R. (ed.) *The Cambridge Companion to Christian Ethics* (Cambridge, UK: Cambridge University Press, 2000).
Glendon, M.A. 'Reflections on the Universal Declaration of Human Rights', *First Things* (April 1998) at www.firstthings.com/ftissues/ft9804/articles/udhr.html
Glendon, M.A. 'Human Rights For All', *Caritas Helder Camara Lecture Series 2002*. at www.catholiceducation.org/articles/social_justice/sj0006.html
Glendon, M.A. *A World Made New: Eleanor Roosevelt and the Universal Declaration of Human Rights* (New York: Random House Trade Paperbacks, 2001).
Goring, R. *The Wordsworth Dictionary of Beliefs and Religions* (Ware, Hertfordshire: Chambers Ltd./Wordsworth Editions, 1995).
Grisez, G. *Living a Christian Life: The Way of the Lord Jesus, Vol. 2* (Illinois: Franciscan Press, 1993).
Grisez, G. and R. Shaw, *Fulfillment in Christ* (Notre Dame, Indiana: University of Notre Dame Press, 1993).
Groome, T. *Educating for Life* (Allen, Texas: Thomas More, 1998).
Gutiérrez, G. *A Theology of Liberation* [1971], (London: SCM Press, 2001).
Gutiérrez, G. *The Truth Shall Make You Free: Confrontations*, English translation. (Maryknoll, NY: Orbis Books, 1990).
Gutiérrez, G. 'Liberation Theology' in J. Dwyer (ed.), *The New Dictionary of Catholic Social Thought* (Collegeville, Minn: Liturgical Press, 1994).

Hannon, P. 'Theology, War and Pacifism' in L. Hogan and B. Fitzgerald (eds.) *Between Poetry and Politics: Christian Theology in Dialogue* (Dublin: Columba, 2003).

Hannon, P. *Moral Decision Making*, 'Into the Classroom' series (Dublin: Veritas, 2004).

Hartnett, D. 'Interview with Gustavo Gutiérrez', *America Magazine*, Monday, March 31st, 2003, online at: www.jesuits-chi.org/whatsnew/news.asp?news_id=172

Hauerwas, S. *Against the nations : war and survival in a liberal society* (Minneapolis: Winston Press, 1985).

Hauerwas, S. *A Community of Character* (Notre Dame, Ind.: University of Notre Dame Press, 1981).

Hauerwas, S. *Performing the Faith: Bonhoeffer and the Practice of Non-violence* (Grand Rapids, MI: Brazos Press, 2004).

Himes, K. *Responses to 101 Questions on Catholic Social Teaching* (New Jersey: Paulist, 2001).

Hinnells, J. R. *The Penguin Dictionary of Religions*, 2nd edition (London: Penguin, 1995).

Hittinger, R. *The First Grace: Rediscovering the Natural Law in a Post-Christian World* (Wilmington, Delaware: ISI Books, 2003).

Hogan, L. *Human Rights*, Christian perspectives on development issues series (Dublin / London: Trócaire / Veritas / Cafod, 1998).

Humphreys, C. *Buddhism: An Introduction and Guide*, 3rd edition [1951 original], (London: Penguin, 1990).

Ingram, D. and J. Parks, *The Complete Idiot's Guide to Ethics* (Indianapolis, IN: Alpha Books, 2002).

Irish Episcopal Conference, 'Prosperity With a Purpose' (1999): www.catholiccommunications.ie/pastlet/prosperitypastoral.pdf

Irving, T.B., K. Ahmed, and M. M. Ahsan, *The Qur'an: Basic Teachings*, revised edition (London: The Islamic Foundation, 1992).

John Paul II, *Veritatis Splendor* (1993) at papal documents archive: www.vatican.va/offices/papal_docs_list.html

John Paul II, *Evangelium Vitae* (1995) at papal documents archive: www.vatican.va/offices/papal_docs_list.html

Johnson, J.T. *Morality and Contemporary Warfare* (New Haven: Yale University Press, 1999).

Jumier, J. *How to Understand Islam*, English trans. J. Bowden (London: SCM press, 1989).

Kanitkar, V.P. and W. Owen Cole, *Hinduism*, 'Teach yourself - World faiths' series (London: Hodder and Stoughton, 1995).

Kellner, M. 'Jewish Ethics' in P. Singer (ed.), *A Companion to Ethics*, Blackwell Companions to Philosophy (Oxford: Blackwell, 1993).

Killingley, D. 'Hinduism' in L. Ridgeon (ed.), *Major World Religions* (London and New York: RoutledgeCurzon, 2003).

King, M.L. 'Letter from Birmingham Jail': www.thekingcenter.org/prog/non/letter.html

Lane, D.A. *Foundations for a Social Theology: praxis, process and salvation* (Dublin: Gill and Macmillan, 1984).

Latkovic, M. 'Capital Punishment, Church Teaching and Morality: What is Pope John Paul II Saying to Roman Catholics in *Evangelium Vitae*?' [both this article and the next two, and details of their publication, are available online at www.aodonline.org/SHMS/Faculty+5819/Faculty+-+Welcome.htm]

Latkovic, M. 'Just War Theory, Catholic Morality and the Response to International Terrorism' [online, see above].

Latkovic, M. 'Eight Principles of Catholic Social Teaching', *Josephinum Journal of Theology* Vol. 7, Nos. 1-2 (Summer 2000) [also online, see details above].

Lebacqz, K. *Six Theories of Justice* (Minneapolis: Augsburg Publishing House, 1986).

McAfee Brown, R. *Liberation Theology: An Introductory Guide* (Louisville, Kentucky: Westminster/John Knox Press, 1993).

Macbeth, F. and N. Fine, *Playing with Fire: Creative Conflict Resolution for Young Adults* (Gabriola Island, BC: New Society Publishers, 1995).

McCann, J. 'Improving Our Aim' in L. Monaghan and N. Prendergast (eds.), *Reimagining the Catholic School* (Dublin: Veritas, 2003).

Massaro, T. and T. Shannon, *Catholic Perspectives on Peace and War* (Lanham, Maryland, USA: Rowman and Littlefield, 2004).

Mautner, T. (ed.), *The Penguin Dictionary of Philosophy* (London: Penguin, 2000).

Meeks, M.D. *God the Economist: The Doctrine of God and Political Economy* (Minneapolis: Fortress Press, 1989).

Miall, H., O. Ramsbottom and T. Woodhouse, *Contemporary Conflict Resolution: the prevention, management and transformation of deadly conflicts* (Cambridge: Polity Press, 1999).

Niebuhr, Richard, *Christ and Culture* (New York: Harper and Row, 1951).

O'Donovan, O. et al. (eds.), *The Just War Revisited*, Current Issues in Theology (Cambridge, UK: Cambridge University Press, 2003).

Palmer, M. *The Times – World Religions: A History of Faith* (London; Times Books, 2002).

Pieper, J. *The Four Cardinal Virtues* (Indiana: University of Notre Dame Press, 1966 – including the original book on *Justice* of 1955).

Pontifical Council for Justice and Peace, *Compendium of Social Doctrine of the Catholic Church* (Vatican City: Liberia Editrice Vaticana, 2004).

Power, J. *Like Water on Stone: The Story of Amnesty International* (London: Allen Books/Penguin Press, 2001).

Preston, R. 'Christian Ethics' in P. Singer (ed.) *A Companion to Ethics*, Blackwell Companions to Philosophy (Oxford: Blackwell, 1993).

Ramsey, P. and S. Hauerwas, *The Just War: Force and Political Responsibility* (Rowman and Littlefield, 2001).

Rawls, J. *A Theory of Justice* (Cambridge, Mass. USA: Harvard

University Press, 1971).

Ridgeon, L. 'Islam', in L. Ridgeon (ed.), *Major World Religions* (London and New York: RoutledgeCurzon, 2003).

Rowland, C. *The Cambridge Companion to Liberation Theology* (Cambridge University press, 1999).

Rowland, T. *Culture and the Thomist Tradition After Vatican II* (London and New York: Routledge, 2003).

Sacks, J. *The Politics of Hope* (London: Vintage paperback edition, 2000).

Sacks, J. 'Judaism's Religious Vision and the Capitalism ethic', *Religion and Liberty* (Nov/Dec 2001) at www.acton.org/publicat/randl/interview.php?id=401

Sacks, J. *A Clash of Civilisations? Judaic Sources on Co-existence in a World of Differences*, (2003) online at www.chiefrabbi.org/ar-index.html

Sacks, J. *The Dignity of Difference*, revised edition (London/New York: Continuum, 2003).

Sandy, L.R. and R. Perkins, Jr., 'The Nature of Peace and Its Implications for Peace Education' *Online Journal of Peace and Conflict Resolution* Issue 4.2, Spring 2002, at www.trinstitute.org/ojpcr/4_2natp.htm

Scott, P. and W.T. Cavanaugh (eds.), *The Blackwell Companion to Political Theology* (Oxford, UK: Blackwell, 2004).

Siddiqi, M.N. *Role of the State in the Economy: An Islamic Perspective* (Leicester, UK: The Islamic foundation, 1996).

Simons, R.G. *Competing Gospels: Public Theology and Economic Theory* (Alexandria, Australia: E.J. Dwyer, 1995).

Smith, J.E. 'The Moral vision of the Catechism' in M. Hogan and T. J. Norris, *Evangelizing for the Third Millennium: The Maynooth Conference on the New Catechism* [May 1996], (Dublin: Veritas, 1997).

Stacey, H. *Let's Mediate: A Teacher's Guide to Peer Support and Conflict Resolution Skills for All Ages* (Bristol: Lucky Duck Publishers, 1997).

Standley, D. 'Opening up the Church's Social Teaching' in

Priests and People (May 2004) at www.priestsandpeople.co.uk/ [follow 'previous articles' link]

Stackhouse, J. 'In the World but ...' in *Christianity Today* (April 22nd, 2002): www.christianitytoday.com/ct/2002/005/8.80.html

Symonides, J. (ed.) *Human Rights: Concept and Standards* (Dartmouth, UK: Dartmouth Publishing/UNESCO, 2000).

Thomson, J.M *Justice and Peace: A Christian Primer* (Maryknoll, New York: Orbis, 1997).

US Catholic Bishops, *The Challenge of Peace* (1983): www.osjspm.org/cst/cp.htm

USCCB, 'Responsibility, Rehabilitation, and Restoration: A Catholic Perspective on Crime and Criminal Justice' (2000): www.usccb.org/sdwp/criminal.htm

Vardy, P. *The Puzzle of Ethics*, 2nd edition (London: Fount, 1999).

Walzer, M. *Just and Unjust Wars: A Moral Argument With Historical Illustrations*, 2nd edition (New York: Basic Books, 1992).

Waltzer, M. 'The right Way' in *The New York Review of Books* (13th July 2003): www.mafhoum.com/press4/ 135P5.htm

Weigel, G. *The Truth of Catholicism: Ten Controversies Explored* (Herefordshire: Gracewing, 2002).

Weigel (George) articles online: www.ratzingerfanclub.com /Weigel/

Williams, J.K. 'Equality', *Religions and Liberty* (Jan/Feb 1992) online at www.acton.org/publicat/ randl/article.php?id=31

Williams, T. and A. Falconer, (eds.) *Sectarianism: Papers of the 1994 Corrymeela Ecumenical conference* (Dublin: Dominican Publications in association with the Irish School of Ecumenics, 1994).

Websites

About Buddhism: www.thebigview.com/buddhism/
Amnesty International (Ireland): www.amnesty.ie/

Archdiocese of St Paul and Minneapolic Office of Social Justice: www.osjspm.org
BBC education website: www.bbc.co.uk/learning/library/
BBC site on human rights: www.bbc.co.uk/worldservice/people/features/ihavearightto/
BBC World Service on World Religions: www.bbc.co.uk/worldservice/people/features/world_religions/index.shtml
Buddha net: www.buddhanet.net
CAIN (Conflict Archive on the Internet): http://cain.ulst.ac.uk/
Cardinal Ratzinger Fanclub archive on just war: www.ratzingerfanclub.com/justwar/index.html
CatholicIreland.net (saints page): www.catholicireland.net/pages/index.php?nd=68
Catholic-pages.com saints' directory: www.catholic-pages.com/dir/saints.asp
Catholic Peace Fellowship: www.nd.edu/~mbaxter/cpf/index.htm
Derechos Human Rights: www.derechos.org/
Development Education Ireland: www.developmenteducation.ie/home.php
Dugan, M.A. 'Non-violence': www.beyondintractability.org/m/nonviolent_direct_action.jsp
First Things online journal: www.firstthings.com/index.html
Gandhi Institute: www.gandhiinstitute.org/.
Gandhi article in *Wikipedia* encyclopedia at: www.campusprogram.com/reference/en/wikipedia/m/ma/mahatma_gandhi.html
Hauerwas online: unofficial internet archive: www.bigbrother.net/~mugwump/Hauerwas/
Himilayan Academy Publiations, 'Hindu Lexicon': www.himalayanacademy.com/books/dws/lexicon/v.html
Hindu Resources Online: www.hindu.org/
Hinduism site: www.hinduism.co.za/
Human Rights Watch site: www.hrw.org/

Human Rights Web Directory: homepage.eircom.net /~hrwd/
INCORE - International Conflict Research: www.incore.ulst.ac.uk/
Islamicity: www.islamicity.com/mosque/Zakat/
Kelly, M. 'Nonviolence.org': www.non-violence.org/
King Center: www.thekingcenter.org/tkc/index.asp
Livefreecritique:www.geocities.com/livefreecritique/acceptprotest.html
McCarthy, C. 'The Class of Non-violence': www.salsa.net/peace/conv/index.html
Mater Dei 'Logos' Site [Junior Cert RE materials]: www.materdei.ie [follow 'Logos' link]
Medellín documents (1968): www.providence.edu/las/documents.htm [following Medellín link].
Multi-faith Net: www.multifaithnet.org/
Papal Documents archive: www.vatican.va/offices/papal_docs_list.html
PBS *Religion and Ethics* weekly: www.pbs.org/wnet/religionandethics/index.html
Peace Brigades International: www.peacebrigades.org/
The Pew Forum: pewforum.org/
Project Ploughshares: www.ploughshares.ca/ index.html
Sojourners – Christians for Justice and Peace: www.sojo.net/index.cfm
The Online 'Journal of Peace and Conflict Resolution': www.trinstitute.org/ojpcr/archive.htm
(issue 5.1, Summer 2003 is at www.trinstitute.org /ojpcr/)
UN Declaration of Human Rights: www.unhchr.ch/udhr/lang/eng.htm
Understanding Hinduism: www.hinduism.co.za/
UNESCO site on peace and non-violence: www3.unesco.org/iycp/
University of Colarado online conflict resolution site:

www.colorado.edu/conflict/peace/overview_pg.htm
Vatican Archive [Bible, Catechism, Vatican II, Code of Canon Law]: www.vatican.va/archive/index.htm
Yahoo Search Directory (Social Science – Peace and Conflict Studies): dir.yahoo.com/Social_Science/Peace_and_Conflict_Studies/
Zenit archive library on just war: www.zenit.org/english/war/index_archive_war.phtml

Notes

1 See J. Pieper, *The Four Cardinal Virtues* (Indiana: University of Notre Dame Press, 1966 – including the original book on *Justice* of 1955), pp. 43-44.
2 As quoted in R. Hittinger, *The First Grace: Rediscovering the Natural Law in a Post-Christian World* (Wilmington, Delaware: ISI Books, 2003), p. 115.
3 This section is indebted to the brilliant analysis by Pieper of justice in *The Four Cardinal Virtues*, especially chapter 5, 'Recompense and Restitution'.
4 See St Thomas Aquinas' famous theology textbook *Summa Theologiae* II-II, Question 58, article 3. The easiest access to this great though demanding work of Aquinas is online. It is available in full online as 'Summa Theologica', at www.newadvent.org/summa/ (homepage and index). All subsequent quotations and references to the *Summa Theologiae* can be accessed from this index. It is divided into the first part (I), the first part of the second part (I-II), the second part of the second part (II-II), the third part (III) and supplement. There are Latin titles for these and other ways of abbreviating them, but the basic structure is actually simple enough. The second part, divided into two subsections, concerns morality. A more up-to-date version, though in some ways a paraphrase, is Timothy McDermott (ed.), *Summa Theologiae: A Concise Translation* (Allen, Texas: Christian Classics, 1989).
5 The term used in the Catholic tradition is 'the universal destination of goods' and there is much on this theme in the social teaching of the Church. See, for example, article six in *The Social Agenda*, a thematic survey of the teaching published by the Pontifical Council for Justice and Peace in 2000. The index for the complete online book

is available at www.thesocialagenda.com/. See also Pontifical Council for Justice and Peace, *Compendium of Social Doctrine of the Catholic Church* (Vatican City: Liberia Editrice Vaticana, 2004), chapter four, part three, paragraphs 171-184.

6   See the *Catechism of the Catholic Church*. The online version is available at the Vatican archive website www.vatican.va/archive/catechism/ccc_toc.htm. The particular paragraphs on the death penalty are at ch. 2, article 5 (dealing with the fifth commandment) in the third section of the Catechism, which deals with morality. It is entitled 'Life in Christ'. It is worth noting that this part of the Catechism was changed from the original translation from the French in 1992. The official Catechism is the Latin edition and it was the basis for a later edition of the Catechism in 1997. This is the version to use. This later edition did not change the teaching substantially, but it did phrase the teaching in a more anti-death penalty fashion, a fact that emphasises how the practice of the death penalty is frowned upon increasingly by the Catholic magisterium. Details of the changes from the 1992 to the 1997 versions are available at www.scborromeo.org/ccc/updates.htm. E. Christian Brugger is one Catholic theologian who argues strongly that the changes from the 1992 to the 1997 Catechism, along with the Pope's approach to the topic in *Evangelium Vitae* in 1995, clearly indicate the beginnings of a decisive change in the Church's position: from a conditional acceptance of its legitimacy to a total rejection. See E. Christian Brugger, *Capital Punishment and Catholic Moral Tradition* (Notre Dame, Ind: University of Notre Dame Press, 2003) and his article 'Catholic Moral Teaching and the Problem of Capital Punishment' in *The Thomist* 68 (2004), pp. 41-67.

7   It should be noted that the hypothetical examples given here of when it might be appropriate to use capital punishment to protect society are my own. The Church magisterium has never to my knowledge specified what conditions would justify the death penalty in practice in modern times.

8   The teaching of the Catholic Church on the wrongness of taking innocent human life is most strongly expressed, indeed infallibly so, in Pope John Paul II, *Evangelium Vitae*, his encyclical letter on the Gospel of Life (1995). See especially nn. 57, 62, and 65 (on innocent life, abortion and euthanasia respectively). The section of this encyclical on the death penalty is nn. 55-56. The whole encyclical is worth studying in full as it is an inspiring combination of biblical,

theological and philosophical argument and reflection on the issue of life and its sanctity.

9 Another Catholic theologian (in addition to Brugger, see note 6 above) who has respectfully argued in detail that the Church position is wrong, and that the death penalty, along with all deliberate killing as an end or a means, is evil in principle, is Germain Grisez. See his *Living a Christian Life: The Way of the Lord Jesus*, Vol. 2 (Illinois: Franciscan Press, 1993), pp. 474-75 and 891-94. A particularly good reference site online for a variety of views and arguments on the death penalty is The Pew Forum at http://pewforum.org/ (homepage). Clicking on the 'Issues' link brings up 'Death Penalty', a subsection that contains numerous articles and debates on the issue. The 'Issues' link also connects to very good collections of material on human rights and religion, and just war theory – highly recommended. This site is an excellent place to find the views of other Christian denominations and other religions on these issues.

10 This argument, admittedly an intellectually demanding one, is outlined in Cardinal A. Dulles, 'Catholicism and Capital Punishment', *First Things* 112, April 2001, available online [follow links from homepage]. More historical evidence would be necessary to demonstrate that the cultural change Dulles claims has taken place has actually occured, but his argument is not implausible and has the merit of helping Catholics to understand how a genuine 'development' of Church doctrine could be possible in the area of capital punishment (rather than a reversal of doctrine).

11 Consider a link with literature dealing with the challenge of developing empathy, in English for example. To mention one instance: many students will have read Harper Lee's *To Kill a Mockingbird* for their Junior Certificate. This is a wonderful fictional exploration, set in the 1930s in Alabama, dramatising the theme of the importance of empathy in understanding people who are different, especially those of different colour or those who are rejected by a prejudiced society.

12 A very clear and concise treatment of the utilitarian approach to justice is found in K. Lebacqz, *Six Theories of Justice* (Minneapolis: Augsburg Publishing House, 1986), ch. 1.

13 The position of Robert Nozick on justice takes this idea and develops the libertarian understanding of justice as defined by fair and lawful processes that lead to ownership of private property. Once it is the case that you own your property then it is unjust to oblige you to give

it away to anyone else. This position and its weaknesses are outlined very clearly in *Six Theories of Justice* (mentioned in the previous note), which devotes a chapter to Nozick and one to each of five other theories of justice. This makes the book an excellent introduction to justice as understood by Utilitarianism, Nozick and Libertarianism, John Rawls, the US bishops' 1986 pastoral and Catholic Social Teaching in general, Reinhold Niebuhr and a general Protestant approach, and Liberation Theology.

14 This is not to deny that the West bears some responsibility for the problems of the developing world, nor that powerful and wealthy countries have a responsibility in justice and charity (love) to help countries in need.

15 For the sake of simplicity, I do not deal in my example with the idea of distribution-with-conditions, such as the offering of aid to developing countries while insisting that healthy economic policies or democratic procedures are implemented by the state receiving the aid. Though distribution of this kind has its problems, it seems better, in some situations at least, than unconditional distribution or unconditional aid. What conditions should be attached to distribution or aid and who should decide them is a huge area of debate and division of opinion – the point here is only that applying *some* conditions may be better than a simplistic application of an equality principle.

16 The analysis of equality in this section is heavily indebted to J. Baker, 'Equality' in S. Healy and B. Reynolds (eds.), *Social Policy in Ireland: Principles, Practice and Problems* (Dublin: Oak Tree Press, 1998), though it does not agree fully with Baker's support for radical egalitarianism. A more detailed account of types of equality can be found in R.J. Arneson, 'Equality' in R.L. Simon (ed.), *The Blackwell Guide to Social and Political Philosophy* (Oxford, UK: Blackwell, 2002). An excellent book-length treatment of the idea of justice as equality is D.B. Forrester, *On Human Worth: A Christian Vindication of Equality* (London: SCM, 2001).

17 The 1948 Declaration, and more, is readily available online at the official UN site. The Declaration itself is at: www.unhchr.ch/udhr/lang/eng.htm while other human rights instruments are listed and available from another page at the official UN site at www.unhchr.ch/html/intlinst.htm. These include in full the International Covenant on Economic, Social and Cultural Rights, and that on Civil and Political Rights.

18 Mary Ann Glendon, *A World Made New: Eleanor Roosevelt and the Universal Declaration of Human Rights* (New York: Random House Trade Paperbacks, 2001). This book has as its appendices the various drafts of the Declaration and the final version, which give a good idea of the continuities and changes in its development.
19 The diagram of Cassin's Portico is in *A World Made New*, p. 171 and the discussion of it is on pp. 173-191.
20 *A World Made New*, pp. 184, 185.
21 See *A World Made New*, p. 187.
22 *A World Made New*, p. 202.
23 *A World Made New*, p. 189.
24 A very useful discussion of the limits of a rights approach to understanding morality is found in Janet E. Smith, 'The Moral vision of the Catechism' in M. Hogan and T. J. Norris, *Evangelizing for the Third Millennium: The Maynooth Conference on the New Catechism* [May 1996], (Dublin: Veritas, 1997) 96-114, available on the 'faculty' link to Smith at the Sacred Heart Major Seminary homepage [at www.aodonline.org/SHMS/SHMS.htm]. Some philosophical or theological approaches to ethics are sharply critical of any reliance on rights; see, for example, Tracey Rowland, *Culture and the Thomist Tradition After Vatican II* (London and New York: Routledge, 2003), where the author strongly criticises the Church's positive attitude to modern culture and in particular its acceptance of rights language. In this, Rowland follows the philosophical analysis of Alisdair McIntyre and the theological approach of David Schindler. Her basic point is that rights language masks the primarily emotivist ethics of modernity, an ethics that reduces justice to exertions of power based on subjectivist or relativistic preferences. In his mainly positive introduction to her book, Aidan Nichols argues that she goes too far in this regard and states that 'rights' are a reflection of 'the objective order of the world' (p. xiv), an approach that echoes that of Pope John XXIII in *Pacem in Terris*.
25 See Aquinas' reply to objection 4 in *Summa Theologiae* II-II, question 29, article 2.
26 The quote is taken from the online site 'Latin American Studies Program' of Providence College, Rhode Island, USA at www.providence.edu/las/documents.htm [following the 'Medellín conference' link].
27 I am very grateful to Annette Honan for checking out my interpretation of the syllabus for this section and for suggesting some

useful examples. See also M.A. Dugan, 'Non-violence', online at www.beyondintractability.org/m/nonviolent_direct_action.jsp. It should be noted that the central term is sometimes spelt 'nonviolence', though here I have spelled it consistently with a hyphen.

28 One site, combining non-violence as protest and lifestyle, with many useful links, is a site run by a Quaker: www.non-violence.org/ The Peace Brigades International site (Protective Accompaniment, Peace Education, Documenting Peace Intiatives) is at www.peacebrigades.org/index.html. A Catholic site run mainly by Michael Baxter is at www.nd.edu/~mbaxter/cpf/index.htm [it has a developing page on saints and martyrs that is worth attention]. A very interesting site, combining nonviolent protest on civil rights issues with non-violent protest against abortion, is 'livefreecritique' at www.geocities.com/livefreecritique/acceptprotest.html. A UNESCO site dedicated to peace and non-violence is at www3.unesco.org/iycp/ The film 'Witness', directed by Peter Weir (1986), would be a useful pedagogical tool. It is an imaginative and highly entertaining exploration of the themes of violence and non-violence in the modern world, dramatising a situation where a New York cop (played by Harrison Ford) has to hide out in an Amish community that is, of course, dedicated to a totally pacifist philosophy (non-violence as lifestyle).

29 For a very detailed treatment of non-violence, see 'The Class of Non-violence' by Colman McCarthy at www.salsa.net/peace/conv/index.html [which includes six detailed lessons, including sections on Gandhi, Dorothy Day and Martin Luther King, Jr.].

30 A good place for material on issues relating to Gandhi is found at the 'M.K. Gandhi Institute' run by his grandson, Arun Gandhi, at www.gandhiinstitute.org/. Another web reference for Gandhi is at www.campusprogram.com/reference/en/wikipedia/m/ma/mahatma_gandhi.html.

31 The King Center website, linked to the actual Center set up by Coretta Scott King in 1967 in Atlanta, is the best place to start here: www.thekingcenter.org/tkc/index.asp [homepage – but also see sitemap link]. The 'Letter from Birmingham Jail' can be found in full in text *and audio* at www.thekingcenter.org /prog/non/letter.html. The site contains a short article on non-violence as a way of life.

32 See www.thekingcenter.org/prog/non/6principles.html for a development of these six principles, including video clips of Dr Luther King.

33 At www.thekingcenter.org/prog/non/6steps.html [again, there is a development of each step in detail at this site].
34 The Program overview is at www.colorado.edu/conflict/peace/overview_pg.htm. Another excellent web resource, also from this University, is www.crinfo.org/v3-menu-about-crinfo.cfm.
35 The glossary can be accessed from the first address in the previous note.
36 For a good good starting point for research on the Northern Ireland Peace process and conflict resolution as it applies there, see http://cain.ulst.ac.uk/, the excellent CAIN site (Conflict Archive on the Internet).
37 This book uses 'Old Testament', rather than using the term 'Hebrew Scriptures', although 'Old Testament' is a phrase frowned upon by some modern writers as discriminatory towards Jews. I am not persuaded, however, that it is unjust for a Christian to write honestly as a Christian, using Christian terminology; nor is 'Hebrew Scriptures' exactly the same as the complete Old Testament canon that is accepted by the Catholic Church. So the term 'Old Testament' is both fair and more accurate than 'Hebrew Scriptures'.
38 This is the central point of J. Donohue, 'Biblical Perspectives on Justice' in J.C. Haughey (ed.), *The Faith that does Justice*, Woodstock Studies, vol. 2 (New York: Paulist, 1977).
39 Reading 'rights language' into this story is something of an anachronism, of course, and should not be taken literally. The text suggests how the Biblical story resonates strongly with the visions of justice and peace already examined in 2.1 and 2.2 above.
40 An excellent place to find out about the Catholic faith's understanding of the Creation and the Fall is in the *Catechism*: see paragraphs 279-384 and 385-421. It is assumed by this book that other elements of doctrine mentioned in this section on the Judaeo-Christian tradition will be researched in the *Catechism*. The various relevant paragraphs and sections are easily found using the contents page or index.
41 There are further theological dimensions to the interpretation of this story, such as the symbolism of the serpent as Satan, but this book omits these aspects for the sake of brevity.
42 UK Chief Rabbi, Jonathan Sacks, has written about this in his recent book *The Dignity of Difference* (London/New York: Continuum, revised edition, 2003).
43 See the 1984 'Instruction on Certain Aspects of Liberation Theology'

(*Liberatatis Nuntius*) from the Congregation for the Doctrine of the Faith, which offered several criticisms of a politicisation of the faith and a reductionistic interpretation of the Scriptures (esp. ch. IV, 3-4 dealing with the Exodus). In 1986, a second document was issued by the Congregation, 'Instruction on Christian Freedom and Liberation' (*Liberatis Conscientia*), this time taking a more positive tone, outlining an orthodox theology of liberation, one highly suited for use in a Catholic school context. It provides for teachers a very accessible and inspiring outline of a Catholic understanding of justice and peace, with a strong emphasis on liberation as an essential theme in evangelisation. Both documents should be read together as a couplet. They can be accessed in full from the Congregation's doctrinal documents page online at www.vatican.va/roman_curia/congregations/cfaith/doc_doc_index.htm

44 G. Weigel, *The Truth of Catholicism: Ten Controversies Explored* (Herefordshire: Gracewing, 2002), pp. 81, 83. Weigel is a Catholic author worth studying. His writings on justice issues from the Catholic perspective are particularly good, and many of them are published online: see www.ratzingerfanclub.com/Weigel/

45 From 'Judaism' in *Britannica* CD©2000 Deluxe Edition 1994-1998, Encyclopaedia Britannica Inc.

46 See on this Matthew Berke, 'A Jewish appreciation of Catholic Social Teaching' in K. Grasso, G. Bradley and R.P. Hunt, *Catholicism, Liberalism and Communitarianism* (Maryland: Rowman and Littlefield, 1995), pp. 235-253.

47 See his online book *A Clash of Civilisations? Judaic Sources on Co-existence in a World of Differences*, pp. 5-6, at www.chiefrabbi.org/ar-index.html [following the 'other articles' link].

48 See Menachem Kellner, 'Jewish Ethics' in P. Singer (ed.), *A Companion to Ethics*, Blackwell Companions to Philosophy (Oxford: Blackwell, 1993), pp. 82-90.

49 An interesting collection of accounts of modern 'saints' who died for the faith (and often for justice too) is S. Bergman, *A Cloud of Witnesses: 20th Century Martyrs* (London: Font paperbacks, 1998) which includes the Jesuits of El Salvador, Oscar Romero, Steven Biko, Martin Luther King, Dietrich Bonhoeffer, Edith Stein, Simone Weil, Maximilian Kolbe, Charles de Foucauld and Maria Goretti. Used judiciously, this would be a good resource for the classroom. Chesterton's works on St Thomas Aquinas and St Francis of Assisi are well worth reading. Also see the saints' page at CatholicIreland.net website at

www.catholicireland.net/pages/index.php?nd=68 and the excellent and very comprehensive 'catholic-pages.com' saints' directory at www.catholic-pages.com/dir/saints.asp

50 This is a major focus of modern Catholicism and is well expressed in *Gaudium et Spes*, 'The Pastoral Constitution on the Church in the Modern World', one of the documents of Vatican II. It's 39th paragraph is worth careful study. The documents of Vatican II can be accessed from the Vatican archives page at www.vatican.va/archive/index.htm , which also links to *The Code of Canon Law*, *The Catechism of the Catholic Church* and *The New American Bible*.

51 A detailed but accessible treatment of the Church's social teaching over the centuries is found in Roger Charles, *Christian Social Witness and Teaching: The Catholic Tradition from Genesis to Centesimus Annus*. Vols. 1 and 2 (Herefordshire: Gracewing, 1998.) Volume 1 deals with the Bible and following centuries; Volume 2 deals with 1891 until 1991 or so.

52 Aquinas' detailed treatment of the virtue of justice is in *Summa Theologiae* II-II, questions 57-122. Though long, and difficult in places, this is well worth looking at (and it's online in full). *A Companion to the Summa* by Walter Farrell is available online at www.op.org/Farrell/companion/ [it can be downloaded in zip format]. Though a little dated in its language and ideas, it is a very accessible comprehensive introduction to St Thomas' work.

53 The original treatment of this typology is in Richard Niebuhr, *Christ and Culture* (New York: Harper and Row, 1951). I am working from a summary of this work in Ronald Preston, 'Christian Ethics' in P. Singer (ed.) *A Companion to Ethics*, 92-93, where it is applied to ethics. Joseph McCann applies the five-part scheme to educational and institutional concerns in his thoughtful contribution to L. Monaghan and N. Prendergast (eds.), *Reimagining the Catholic School* (Dublin: Veritas, 2003). There are essays critiquing the typology by John Stackhouse in *Christianity Today* (April 22, 2002) online at www.christianitytoday.com/ct/2002/005/8.80.html and by George Marsden in *Insights: The Faculty Journal of Austin Seminary*, Fall, 1999 online at www.religion-online.org/cgi-bin/relsearchd.dll/showarticle?item_id=517 .

54 This book focuses mainly on the Catholic tradition, though its primarily biblical approach may appeal to other Christian traditions too. For scholarly treatments of some major Protestant thinkers see P. Scott and W.T. Cavanaugh (eds.), *The Blackwell Companion to*

Political Theology (Oxford, UK: Blackwell, 2004). It offers chapters on the Reformation, Karl Barth, Dietrich Bonhoeffer, William Temple, Reinhold Niebuhr, Jurgen Moltmann, Stanley Hauerwas (and also Catholic, Eastern Orthodox, Islamic and Jewish approaches to political theology).

55 Preston, "Christian Ethics", 92.

56 The statements of the American bishops are a rich source of applied Catholic Social Teaching. Their statement on crime and punishment issues is directly relevant to this syllabus. It is found in full at www.usccb.org/sdwp/criminal.htm. Closer to home, the Irish bishops publish CST documents regularly too, though they do not tend to get a lot of media attention. See *Prosperity with a Purpose* from 1999, available online at www.catholiccommunications.ie/pastlet/prosperitypastoral.pdf

57 'Eight Principles of Catholic Social Teaching' in the *Josephinum Journal of Theology* Vol. 7, Nos. 1-2 (Summer 2000): pp. 54-70, available online at Latkovic's website, accessed from the 'faculty' links of the Sacred Heart Major Seminary homepage at www.aodonline.org/SHMS/SHMS.htm

58 Given in DCU as part of the spring Lecture Series for the Centre for International Studies – School of Law and Government (25th Feb 04), organised by Dr Peadar Kirby of DCU.

59 Linda Hogan, *Human Rights*, Christian perspectives on development issues series (Dublin / London: Trócaire / Veritas / Cafod, 1998), pp. 44-45. A brief, positive outline of liberation theology is given by G. Gutierrez in the entry 'Liberation Theology' in J. Dwyer (ed.), *The New Dictionary of Catholic Social Thought* (Collegeville, Minn.: Liturgical Press, 1994). Gutierrez's classic book is *A Theology of Liberation* [1971], (London: SCM Press, 2001). See also a recent interview with Gutierrez by D. Hartnett at www.jesuits-chi.org/whatsnew/news.asp?news_id=172 (published originally in *America Magazine*, Monday, March 31, 2003.)

60 Grisez, *Living a Christian Life*, p. 362. Grisez's treatment of justice in chapter 6 is particularly good, especially his integration of mercy and justice (and see also parts of chapters 7, 8, and 10).

61 In this regard, I highly recommend the book in this series on section C (*World Religions*) by Philip Barnes (Dublin: Veritas, 2003), and its treatment of both Islam and inter-religious dialogue. Also, section E of the syllabus and the book on it by Sandra Cullen, *Religion and Gender* (Dublin: Veritas, 2004) offer an opportunity to examine the

treatment of women in Islam and other religions.
62 'Islam', *Britannica* CD©2000 Deluxe Edition 1994-1998, Encyclopaedia Britannica Inc.
63 T. Ballantine Irving, K. Ahmed, M. M. Ahsan, *The Qur'an: Basic Teachings* (London: The Islamic Foundation, revised edition, 1992), p. 23.
64 *The Qur'an: Basic Teachings*, p. 151. The words in brackets are interpolated by the authors. Another excellent source of Qur'an translations, in fact to several versions, is at the Islamicity website at www.islamicity.com/mosque/quran/
65 *The Qur'an: Basic Teachings*, Editors' comments in its glossary, pp. 270-271.
66 J. Jumier, *How to Understand Islam*, English trans. J. Bowden (London; SCM press, 1989), pp. 62-63.
67 *How to Understand Islam*, p. 62.
68 See www.islamicity.com/mosque/Zakat/. There are many excellent articles here, following the menu 'Education Centre' and then 'Islamic Education', for such titles as 'Charity and Distributive Justice' (under 'Political and Economic Aspects') and two very useful 'Zakat' talks (which are found under 'Core Beliefs').
69 The following paragraph is indebted to L. Ridgeon, 'Islam' , in L. Ridgeon (ed.), *Major World Religions* (London and New York: RoutledgeCurzon, 2003), pp. 258-259.
70 V.P. Kanitkar and W. Owen Cole, *Hinduism*, 'Teach yourself – World Faiths' series (London: Hodder and Stoughton, 1995), p. 76.
71 'Hinduism', *Britannica* CD©2000 Deluxe Edition 1994-1998, Encyclopaedia Britannica Inc. According to Hindu thought, the 'Perusa' is the primeval man from whom the universe developed.
72 There seems to be two ways of spelling this term: "Ksatriya" and "Kshatriya". This book follows the first.
73 From a Hindu 'Lexicon' at www.himalayanacademy.com/books/dws/lexicon/v.html .
74 See D. Killingley, 'Hinduism' in L. Ridgeon (ed.), *Major World Religions*, p. 44.
75 See previous note.
76 Taken from one Hindu scripture, The *Mahabharata* - Santi Parva, section CLXXXVIII, cited at www.hinduism.co.za/newpage8.htm. This web page contains several quotations from Hindu scriptures related to the issue of Varnas. The home page, containing many excellent resources on Hinduism, is at www.hinduism.co.za/ [and see

also www.hinduism.co.za/dharma.htm]. The 'Dharma' and 'Untouchables' links are two examples relevant to the course.
77 From The *Mahabharata*, Anusasana Parva, section CLXIV at website: see previous note.
78 I am particularly grateful to Bruno Breathnach, MA, HDE Director of Rigpa Dublin, Tibetan Buddhist Meditation Centre, for reading this section and sending me very helpful material from which I have quoted extensively.
79 An excellent website dealing in detail with Buddhism, including the Noble Eightfold Path and the Five Precepts, is found at www.thebigview.com/buddhism/. See also C. Humphreys, *Buddhism: an Introduction and Guide*, third edition [1951 original], (London: Penguin, 1990), pp. 110-111, for a concise introduction to the eight paths.
80 *Buddhism*, pp. 110-111.
81 *Buddhism*, p. 109.
82 *Buddhism*, p. 19.
83 *Buddhism*, p. 19.
84 M. Palmer, *The Times – World Religions: A History of Faith* (London: Times Books, 2002), p. 105.
85 These points were emphasised in Bruno Breathnach's correspondence with the author.
86 *Times World Religions*, p. 106.
87 *Times World Religions*, pp. 110-111, emphasising the non-violence of Buddhism.
88 Worth studying on 'Buddhist Ethics' is http://buddhanet.net/e-learning/budethics.htm. Also, for this topic see http://buddhanet.net/e-learning/buddhism/bs-s09.htm which is unit eight (of a secondary school syllabus) of 'Contemporary Issues and Buddhism'. Zipped files are at http://buddhanet.net/ftp03.htm. On 'socially engaged Buddhism' see http://www.buddhanet.net/filelib/genbud/eng_bud.txt. Also, highly recommended, see 'Lecture on Vesak Day' by Ven. Bhikkhu Bodhi (United Nations, 15th May 2000) at http://buddhanet.net/budmsg.htm and 'Buddhism in a nutshell' by Narada Thera at http://buddhanet.net/nutshell04.htm.
89 See *Summa Theologiae* I-II Question 96, article 4.
90 See 'Latin American Studies Program' of Providence College, Rhode Island, USA, as in note 23 above.
91 A good online site to start looking into Hauerwas' thought and reading some of his work is at www.bigbrother.net/

THE CONCEPT OF JUSTICE AND PEACE 237

~mugwump/Hauerwas/. His most recent book, at time of writing, is *Performing the Faith: Bonhoeffer and the Practice of Non-violence* (Grand Rapids, MI: Brazos Press, 2004), which deals with many of the issues looked at in parts 2.2, 2.3 and 2.4 of this course.
92 See Baxter's very provocative and suggestive article, 'Just war and pacifism: A 'pacifist' perspective in seven points' at www.cjd.org/paper/baxpacif.html.
93 In listing the conditions, this book follows the US Catholic Bishops' 1983 Pastoral Letter, *The Challenge of Peace*, paragraphs 85-110, available online at www.osjspm.org/cst/cp.htm (though 'comparative justice', which the bishops include but which does not appear in all versions of the theory, is not treated here).
94 A philosophical and theological critique of utilitarianism (or proportionalism or consequentialism, as it is also known) is found in G. Grisez and R. Shaw, *Fulfillment in Christ* (Notre Dame, Indiana: University of Notre Dame Press, 1993), chapter 6. (This is a popular version of Grisez's more thorough *Christian Moral Principles*.) Pope John Paul II has rejected the utilitarian approach as incompatible with the Catholic faith, in his encyclical *Veritatis Splendor* (1993), especially pars. 71-83, available at the Vatican website archive of the Pope's writings at www.vatican.va/holy_father/john_paul_ii/
95 A particularly good, short treatment of the issues is given by another author in this series, Pat Hannon, in 'Theology, War and Pacifism' in L. Hogan and B. Fitzgerald (eds.) *Between Poetry and Politics: Christian Theology in Dialogue* (Dublin: Columba, 2003), pp. 117-134. A book-length analysis of the Catholic tradition is found in T. Massaro and T. Shannon, *Catholic Perspectives on Peace and War* (Lanham, Maryland, USA: Rowman and Littlefield, 2004). Robert Gill and R. John Elford have some interesting points to make in their contributions on Christianity, war and the arms trade in R. Gill (ed.) *The Cambridge Companion to Christian Ethics* (Cambridge, UK: Cambridge University Press, 2000). There is a veritable library online (275 documents!) relating to 9/11 and the fight against terror at the zenit archives: www.zenit.org/english/war/index_archive_war.phtml. Another even better online library is found at www.ratzingerfanclub.com/justwar/index.html, which contains many excellent articles on just war in general and the Iraq war in particular. Several books on the topic are mentioned at the end of the chapter above. Particular mention must be made of those by Paul Ramsey, James Timothy Johnson and Michael Waltzer. Waltzer has a very interesting article,

'The Right Way', *The New York Review of Books* (13th July 2003) [www.mafhoum.com/press4/135P5.htm].

3

The Religious Imperative To Act For Justice and Peace

A specific area
This part focuses on a very specific area for application of justice and peace principles: the environment. Other specific areas, such as just war, have already been treated. As with the first chapter, the approach taken here is to discuss the main concepts and issues in some detail and to suggest further references to extend the exploration. This is an area where interpretation of the facts can change quickly, at least when large claims or long-term predictions are being made. Teachers should liaise closely with colleagues who teach science, geography, economics and other relevant subjects while also keeping an eye out for items on TV and in newspapers and magazines. The source of any information in the media should always be carefully noted. Claims or conclusions presented there might be simplified, with the scientific nuances and limitations glossed over for popular consumption. It may be tempting for some teachers to emphasise dramatic claims and frightening scenarios to gain the attention of students, but this is usually not advisable. Students and teachers should take the more outlandish claims and predictions in this area with a grain of salt, though not in a way that dismisses the importance of the issues. It is not for nothing that the term 'imperative' is used

in the title of this part of the section. The environment is not something we can afford to neglect or abuse.

Aims

The aims for this part (syllabus, p. 64) overlap with the previous parts considerably. There continues to be a concern with knowing 'the variety of perspectives on justice and peace' and understanding the links between religious faith and commitment to act for justice and peace. There is a continuing emphasis on 'openness to and respect for' those who campaign for justice, including those who do so 'out of religious conviction'; also emphasised is an appreciation for and sensitivity to issues of justice and peace in given situations, including students' own lives.

A religious focus

One completely new aim is mentioned: to 'have an understanding that the current environmental crises compel many religious believers to act and campaign on environmental issues'. The idea here is that the critical nature of the environmental problems we face can move us to act to improve the situation. One major aim of this part, therefore, is to show how religious faith motivates and shapes this action. The present book is not mainly concerned to summarise or evaluate all the detail of the scientific data on the various crises. This is clearly an important task, but, like the task of social analysis in part one, it is not a specifically religious task – or 'skill' to use the syllabus term. Several references are mentioned in this chapter, however, that give detailed scientific information on the various issues. What mainly concerns us in this chapter is how the religious believer, in particular the Christian, is going to deal wisely and justly with the information, claims and debates in the light of religious faith and philosophical reasoning. Dealing with the environment and its crises is potentially interesting and fruitful as an area of teaching, but it is also an area where one might succumb to faddish or even bizarre theories and ideas.

Structure
The structure of this part (and chapter) is simple:
1 A general introduction to the area of the greening of religion (focusing on the concept of 'greening of religion', a major religious commentator on it, and a religious group living by it).
2 Treatment of four specific religious approaches to environmental issues (broadly: Judaic, Christian, Buddhist and Islamic).

As well as explaining concepts and providing information and references, this chapter includes some ideas on how to teach, and how not to teach, this area.

3.1 RELIGION AND THE ENVIRONMENT

(i) The 'greening' of religion

Environmentalism
The first area specified in the syllabus is to understand the general connection between environmentalism and religion. 'Environmentalism'[1] refers to a relatively recent phenomenon, the wide-spread interest in issues to do with how we are treating the natural world – animals, trees, the soil and the land, the seas, rivers and lakes, the air, and the Earth as a whole. Political parties (the 'Greens') have been established in light of this new movement, and other political parties have taken its issues on board in their own policies.[2] What has caused this huge increase of interest in things environmental? Some aspects of an answer are outlined here.

Historical factors in the rise of environmentalism
In the twentieth century, the world experienced two massive wars, which included the development of highly destructive

weaponry, and in particular the development and use of the vast destructive power of atomic bombs. Even 'peaceful' atomic energy risked huge destruction caused by nuclear accident or terrorist attack. The world was faced for the first time with the possibility that we could destroy our civilisation and perhaps even our planet. Science has also given us new knowledge of potential massive natural disasters, often linked to our developing technology and its effects on the world we live in, particularly effects on climate. Global warming, the gradual but accelerating reduction of the ozone layer protecting the earth, widespread depletion of (and even elimination of) many species, the destruction of huge areas of forest and arable land, the spread of deserts, heavy pollution – all these and more have become part of our daily thinking, part of our common concern. Our culture has even become somewhat apocalyptic in reference to this. The media has sometimes facilitated this apocalyptic mood. One example is a film inspired by fears of global warming and its effects, 2004's *The Day After Tomorrow*, which dealt with the catastrophic effects of global warming in very vivid terms (a huge tidal wave engulfing Manhattan, global freezing conditions, and so on). Though fiction, this film feeds off (and into) a cultural fact: many people are deeply fearful about our future on the planet and the many perceived and genuine threats to it. Note the nearness of the catastrophe implied in the film's title.[3]

As well as the negative reasons for the rise of environmentalism, there are positive reasons too. Since we have gone into space and even to the moon, we have been able to look back on the earth and see that it is a distinct home. The photograph of the earth taken from the moon has become an icon of our age. The growth in communication technology and the increasing mobility of people has led to the now clichéd idea of the earth as a 'global village'. We are used to thinking in global terms and have a more scientific understanding of our environment, our ecology, our global home.

What is the ideal state of the world?
What is the ideal state for the earth? Is the answer a 'natural paradise', with little, or even preferably *no*, human and technological impact? Some people may be inclined to see cities, roads, cars and other man-made things as inherently less-than-ideal, as human impositions on a nature that is pure in its own innocence and integrity. Some have become quite cynical and pessimistic about human 'progress' and 'development'. Even if we see the need for roads and 'developments', we still tend to think of them as necessary evils, not necessary goods. Perhaps this is because we tend to share the assumption that nature is innocent and pure in itself and that we humans have sullied this by our scientific and economic activity, at least insofar as this activity is exploitative and destructive. As a result, nature is perhaps fighting back and we are going to pay for our 'sins' against it.

Maybe this is somewhat over-stated, but it reflects accurately at least some of our common assumptions. Along with this assumption about the 'integrity'[4] of nature, however, there can be other emotions and thoughts. We know that nature is often 'red in tooth and claw'. We spend much of our wealth protecting ourselves from nature's destructive forces.

In spite of our mixed feelings about nature we can be sure that action to conserve and protect the environment is needed, and this idea is supported by the writings and protests of environmentalists. This concern for the environment is not difficult to connect to our belief in God the Creator and our responsibility to care for his creation. Religious faith can strengthen our commitment to listen to environmentalist warnings, to assess them carefully, and to act justly to improve matters. The ideal state of the world will include humans living lightly on the land, pursuing development in a way that respects nature and does as little damage to it as possible.

The Greening of Religion
Religions have responded to the growth of environmentalism by including its broad concerns in their own teachings. Religions have become more 'green' in response to the negative and positive factors mentioned above, just as society more generally has become more 'green' in response to them. This is not just a matter of religious bodies trying to be 'relevant' to modern concerns, though there is always the danger of a superficial 'jumping on the bandwagon' regarding the latest fad or fashion. The greening of religion is much more than this and religions have great potential to contribute to the environmental cause.

Religion can contribute to the environmental cause
Gary Gardner has listed five areas where religion can powerfully help the cause of creating a more just and sustainable world. These five points could form a useful structure for approaching this topic in class discussion and research:[5]

1 Religions have the capacity to shape *world views* (cosmologies) that support a positive view of nature and our connection to it.
2 They can develop environmentally friendly and ethically inspiring *moral teachings* flowing from these cosmologies, teachings communicated by leaders with strong authority.
3 Religions have large numbers of *adherents* who can respond to these teachings in a way that practically aids environmental programmes and movements.
4 They also have *material resources* such as buildings like churches and hospitals, and financial activities such as investment, that can be utilised in a publicly evident, environmentally supportive manner.
5 Finally, religions have a tremendous power in *forming communities*, and the environmental movement needs community for it to be effective.

Gardner thinks that the environmental movement has only just begun to acknowledge the importance of religion and its potential. A 'budding rapprochement' between the two communities has started, as the potential of religion to motivate environmental activism has been increasingly appreciated and religious bodies have responded positively in their turn to environmentalist concerns.[6]

Pantheism and the rejection of a transcendent God
'Green' religion can be a great support for environmental concern, but, as understood from within the Catholic tradition and the broader Christian tradition, it needs to be an orthodox religious faith that thinks clearly and sensibly about the issues in the light of God's revelation.[7] Some approaches to environmentalism can be pantheistic, however, seeing nature as a type of divinity or god. (Feminist environmentalism may speak here in terms of a nature 'goddess' rather than a god and blame wide-spread and deep-rooted 'patriarchy' for our problems, including environmental crises.) Pantheism is suggested by references to the earth or the universe as a kind of living organism, for example, in the well-known 'Gaia' hypothesis of James Lovelock. It is implied more particularly by a close connection of some environmental thinking and action with mystical traditions and ideas that eschew the doctrine in Judaism, Christianity and Islam of a transcendent Creator God distinct from his creation and opt for a more immanent god who lives in nature as its soul, so to speak.

These kinds of ideas are good examples of the greening of religion and they provide many people with 'meaning and value', to echo the title of the introductory section of the syllabus. This is something that ought to be acknowledged. Religions that are centred on belief in a transcendent God, however, will logically find themselves in a somewhat critical relationship with such ideas. It is a particularly interesting question which is the more 'friendly' towards environmental concerns: belief in a transcendent God or belief in a more immanent god. As mentioned in the introduction to this book, my overall approach is firmly grounded in the Christian faith, with a view to the syllabus being taught in a way that is consistent with the religious ethos and character of particular schools (which in Ireland will tend to be Catholic schools), but it is still necessary to acknowledge and understand other religious approaches to the environment and its problems, as is done in this chapter and its references.

Some would say that belief in a transcendent God is the less friendly approach towards environmental justice. One accusation that has been levelled at 'religion', and in particular at Christianity, is that it is a major source of the environmental problems we face. It is claimed such religion has helped cause the crises because it has fed human arrogance and pride. It has taught man that he has a God-given right to dominate and use nature for his own purposes. It has preached that man is superior over all animals and plants and the earth itself. It has supported the rise of an interfering science and an imposing technology. The book of Genesis chapter one, verses 26-29 is the main culprit here. The 'offending' phrases include:

> Then God said, 'Let us make humankind in our image, according to our likeness; and *let them have dominion over* [the world] ... and God said to them, 'Be fruitful and multiply, and fill the earth and subdue it; and have dominion over the fish of the sea and over the birds of the air and over every living thing that moves upon the earth. [Italics my own.]

The Bible can therefore be accused of teaching that man is superior over all earthly nature and therefore can do what he likes with it. It can be shown that this is not a very accurate interpretation of the biblical text (as will be discussed in some detail in part 3.2 below, looking at the concept of stewardship-dominion). It is an interpretation that has gained some currency in environmental circles, at least until recently.[8] It may account partially for what Gardner describes as the gap between the religious and environmentalist communities.[9]

Efforts to answer the criticisms levelled against the Bible are among the factors that have led to the 'greening' of religion, as Church organisations and theologians have emphasised the pertinence of religious faith to environmentalist concerns as one element in a policy of defending religion from being seen as hostile to the environment or irrelevant to modern concerns.

Finding out the scientific facts: GEO 2000
Turning now to the scientific angle of the topic, one of the first tasks is to find out the accurate scientific facts on the environment and the crises it faces. The reader will find useful authors who acknowledge that there are difficulties in measuring and interpreting the scientific findings and in working out what to do about the issues raised.[10] One of the most reliable, official sources of information on the global environmental situation, and one readily accessible online, is the *GEO 2000 report of the UNEP* (United Nations Environment Programme).[11] This is a detailed study of regional and global issues 'based on contributions from UN agencies, 850 individuals and 30 environmental institutes [that] outlines progress in tackling existing problems and points to serious new threats. It concludes its report by setting out recommendations for immediate, integrated action.' Its press release summary reads:

> According to GEO-2000, full scale emergencies now exist in a number of fields. The world water cycle seems unlikely to be able to cope with demands in the coming decades, land degradation has negated many advances made by increased agricultural productivity, air pollution

is at crisis point in many major cities and global warming now seems inevitable.

Tropical forests and marine fisheries have been over-exploited while numerous plant and animal species and extensive stretches of coral reefs will be lost forever – thanks to inadequate policy response.

In a survey conducted by the Scientific Committee on Problems of the Environment for GEO-2000, 200 scientists in 50 countries identified water shortage and global warming as the two most worrying problems for the new millennium. Desertification and deforestation at national and regional level was also a frequently cited concern.

Its recommendations focus on the concepts of 'sustainability' (taking a long-term view) and 'integration' (making sure that environmental concerns are central in people's thinking and planning at all levels):

At the core of GEO-2000's recommendations is a reinforcement of Agenda 21's call for environmental integration. 'The environment remains largely outside the mainstream of everyday human consciousness and is still considered an add-on to the fabric of life,' says GEO-2000.

'... Integration of environmental thinking into the mainstream of decision-making relating to agriculture, trade, investment, research and development, infrastructure and finance is now the best chance for effective action,' says GEO-2000.

Additional sources of information
Also online, the Development Gateway website has a very good section on environmental issues in a global perspective.[12] Teachers and students should study the Irish Department of the Environment and Local Government website. Two Irish

publications (both available in full online) are especially relevant. One is *Sustainable Development: A Strategy for Ireland* (1997) and the other is *Making Ireland's Development Sustainable* (2002).[13] The Environmental Protection Agency provides essential reading.[14] (There is so much information at these sites, it can be overwhelming. It would be advisable to divide up the topics, or at least a manageable portion of them, among students.)

Read the critics too: Lomborg

It is also good to study writers who are critical of environmentalist claims, who argue that the scientific case for the environmental crisis needs to be assessed more carefully and priorities specified more wisely. The best example of such a critic of the environmentalist 'agenda', in my opinion, is the Danish writer Bjørn Lomborg, author of *The Skeptical Environmentalist* (2001). He considers himself to be an environmentalist, but one critical of what he argues are numerous exaggerations and errors in the usual environmentalist claims, warnings and recommendations. Using statistical analysis on the figures from reputable sources (the same sources used by the environmentalists he criticises), Lomborg puts forward a detailed argument that 'the state of the world' is not as bad as commonly portrayed and widely believed. He argues that things are getting better, though they are not necessarily good enough yet. He is highly critical of Greenpeace, Earthwatch, Paul Ehrlich, and other well-known environmentalist organisations and writers. His first chapter is online in full and provides a comprehensive overview of his book.[15] An attentive reading of his book and website will invite people to reassess what they've come to assume about several issues relevant to this topic, though one might not be fully convinced by his arguments and figures.[16]

It is possible to follow the responses by Lomborg to criticisms of his work on his website. He includes links to the original critical texts on his site, with his own responses, so it is possible to see both sides of the 'debate' that is taking place. It is a fascinating example of how controversial this area of environmental science and ethics is – and how careful a teacher needs to be in teaching it.

An approach that includes a 'skeptic' such as Lomborg, and brings his arguments into dialogue with opposing views, may encourage critical thinking in one's pupils and so contribute to a thoroughly educational approach to teaching this syllabus. Also, such an approach will help to avoid problems that may occur if overstated claims are made as part of environmentalist arguments and later uncovered as unreliable by informed students, with the authority of the whole environmental cause (not to mention one's teaching) thereby weakened.

(ii) A Religious Commentator on the Environment

Fr Seán McDonagh
The syllabus asks us to outline the life and ideas of a commentator on religion and the environment. The most impressive example to come to mind here is Fr Seán McDonagh, an Irish priest of the Columban order, consultant to the General Council of the Columban Fathers on ecology and environment. He worked among the T'boli people of Mindanao, Philippines for twenty years. His experience led him to become aware of the link between environmental and poverty issues. He has written much on environmental issues, both in an applied way (focusing on specific practical problems) and in a more theoretical way (looking at the Christian theology of environmentalism). He has focused on both global and national issues. His books explain the link between religion, particularly Christianity, and right relationship with our world. One basic theme is 'creation', especially in relation to the book of Genesis, chapters 1-3, but there is a great deal more, including Christology.[17]

His books include
- *To Care For the Earth* (1986)
- *The Greening of the Church* (1990)
- *Passion for the Earth* (1995)
- *Greening the Christian Millennium* (1998)
- *Why are we Deaf to the Cry of the Earth?* (2001)
- *Dying for Water* (2003)
- *Patenting Life? Stop!* (2003)
- *The Death of Life: The Horror of Extinction* (2004)

Some of his articles can be found at the Columban website, under the heading 'MA in Ecology and Religion'.[18]

His life and message were recently summarised in *Reality* magazine.[19] The following are some excerpts:

> After ordination in 1969, [Fr McDonagh] spent the next years in parish and teaching ministry in the Philippines as a Columban missionary. From 1980 onwards, he worked among the T'boli people of South Cotabato, and it was during this time that his concern for the destruction of the environment grew.... At the moment, he is co-ordinator of the Justice, Peace and Integrity of Creation Programme of the Columban Missionary Society worldwide, as well as chair of the Irish environmental organisation, VOICE. [Fr McDonagh says,] 'During my 20 years as a missionary in the Philippines, I witnessed enormous destruction of the rainforest, mangrove forests, rivers, lakes and the soils of the country. A city like Manila was, and is, choking with air pollution and smog. It faces major problems supplying basic services like water and sanitation to its citizens in the coming years. During my time in the Philippines, I became involved in environmental issues. I worked with groups who were trying to protect what was left of the

rainforest, and at the same time, replant in suitable places.'

McDonagh sums up his message thus:

> Everyone will admit that greed, covetousness and other commonly recognised human vices have undoubtedly contributed to our present crisis. Nevertheless, the principal cause of ecological devastation in our world today has been the unrelenting pursuit of what many people consider a good and desirable thing – the modern, growth-oriented, industrial model of development. What many people long for is in fact destroying the world. There is very little appreciation that this generation has obligations to future generations. The challenges of inter-generational justice are seldom discussed. As a people we seem to be very insensitive to the environmental maxim that 'we do not inherit the earth, we borrow it from our children.' Given that the Christian churches have arrived at these challenges a little breathless and a little late, they must now make up for lost time and, in co-operation with other faiths, throw all their energies into urgently addressing the challenge of justice, peace and the integrity of creation. Unless this awareness is gained in the very near future, human beings and the rest of the planet's community will be condemned to live amid the ruins of the natural world. The first and most important contribution that the churches could make to the present ecological crisis would be to acknowledge the magnitude of the problem and urge people to face it with courage.

It is interesting to see McDonagh highlighting the essentially ethical nature of the problems faced by the human race, particularly the dimension of vice. It would be very useful to discuss in class what exactly 'greed' is and how are we to know when we have enough of the earth's goods. What are the virtues we need to defeat vice? Should humans be more content with what we already have? Another emphasis in McDonagh's analysis is the centrality of 'intergenerational justice', the moral principle of giving to our children and our children's children what they are due – a healthy environment to live in. This clearly ties in a concern for the environment with a focus on justice.

The first chapter of McDonagh's recent *Dying for Water* is available online in full.[20] It adds more biographical information and provocative arguments. McDonagh's books and online articles provide much food for thought and action in relation to the link between religious faith (specifically, Christian) and environmental justice. In addition, his accessible accounts of the details of many specific environmental problems provides a confident reply to the skeptical approach of writers such as Lomborg. It might be worth bringing these two writers into some dialogue in the classroom in relation to some issue, such as global warming or species extinction.[21] The juxtaposition of their opposite arguments and the process of resolving the tensions raised by this juxtaposition could be highly educational. I would regard his work as a substantial contribution to the area of environmental Christian ethics and would recommend that students be encouraged to read widely among his many writings.

(iii) A Religious Environmental Group

An Tairseach
The syllabus also requires study of 'a religious group or organisation with an environmental commitment or lifestyle' (syllabus, p.65). Again, the present book proposes an accessible Irish option as our example: 'An Tairseach' (the Dominican Sisters' Farm and Ecology Centre in Wicklow).[22] Established in

1998, this comprises an organic farm, a conservation area and a centre for ecology and spirituality, all of which are described on its web homepage. Its website explains its Irish name thus: 'An Tairseach, meaning threshold, gives this project its name. It suggests a new beginning, an alternative and more sustainable way of working with the land and also a renewed relationship with the whole community of life, human and non-human.' This emphasis on all of life as a unified community is central to their philosophy. In several places on the site it is clear that their main inspiration is a kind of creation spirituality, shaped by the thought of Brian Swimme and others who have developed a poetic view of the evolution of the universe and who see the Earth as an organic unity. Unlike the work of Seán McDonagh outlined above, there does not seem to be a specifically Christian theology behind the project. As far as I can see, there seems to be little or no mention of Christ, sacraments or Church; the emphasis is all on a creation theme. It is an interesting question, in my opinion, how a creation-based focus on the environment might be developed into one that includes an explicitly Christological focus, as Christ is the centre of Christian faith. Perhaps this is an area that An Tairseach and/or other Christian groups might develop in the future, to add to the inspiring, poetic creation spirituality.[23] Other Christian groups who follow a 'green' approach to life include the Franciscan, Benedictine and the Columban religious orders.[24]

Greening of Religion – Overview

Some methodological issues
Dealing with global issues of great weight and seriousness can become a bit unreal unless you keep your feet firmly on the ground. So, some kind of local focus would be good perhaps. It makes little sense, for example, to be talking in class about saving the world from pollution whilst the students are littering the school yard during lunch break! The structures of

behaviour in school (and at home too) will naturally come under scrutiny if this section is being taught well. Is there any place for recycling? Is there any attention to the beauty of the surroundings and the pleasantness of the school environment itself? What is the level of needless waste? Is a long-term or a short-term view the norm? How do our liturgies include and express respect for nature and the natural? In relation to teaching the curriculum itself, it may be worth considering integrating the work with literature (especially poetry) and art. Teachers may wish to organise poetry or story writing, song composition, and/or art project work on the topic of ecological concerns to accompany and enhance this course. It would be very appropriate to decorate the RE room with posters, charts, and so on, especially ones produced by students studying the course. Documentaries on ecological issues are often on TV and it would be worth keeping an eye open for them.[25] (This is not to neglect radio, though it is harder to work with purely audio media in class.) Finally, speakers with expert knowledge on environmental issues are always a good option, if available; perhaps this might be organised in conjunction with the science teachers also dealing with ecology issues.

Further examples of religious links to environmentalism
In addition to the individual and group presented above, there are many others involved in linking faith, justice and peace, and environmental concern.[26]
- In 1988 the World Council of Churches (WCC) started a 'Climate Change Programme' that lobbied governments and international organisations to deal with structures and lifestyles that have contributed to the current climate crisis.
- The Parliament of World Religions issued statements in 1993 and 1999 on the ethical challenge of caring for the world.
- In 1996 the World Wide Fund for Nature (WWF) organised a conference in Assisi, Italy, where representatives of five of

the world's faiths discussed strategies for helping their communities to work to protect the environment.
- Harvard University organised a series of conferences on 'Religions of the World and Ecology' from 1996 to 1998, from which nine volumes were published and The Forum on Religion and Ecology established to continue the discussions.
- In 1994, 1997, 1999 and 2002, Eastern Orthodox Ecumenical Patriarch Bartholomew I convened a series of shipboard symposia, involving scientists, policymakers, religious leaders and journalists, focusing on regional water-related environmental issues.
- The Millennium World Peace Summit of Religious and Spiritual Leaders brought together more than 1,000 participants at the UN, where the environment was an important topic of discussion.[27]

Catholic Church Teaching on the Environment

What about the Catholic Church? Seán McDonagh has criticised it for not being quick enough or radical enough in its response to the environmental crises we face. He has a point. The Church has spoken on this issue more than one might think, however, as can be seen in the number of magisterial statements since 1972 (found in Sr Margorie Keenan, *From Stockholm to Johannesburg*). The main papal documents are:

- 1979 *Redemptoris Hominis* (8, 15, 16)
- 1981 *Laborem Exercens* (4, 25)
- 1987 *Sollicidudo Rei Socialis* (26, 29, 39, 34, 48)
- 1990 'Pope John Paul II Message for World Day of Peace – *Peace with God the Creator; Peace with All of Creation*'
- 1991 *Centesimus Annus* (37, 38, 40, 52)
- 1995 *Evangelium Vitae* (27, 42)
- 2002 'Common Declaration of Pope John Paul II and the Ecumenical Patriarch Bartholomew I – Rome-Venice, 10th June 2002'

- 2003 'Pope's Message to Patriarch of Constantinople on the Environment' Vatican city, 11th June 2003.

The 1990 document is the only lengthy treatment devoted by a pope to environmental concerns, and as such deserves special attention. One should also mention *The Catechism of the Catholic Church* (especially 299, 349, 354, 376-8, 2415-2418, and 2450-2457). A particularly good Catholic website, fully orthodox and containing numerous links to articles and documents, including the ones just listed, is the 'Catholic Conservation Center' run by Bill Jacobs.[28] There have been several letters by bishops in various places on environmental themes. One of the earliest was 'What is Happening to our beautiful land?' by the Bishops of the Phillipines (1988).[29]

3.2 RELIGIOUS TRADITIONS AND THE ENVIRONMENT

Structure
Four topics are to be studied here:
- Judaism: Sabbath, Schmittah and Jubilee
- The Genesis creation texts: the concepts of stewardship and dominion
- Buddhism: the Five Precepts
- Islam: the concept of vice-regent of the earth.

Christianity is not directly specified nor is Christ mentioned, but they can be incorporated appropriately into one's teaching of the stewardship-dominion concept, as suggested below. (Hinduism is not mentioned in 3.2.) Particular empirical facts and figures relating to the crises themselves are not detailed below; rather, the meaning of the religious concepts are clarified, and it is indicated how they might be appropriately applied to specific issues.

(i) Judaism: Sabbath, Schmittah, Jubilee

These three concepts express a deep appreciation that the Earth is the Lord's and human persons should not be arrogant and selfish about it.[30] Though they are Jewish concepts originally, they have universal significance.

Sabbath

Exodus

There are two versions of the Decalogue (Ten Commandments) – one in Exodus 20 and the other in Deuteronomy 5. The Exodus commandment regarding the Sabbath (Ex 20: 8-11) links the Sabbath to Creation. It emphasises that all, including slaves, strangers and even animals, should rest from work on that day because God rested from his own work of creation on the seventh day. This suggests a universal significance for the Sabbath. Though it is intended directly for the Jewish people (and for Christians in a modified form after Easter Sunday), the Sabbath can teach all people about the importance of rest and the relationship of God to his creation. There is also perhaps a parallel with the rainbow sign of the universal covenant made by God with all mankind after the flood and at the new beginning (see Gen 9). Later in Exodus it is written that the Sabbath will be an everlasting sign of God's covenant with his people (see Ex 31: 12-17).[31]

Deuteronomy

The Deuteronomy Sabbath commandment (Deut 5: 12-15) is similar to the one in Exodus, but also quite distinctive. Although once again the emphasis is on rest for all, including slaves and farm animals, this version links the Sabbath to the exodus from slavery in Egypt and the subsequent Covenant, rather than to Creation. The reason given is that the Israelites were once slaves, but God saved them. This suggests a social reason for the Sabbath rest – the human importance of resting for people who work hard and who suffer. It also suggests a kind of equality between slave and master: both must obey God's law of Sabbath rest (and the master must facilitate this). Also, God's great actions in delivering Israel are emphasised. In memory of finding their place of rest in the promised land, the Israelites are to rest on the Sabbath (cf. Deut 12: 9; Ps 95: 11). The Sabbath has an inherently religious purpose – it is not just a time to rest, it is a time to remember God and to worship him.[32] The notion of resting from work is central, however, as is suggested by the root of the word, *Shabbat*.

Application to environmental concerns
The Sabbath can be related to environmental crises by the way it relativises human work. The Sabbath puts into religious perspective all human work, profit-making, 'development', and 'progress'. None of these are to be our 'gods'; we are not to commit ourselves ultimately to human work, human achievements, human projects. The ultimate context for everything is God, his relationship with us and his laws. Nothing takes precedence over these. Thus, religious faith prevents the profit motive from dominating us and making us slaves to wealth creation. Insofar as one sees our being 'slaves' to wealth creation and profit as the root of our environmental problems, and it is undoubtedly a major factor, the religious institution of the Sabbath is a valuable reminder of where our priorities should lie. Added to this is the principle that all human beings, including the 'slaves' and 'strangers', are due a regular period of rest so that they can be refreshed (and so worship God in peace and holiness). In fact, even animals are due a rest according to the Biblical law – this is a reminder that God wishes us to treat animals with respect (see Pr 12:10). This is true even though the Bible does not outlaw the sacrifice of animals nor their use as food.

A final thing to note is that the Sabbath was an obligation from God. Many have lost their sense of an obligatory rest on the Sabbath. The religious, social and environmental value of this rest has to be restored somehow. It could be a good idea to discuss in class how this might be achieved practically. For example, ought the Church to teach more firmly in this area? Has the civil law any role to play? Insofar as it is left totally up to our own choice, it would seem that we are happy to let the Sabbath become just like the other days – a day for being busy making money or spending money. Originally, the Sabbath was a Divine law, not a human option. It was a law that brought joy and freedom, but it was nonetheless a law. God's will (for our good) was always seen in the biblical perspective as a constant, necessary restraint against human arrogance and greed and forgetfulness, sinful qualities that lie behind our mistreatment of nature today.

The Sabbath seeks to free people from themselves in their inmost being, and in this respect it can also play a vital role in the present-day world. Modern man is moved by the unbridled pursuit of profit, a quest for material advantage and constant progress. To restrain this disastrous course, it is necessary to follow the divine example put before us by the Bible; in order not to succumb to temptations of unlimited growth, not to allow oneself to be entirely taken over by material things, human beings, like God, must know how to say 'Enough is enough' since the world may well be destroyed if such growth takes on excessive proportions.[33]

Schmittah

Sabbatical year

This refers to the sabbatical year, every seventh year (the end of every 'week' of years), when all slaves were to be set free and the fields, vineyards and olive groves left fallow and their produce left for the poor. Biblical references: Ex 21: 2-6; and 23: 10-11; Deut 15: 1-18 and 31:10. (The Ex 23: 10-11 law about land is not found in Deut, but is in Lev 25: 18-22.) Again, the idea seems to be one of Divine restraint on human immersion in work and wealth creation, immersion that causes various kinds of human slavery. 'The Shemitah Year, the seventh year, is analogous to the seventh day, the Shabbat, in that it is a "year of rest" for the Land. No planting or harvesting may be done that year; the population has to rely on the produce of the sixth year for three years, including the eighth, because no planting is permitted in the seventh, which the Lord promises to supply with abundance (Lev 25, 20-21).'[34]

Application to environmental concerns
The concept of *schmittah* comes from the word for 'remission' and refers to both the leaving of the land fallow and the remission of debts. The idea that the land needs to be given a rest is easily related to environmental concerns today. We are too taken up, it can be argued, with the notion that we must get the most out of the land (and other natural resources) as effectively and quickly as possible, to make profit and to contribute to 'progress' and 'development'. This can lead us to mistreat the land and nature itself, to exploit it rather than use it wisely and justly. The biblical idea in the sabbatical year, the Schmittah, is that our relationship to the land is not one of total ownership and subsequent rights to exploitation. Our land is a gift from God and it is not ours to use all the time. Every seventh day we must rest and every seventh year we must rest. The land is God's: we have it on loan, so to speak. We need to trust God's gift, that it will produce enough for us to live on even if we leave it alone for a while to recover its freshness. We need to be content with what is sufficient, rather than striving to get more and more. This idea is supported by the fact that the produce of the land is for the community, especially the vulnerable and needy, not just the individual owner, and so the produce must be left for the poor during the sabbatical year.

The concept of Schmittah may not have been carried out in history (the details on this issue are not fully known), but it nevertheless remains a powerful symbol of how people are called to trust God and respect the land and its resources. We must not over-exploit the land and plunder its riches in such activities as excessive mining, fishing, and farming. Also, our work on the land should be for the good of all, including the poor. Social solidarity and respect for the land go together.

Jubilee

A 'super-sabbatical' year

'Jubilee' will be linked in many minds with the recent and ongoing campaign to cancel Third World debt. It will also call up memories of the Millennium/Jubilee year of 2000. Its biblical roots are in Lev 25: 8-17, 23-55, (several parts of which apply to the sabbatical year seen above). It was a 'super-sabbatical' year. This is how De Vaux describes it:

> It was a general emancipation [...] of all the inhabitants of the land. The fields lay fallow: every man re-entered his ancestral property, i.e. the fields and houses which had been alienated returned to their original owners [...] Consequently, transactions in land had to be made by calculating the number of years before the next jubilee: one did not buy the ground but so many years of harvests. Finally, defaulting debtors and Israelite slaves were set free, so the purchase price of these slaves was reckoned from the number of years still to elapse before the next jubilee. Religious grounds are given for these measures: the land cannot be sold absolutely, for it belongs to God; Israelites cannot be cast into perpetual slavery, for they are the servants of God, who brought them out of Egypt.[35]

Application to environmental concerns

The passages in Leviticus on Jubilee imply that no-one can accumulate large amounts of land indefinitely – it must return to its original owner in the Jubilee year. Thus, the right to own property is not abolished, but is given an ethical dimension. This, alongside the freeing of slaves, is a kind of prevention of unrestrained wealth accumulation and exploitation of the poor by the powerful rich. The idea of emancipation is central to the biblical institution of Jubilee, hence there is an application to the cancellation of the debts of the developing countries. Social justice principles can ground the call for a cancellation of the heavy debt burden carried by the poorest countries; certainly the biblical principle of mercy can.[36] Concern for the environment includes concern for people who are part of the ecology of the planet. In addition, efforts by the poor of the developing world to meet heavy debt repayments by environmentally destructive production can lead the people of poor countries to take the purely short-term view of repaying the debt. One thinks here, for example, of poor use of land leading to deforestation or desertification, two areas of concern often mentioned in reports on the state of the planet. Debt reduction or cancellation can thus be an important aspect of environmental justice.

Sustainability

Mention of short-term versus long-term perspectives leads to a broader way of linking Jubilee (and the other Jewish concepts) to environmental concerns. One very important concept in much environmental thinking is 'sustainability'. This refers to the necessity of taking a long-term view of all that we do in economics and politics and social policies so that the needs and rights of future generations of human beings will be respected. This is a particularly important value in judging an issue such as our energy usage and its effects. Global warming is another related current environmental issue that needs to be judged in a long-term perspective. These three Jewish/Biblical concepts – Sabbath, Schmittah, Jubilee – draw our attention to the importance of time and the long-term perspective. They all concern how the human community, following God's direction, can shape time in such a way that we gain a healthy perspective on life and values, including the value of the land and its resources, and the value of work and rest. Jubilee, especially, is a concept that emphasises the need to look ahead when planning what to do now, because there will come a time when the land must be 'returned' to God and one's workers (slaves) set free. The religious institution of Jubilee expresses the belief that we live in a framework of time stretching into the future, where our descendents will live on the same land we look after now. We do not merely live in the present moment – we live in God's time and on God's land. As the Psalm says, 'The earth is the Lord's and all that is in it, the world, and those who live in it' (Ps 24: 1-2). It is up to us to use the time and land well, not only for our own benefit, but for the good of the poor now and the good of future generations too.

(ii) The Genesis Creation Accounts: Stewardship and Dominion

Is the message of Genesis anti-environmental?
The treatment of part 3.1 above mentioned the fact that the creation accounts in Genesis (chs 1-3, but mainly 1:26-30) have been accused of teaching an anti-environmental message. This message is that human persons are created by God as beings superior to the rest of nature with divinely-given authority to dominate it. Such an interpretation of Genesis is both inaccurate and unnecessary. What the Creation accounts (in the context of the Bible and the Christian tradition as a whole) tell us is that we are created in God's image to be stewards of creation. We are to exercise a loving and just dominion over nature directed by God's will for the universe. Humans are not given carte-blanche to do whatever we like with nature, exploiting its resources for our own selfish and short-sighted

ends. Perhaps a narrow and inaccurate reading of the Bible has contributed to man's mistreatment of the environment, but it is doubtful that many who exploited the earth's resources were actually led by the Bible to do so. A mixture of good and bad reasons can more plausibly explain how we got to be in the critical position we are in – including pride and greed, but also individual and social needs for food, energy and other necessities. It could be said, too, that the scientific revolution of Galileo and those who followed after him led to our view of nature as a mechanistic set of items to be probed and used with impunity, rather than an organic 'creation' with its own integrity.

Stewardship

What do we mean by 'stewardship'? The image suggested is this: A steward is a person who is placed in charge of a property or estate by the owner, to look after it and protect it on the owner's behalf. The steward does not own the property, though he may have a portion of it as his own to use (to live on, for example).[37] The steward acts only on the authority and under the direction (implicit or explicit) of the owner; he does not act on his own authority or according to his personal ideas or plans unless allowed to do so by the owner. The steward is always accountable to the owner for his stewardship.

Dominion 'in God's image'

All this is implied in the biblical truth that man – male and female – is made 'in God's image'. God is the creator, the 'owner' of all that exists. Humans are placed on earth by God to be stewards looking after his creation. Our dominion over nature is qualified and specified by this truth about us: we are made in God's image and called to act always according to God's will. We are never totally autonomous. We are dependent on God and bound by his will, not just because he is a powerful god, but because he is 'almighty and ever-loving

God'. His wise and loving will is for our good and the good of all his creatures. The Genesis 1 creation account emphasises that God sees his creation as 'good' – notice how often the phrase 'God saw that it was good' is repeated.[38] In Genesis 2, the Garden is a paradise, our original home a wonderful place to live created for us by God. The animals are created to be companions for the man. Even though they are not entirely suitable (only woman is fully man's complimentary equal), it is still notable that the animals are not portrayed as mere things.

Noah and the Ark

The story of Noah and the Ark (Gen 6-9) emphasises this point also, in that God saves the animals, not just the good people. In this new creation of sorts, God makes sure that the future of the planet's animal inhabitants is assured by saving pairs of all animals from the flood. Though some teachers may wish to avoid the Noah story because of difficulties regarding its historicity, it is well worth 'recovering' it and linking it to the earlier creation accounts in its environmental significance.

Original sin

The original parents of the human race failed to be good; they failed to respect the in-built limits of God's creation. They ate the fruit of knowledge of good and evil, spurning their essentially created nature and doubting God's wise design. This original sin spoiled the original harmony between man and woman, between human persons in general, and between man and God. It also spoiled the original harmony willed by God between man and nature – the soil becomes hard for the man to work, childbirth becomes painful for the woman, death becomes part of humanity's lot, the man and woman are evicted from the Garden into a more difficult world. Sin spreads and disharmony reigns. Later, even God's specially chosen people were unfaithful to the Covenant and the land itself 'suffered' because of their sin (see Isaiah 24: 1-6). However, the story does not end there.

Incarnation and Redemption: the cosmic dimension

God becomes 'part' of his creation through Christ's Incarnation. The Word ('Logos') that created the universe became man (see John 1, especially vv 3-4 and 14). This can be seen as a resounding divine endorsement of the goodness of creation, of nature, of 'ecology' and the 'environment'. The only Son of the Father became 'a man like us in all things but sin' (as the Eucharistic prayer puts it); the eternally-begotten was born of the Virgin Mary (as it says in the Creed). By his free acceptance of death, by his 'obedience unto death', Christ redeemed us and all creation. He fully made up for the original sin that spoiled God's original plan for creation's harmony and fulfilment, and for all subsequent sins. We are inclined to see the Redemption won by Christ mainly in terms of its value for the human race, and this is in fact the main message of the Bible and Sacred Tradition. There is a 'cosmic' dimension to the Redemption, however, that risks being lost in modern theology and RE, particularly with any narrow focus on the 'historical Jesus'. Several passages in the NT that highlight the wider 'trans-historical' dimensions of the salvation won by Christ are worth careful study. These passages include:

- Romans 8: 19-23,
- Ephesians 1: 20-23,
- Colossians 1: 13-23
- Revelation 21-22.

These passages imply that the Paschal mystery has an effect on the whole of creation. Christ's Incarnation, Redemption, Resurrection and Ascension have vindicated God's original creation (Genesis 1 and 2) and rescued it from the Fall (Genesis 3) and the sinfulness that followed. The Bible presents an incredibly positive message about the goodness of nature, even as it indicates that nature is not sufficient or complete in itself, but stands in need of redemption and transformation by grace.

Christ is the true image of dominion and stewardship
When we seek to know what kind of 'dominion' we are to exercise over nature (see Gen 1: 26, 28), we might be tempted to see it as a proud superiority over 'brute' matter or 'brute' animals. The best way to understand our 'dominion', however, is to see it in terms of our acting according to our nature as God's image. The best way of understanding being made in God's image is to look at Christ. He is the true image of God. Precisely by being the true image of God, he is the true image of what it means to be a man, to be a human person. (In this way, Christ is the personification of the natural law too.) So, to understand correctly what our 'dominion' means, to grasp what it means to be a 'steward of creation', we need to contemplate Christ, to have within us the mind of Christ.

This means, and this is a most important point, that everything that helps us to contemplate Christ, and so become united with him, is directly relevant to being environmentally just and loving. Such aids include the Sacred Scripture, sacraments, liturgy, prayer, penance, and all elements of Christian living. The Eucharist – and the communion in Christ that it makes possible – is central to this grace-led endeavour.

The image that should shape our imagination and our response to environmental issues is not one of a detached scientist in a white coat, or an arrogant rich executive in a fancy car, or a calculating politician in a smart suit. Our image should be Christ, who did not grasp onto his divine power or even his human life, but emptied himself serving others selflessly, always faithful to the will of his Father, ready to sacrifice himself for the good of the human race and the whole of creation (see Phil 2: 5-11). This is the Christ who lay in a simple manger in a stable, who had nowhere to rest his head, who was hung naked on a cross, who was buried in a borrowed tomb. Such images can purify human hearts and make them like Christ's and enable human beings to love one another, and all creation, as he loved us (this is the New Commandment). The saints, with the Virgin Mary in the pre-eminent place of honour, 'imaged' Christ in various ways. Getting to know the saints can be a powerful way of growing in our knowledge of Christian stewardship. The main saints in relation to the environment include Francis of Assisi, Thomas Aquinas, Benedict, and Hildegard of Bingen.

Application to environmental concerns
The concept of stewardship-dominion can be applied readily to any of the environmental issues, as it implies a just and loving, humble and courageous attitude towards all of one's choices and plans, even in the face of difficulties and sacrifices. It is difficult to set out absolute moral rules regarding the environment, in the light of Christian tradition, but the following are some basics.

Any cruelty towards animals is wrong, though use of them for food, clothing and scientific experiments is not outlawed by Church teaching. Animals are not seen by Christianity, Judaism or Islam as beings equal to man, beings made in God's image as man is, but they are seen as part of God's creation, and deserving of respect.[39]

Intending to cause damage to the environment (for example, vandalising trees) is simply wrong. Carelessness about damaging the environment and negligence about the effects of one's behaviour on nature are immoral also, even if one does not intend any direct harm. Damage to the environment may be accepted as a side-effect of a good action, but only under certain conditions. These conditions are analogous to the conditions for just war, examined above at the end of chapter two. One should try to find less damaging alternatives, for example, and one should be acting for truly just motives, not selfish greed.

Negative effects on the environment are virtually impossible to avoid totally, but people should do what is reasonable to minimise them. So, for example, one should support recycling policies and avoid using one's car more than necessary. Businesses should try to avoid any unnecessary harmful effects on the environment and support environmental impact studies that will aid them in doing this. Obviously, unnecessary or excessive pollution ought to be avoided. What exactly counts as unnecessary harmful effects on the environment is a matter of some debate. Some people would support radical ideas such as the abolition of cars, or at least a substantial reduction in their use, and maybe even a reversion to a more village-based style of economy and society. Is this a requirement of justice or simply a good suggestion?

One basic moral principle to use in working out if a behaviour or policy regarding the environment is fair or just is the Golden Rule. The moral agent should ask if he or she would rationally accept the effects of the behaviour or policy if he or she was one of those affected. This requires a high degree of prudence and impartiality. In some case, it may be extremely difficult to reach a conclusion because there are diverse persons or groups of persons affected by a behaviour or policy, and it can be hard to compare the diverse effects of an action. Some of the requirements put forward to counter global warming, for example, are controversial precisely because they may have several effects, including reducing the degree of warming, but also badly affecting economic progress and well-being. Here, a vital issue to resolve is just how necessary it is to suffer possible negative side-effects of a policy for the sake of a good effect. Accurate working out of the various effects is central to this resolution, as well as a willingness to take an impartial, long-term view of what is best for humankind as a whole. In other words, both science and virtue are needed.[40]

One issue in more detail: population control

This section briefly reflects on a particularly difficult issue: population control. This is an issue that constantly comes up in environmental writings and is likely to arise in the questions of students. It is a highly controversial area and a very important one. The reference in the syllabus to the Genesis creation accounts and to the concepts of stewardship and dominion are directly relevant to the issue of population control. What is said in this section, or some of it, will be shared by many Christians, Muslims, Orthodox Jews and also some non-religious thinkers too.[41] The Catholic approach, which is arguably the most strict and the most developed, is outlined here. Some of the main concepts here will overlap considerably with material from section D: *Moral Decision Making* (especially parts 3.2, 4.1, 4.2 and 4.3).

Is procreation good or bad?
The original passage in Genesis 1 directly links the creation of man as God's image with the call to be fruitful and multiply (see v. 28). Just as God is creative, man as male and female is called to be creative. One primary reference for this in the biblical account seems to be procreation, having children. For some environmentalists, procreation is seen almost as something bad, something to be reduced or eliminated altogether, as a major part of humanity's effort to protect the environment and achieve justice. The assumption is that population growth poses a serious ongoing threat to the environment as it is exploited and plundered to cater for the increasing numbers of humans added to the planet day by day. Space and resources are rapidly running out, it is claimed. It is as though the earth were a life-boat or a spaceship humans are crowded onto, to mention two well-known images. The Catholic Church is sometimes thought to be an *enemy* of justice and environmental protection because of its opposition to family planning, abortion, contraception, and women's 'reproductive rights'. Added to this is wide-spread puzzlement at, and hostility towards, the Church's rejection of condoms as the primary method of combating the spread of HIV/AIDS,

especially in the developing world. Many Catholics share these views. How can support for population reduction not be a necessary part of responsible stewardship of creation?

Ends and means
A few factors can be outlined here to begin to clarify matters or at least to provoke thinking and discussion. This is certainly not intended as a comprehensive treatment of all aspects of these very complex issues. Readers are invited to study these matters further.

To begin with, we should distinguish between 'ends' and 'means'; this is an important distinction in all ethical debates, especially those concerning justice. The overall aim or end of family planning, whether by individual couples or by government or other agencies, is distinct from the methods to be used as means. The Church is not against family planning as such, as many incorrectly assume. However, it does have some things to say about the moral principles that should shape responsible parenthood as an 'end'. It also has some specific things to say about the methods that are ethically correct as a 'means' to this end.

Avoid panic or exaggerations
According to Church teaching, it is the moral right of the couples involved to decide responsibly how many children to have.[42] The Church does not set down what the number should be, but teaches that the decision should be generous and prudent (as indeed all human choices ought to be),[43] taking into account all the relevant circumstances, which one assumes can include wider national and international population issues as well as personal ones. The Church and others are critical of any government coercive or invasive strategy or policy that seeks to make couples have a set number of children; China's one-child policy is a well-known example. In addition, some people have remarked on how hypocritical and unjust it appears for the

affluent and comfortable, but wasteful and exploitative, North to demand of the South that it stop having children in such numbers.[44] It has been argued that world population is not dangerously out of control. UN predictions of population growth have tended to come down in the last couple of decades, and so the population panic that characterised the environmental writings and conferences of the 60s and 70s has abated somewhat. It now looks like world population will level off at around 11 billion by the year 2200.[45] There will not be a devastating population 'explosion' or 'bomb' as predicted by environmentalists such as Paul Ehrlich. In some parts of the world, such as Europe, the problem is actually population decrease, or an ageing population, and this is something that may change our whole approach to this area in the next few years.

Critiquing some common assumptions
It is worth questioning some of the common assumptions behind the idea that population growth is always a bad thing in itself and must be stopped. Population growth means that relatively fewer people, including babies, are dying than used to, and all over the globe people are living longer on average.[46] This is a sign of human progress and is something to celebrate, even as one remains aware of the serious needs of the many people who continue to live in extreme poverty or who suffer very poor standards of living.

Each human person is unique and has an inherent dignity; 'made in God's image' is how this is expressed in the creation accounts of Genesis 1 and 2. Also, each individual can contribute to the human race and can be seen as primarily a 'resource', not as a drain on resources, although this entails a commitment to making sure that all people are supported by appropriate social justice measures in the development of their personal and social potential. It is not actually known at present how many natural resources the world has left, although educated guesses can be made. It has been argued that it is not strictly accurate to claim that we are on the verge of running out of oil, gas, and other non-renewable resources, and ruining all the renewable ones, such as water. We simply do not know that we have reached the limit of our growth, although, and this is an important point, this is not an excuse to waste the resources we have. Waste of resources is immoral in itself and should be avoided, even if we have plenty for our own needs. It has been argued that space, though obviously limited, is not rapidly running out either – the image of earth as a crowded life-boat is misleading. (Of course, there are many who would argue that natural resources and/or space *are* in crisis right now, and that what I have just written is far too sanguine. My point here is at least to raise a question mark over a simple acceptance of such a very grim diagnosis.)

There is no ethical requirement to have as many children as possible, although some people may think that this is Catholic teaching. Even if children are a priceless good, we do not have to maximise everything that is good, as the inadequate utilitarian approach would have us believe. Parents have a responsibility to have the number of children they honestly judge they can care for adequately and bring up well: this is a primary principle of responsible parenthood. Whether or not governments can decide how many children families should have, or even advise on the matter, is questionable. Catholic social teaching (CST), outlined in chapter two above, states that the family is the basic unit of society, prior to the state, and so has its own rights and responsibilities, which are not to be taken from it (except in rare, extreme circumstances). Also, the principle of 'subsidiarity', which is a basic principle of CST, requires decisions and actions to be the responsibility of those at the most local level of an issue, if this is reasonable, so that individuals and families (and other social groups) can participate in living their lives in society without the state or large organisations taking over. This suggests that the decision on how many children to have should normally be taken by the parents, not by the state or by any larger organisation such as the UN, EU or US.

At the same time, the Church supports *some* state intervention to help people to live good lives; it is not an advocate of a totally minimalist state.[47] Could it ever be necessary or advisable for the state or others to step in and decide the number of children, whether by coercion or by strong persuasion and incentives? Could this ever be just? Some argue that extreme circumstances of overpopulation lead to affirmative answers to these questions. It is my impression that many, if not most, of the world's environmental activists and organisations support this line to some extent, though most will favour state persuasion rather than coercion. Others, particularly those who criticise any kind of 'command economy' style of state as inefficient and unethical, say that the state does not have the right or the competence to intervene in this area. Parents should be trusted to make appropriate decisions in light of their own circumstances. In my opinion, the Catholic Church does not teach strictly that the state must stay completely out of the area, but it remains very wary of allowing it in too far. In any case, it clearly teaches that the state must never promote objectively immoral means of family planning.[48]

It is worth mentioning another easily neglected dimension of this issue. We should always remember that 'population' refers to human persons, not statistics, and every human person is a priceless, intrinsic good. There is a real difficulty, therefore, in speaking of a population *problem*. Christopher Derrick puts it like this:

> 'The population problem' is an ambiguous expression. It is undeniably true that where population increases, certain new problems arise while certain old problems are exacerbated: a Christian may thus speak without

hesitation about 'the problems consequent upon rapid population growth', and should regard them as matter for concern and for any help that may be possible. But he then speaks of problems that people *have*. He crosses a fatal Rubicon if he starts to speak of the 'problem' that people *are*, or will be in some foreseeable future. The existence of human beings does not come under our judgement.[49]

Regarding the issue of population control as an aim or end, it can be argued that the problems of hunger and ill health faced by the developing world are caused by such things as corrupt governments, unnecessary wars, ineffective farming techniques, unfair trade rules and procedures, unjust distribution of wealth, and so on, not population growth as such. Justice requires us to focus on these causes of hunger and suffering, in the context of population growth (or decline), rather than seeing people as the problem. These are points made frequently by Church representatives at the various UN conferences on world development issues.[50]

Criticising means: abortion
As well as looking at the issues of the nature and extent of a population problem and whether the state should involve itself in trying to solve it, it is also necessary to look at the possible means to be used to address population issues. The issue of means is distinct from the issue of ends. Even if we agree, for the sake of argument throughout this section, that population ought to be reduced, and couples encouraged (without coercion or manipulation) to have smaller families, it would still matter what methods were to be promoted and used. Firstly, in this respect (and all respects) the Catholic Church rejects abortion completely. It can come as a shock to a Catholic or any pro-life person reading around this environmental area, and the justice and peace area in general, to find that many writers who

are keen supporters of justice, human rights and the environment, also support legalised abortion, sometimes enthusiastically. Abortion is promoted by some as a human right. This is not acceptable in the light of faith for a Catholic (and for many other Christians, Jews, Muslims and others). It can also be rejected in the light of the natural law: abortion is always the deliberate destruction of innocent human life and is therefore an injustice. It is always an unjust means, even if used for a worthy motive or end. It can be difficult to see how abortion could be wrong in certain extreme circumstances, such as after a rape or in the face of massive overcrowding of a city, province or state, but to call abortion an 'intrinsic' wrong is to say that it is always unjust, always wrong, no matter what the circumstances. The circumstances may certainly mitigate the personal guilt of the person who chooses or performs an abortion, and so abortions may vary in this regard, but if it is an intrinsic evil as the Church teaches, then it is always objectively wrong.

One way of explaining this is to look at what is involved centrally in every abortion under the headings of 'equality' or 'discrimination', two important concepts in this RE course. If all human beings are equal, then the primary reason for the wrongness of a 'selfish' abortion (abortion used as a kind of safety net for casual failure to exercise responsible parenthood, for example) is the same reason for the wrongness of abortion after rape. The exact same evil is done in both cases, in terms of the abortion in itself: an innocent human being is deliberately killed. Other aspects of abortion may vary, and this can add to the wrong done in abortion (when it is simply selfish, for example) or lessen the personal guilt of those involved (if they are under extreme pressure, for example, or if they genuinely believe abortion is sometimes justified). Under the heading of discrimination, abortion is unjust discrimination against the unborn human being who is conceived after rape; it is treating him or her as less human than another human being conceived after loving intercourse. All human beings are equal when they are conceived and all deserve in justice to be allowed to live, indeed to be helped to live. This is why the Church sees abortion as always an unjust means, always a wrong way to achieve an end, even a noble end. This is not to deny in any way that rape is itself an intrinsic evil and is always a seriously wrong action deserving of punishment for one who is guilty.[51] Abortion is never this imposition of justice on a rapist.

It is not too difficult then to see why the Church rejects abortion as a means of family planning, even in a situation where there might be great perceived need for effective family planning. Even if chosen for an unselfish reason, abortion is incompatible with loving one's neighbour as oneself, with treating others as you would like to be treated, and ultimately with loving God. It is objectively an evil means. Even if there were an evident necessity to limit population growth in order to protect the environment, abortion could not be morally accepted as a means to this end.

Criticising means: contraception and natural family planning
Secondly, what about contraception? (I am including sterilisation in my treatment of contraception.) This, too, is rejected by the Catholic Church as an ethical means of responsible parenthood, though not for the same reasons as its rejection of abortion. This is a very controversial area, perhaps one of the most controversial in this book, but it is bound to come up in any classroom treatment of justice and peace issues, especially related to the environment and population, so it is an area that ought to be examined. The aims of this section are quite modest. Some of the main concepts and arguments are outlined, with a view to clearing up some of the most common misconceptions around the topic, and further reading is suggested to find more thorough treatments of it. It is not expected that this short treatment of this complex issue will answer all objections or fully convince the skeptical.

The primary point to be made at the start is that the Church's position on contraception is grounded in a very positive understanding of the human person and of sexual intercourse. The Church sees sexual intercourse as a God-given embodiment of marriage, a powerful symbol of married love. This is based on the fact that sexual intercourse can unite a man and a woman as one body in a way that can lead to the creation of children. This understanding is based on observation, of course, but it is found also in the creation accounts in Genesis 1 and 2, the biblical references at the centre of this section of the syllabus. It is also found in the teaching of Christ on marriage, which refers to the Genesis accounts:

> [Christ said:] But from the beginning of creation, 'God made them male and female.' 'For this reason a man shall leave his father and mother and be joined to his wife, and the two shall become one flesh.' So they are no longer two, but one flesh (Mk 10:6-8).

The Church sees the unitive and the procreative dimensions of sexual intercourse as intrinsically connected: the kind of love expressed is objectively one that is related to the creation of new life, and the kind of procreation possible is one linked to the union in love of the parents. In other words, sex means marriage and nothing less. This is a view that is increasingly less accepted, or even considered, in our society today and part of the reason for this, in my opinion, is that 'contracepted' sex does not naturally symbolise marriage in the same way as 'uncontracepted' sex does. The implication of the Church's teaching is that the meaning of sex has been changed for the worse by contraception (among other factors). The 'moral ecology' of society has been affected and it is very difficult now to grasp the truth of the whole of the Church's teaching on marriage and sexual ethics, not to mention living by that truth.[52] This is a concern for our own society, but also for societies in developing countries, who face moral and cultural, as well as economic, challenges.

Many people hold inaccurate ideas about this teaching. The Catholic Church's position is not, for example, that women should have as many children as possible. Nor does the Church believe that people should have sex exclusively for the purpose of having children, although many assume this is its belief. The Church supports the use of Natural Family Planning (NFP) to help conceive children or to limit the number of one's children. The reason the Church supports NFP methods, however, is not because of some supposed unreliability in the methods, which leaves them 'open to life'. NFP can be reliable if used correctly.[53]

Neither does the Church reject contraceptives because they are chemical or man-made or 'artificial', as such, although this is commonly assumed to be its reason. It is not in principle against man's modifying nature or natural processes. However, the Church holds that intervention in nature should always be for the good of the human person, avoiding unnecessary risks to health, and respecting the goodness of nature. This generally means aiding natural processes to work properly, for example heart-transplants.[54] It could be argued that contraception does not enable nature to work, but prevents it from working. In this way, contraception expresses a kind of negative attitude towards nature.

The Church position and stewardship
The Church's teaching on contraception, therefore, fits in very well with the concept of loving and just stewardship of nature, with respect for the integrity of creation. It is not just that contraception thwarts a natural process but that it directly stops a natural process, that has the specific potential to link humans with God in creating a new human person. It is crucially important to grasp the nature and value of the good at stake here. The good of this natural process is far more than a merely biological or physical event or outcome. The Church's

position does not grant 'mere' biology a privileged value, as some have supposed. The good of procreation is an incomparable, multi-faceted good, that includes a biological dimension, but much more – because human beings are biological, but much more. You could say that contraception is a kind of vote against human life (though certainly not to the extent of abortion) in that it specifically intends to make a potentially procreative action *un*creative. No-one can choose to 'contracept' without deliberately choosing to make sex uncreative.[55] In a way, then, it is a vote against nature.

The Church's teaching goes further still. Following natural law in the light of faith, the Church considers human sexuality and sexual intercourse to have a natural significance 'built in' by God. As contraception disrupts the natural integrity of sexual intercourse, it contradicts the objective symbolism or meaning of sex. Sex can no longer objectively unite man and woman fully as 'one body'; sex is no longer unconditionally giving and receiving; sex is no longer a complete acceptance of our masculinity and femininity as bodily persons. The unity between sex and marriage is therefore greatly weakened: it is not surprising that we find it so hard now to see sex and marriage as intrinsically and exclusively connected. All these negative effects can happen in spite of the best intentions of the couples who use contraception for loving motives. The Church is certainly not saying that all people who use contraception are doing so selfishly or in bad faith. Probably, many people, through no fault of their own, are unaware of the issues outlined here and are conscious only that the Church, or perhaps, merely the 'official' Church, rejects contraception. The Church needs to communicate its teaching better if it wants to convince people it is true and to help them to live by it.

Another problem is that most people do not understand why the Church accepts NFP while rejecting contraception. The two methods are seen as the same, because both can be chosen for the exact same good end or motive: responsible parenthood. Therefore, those who consider ends to be the primary issue, or even the only issue, will see both NFP and contraception as morally identical, at least after questions of their effectiveness, safety, and practicability are answered. The two methods are actually quite different means, however, and so they can differ morally as means, even if they are chosen for the same good end.

NFP for family limitation[56] involves fertility awareness and an age-old method: abstinence. In the case of NFP, it is more accurate to speak of 'periodic abstinence'. The couple involved do not make sex infertile during the infertile period of the cycle; it simply *is* infertile due to factors totally outside the control of the couple. Even if they wanted to, the couple could not make sex fertile during the infertile time. They can neither make sex fertile or infertile then. In the case of contraception, by contrast, the couple do something specific to make possibly fertile sex infertile.[57] They do something to separate the procreative dimension of sex from the unitive dimension, and 'discard' the procreative dimension of that act or series of acts. What about NFP couples who abstain during the naturally fertile time (around ovulation)? Are they not making sex infertile in doing this, just like those using contraception make sex infertile? The answer is no, because you cannot make sex infertile unless it is actual or probable, and there is no actual or probable sex in abstinence. Couples who choose to abstain during the fertile period could be acting immorally only if there were some obligation on them to have sexual intercourse during that time. There is no such obligation: couples are not obliged to have as many children as possible or to have sex whenever it could possibly procreate children. The Church's position is that it is God's will that whenever we choose sexual intercourse (which should always be an expression of married love), we ought to accept its natural potential, without closing it off from life or rejecting any dimension of its full significance. NFP users do this; people who choose contraception do not.

The Church regards contraception as a contradiction of God's will for us. This is why she does not accept it as a moral means. Therefore, contraception cannot be rightly chosen or promoted even for a good cause, a moral end, such as environmental protection by population reduction (assuming for the sake of the argument that this is a truly good cause). Both abortion and contraception are considered by the Church to be objectively immoral and so they can never be rightly chosen or promoted as a means of justice or love.[58]

Means: HIV/AIDS prevention by condom use
What about HIV/AIDS prevention? Condom use here is more accurately described as 'HIV/AIDS prevention' than 'contraception', even though these are often assumed to be the same because both can involve using condoms. This topic is not really a matter of population control, then, but it is an issue that will probably be raised if population, contraception and religion are being looked at in the classroom. It is an issue related to the theme of justice, especially the public policy dimension.

Strictly speaking, in terms of analysis of the intentionality of human action and morality, HIV/AIDS prevention is distinct from contraception. Even a permanently infertile person (who knows of his condition), for example, could use condoms for HIV/AIDS protection, although it could not be contraception for that person. Protection against the disease is the primary purpose of the act; sometimes it is the only purpose. In other words, contraception can be a side-effect of condom use for HIV/AIDS protection. If so, the ethical principles guiding the evaluation of side-effects apply to this situation, rather than the ethical principles for judging contraception in itself.[59] Indeed, often in environmental issues generally, the main ethical question will be how to judge the morality of bad or unwanted side-effects of choices that are aimed at the good of people. The principles governing the acceptance of side-effects include the following:

- the end intended must be genuinely good;
- no better alternative choice must be available;
- the bad side-effect must not be a means to the good effect;
- we must follow the Golden Rule and other relevant moral principles that prevent us from choosing unfairly or unlovingly towards other people.

This way of analysing morality is sometimes spoken of as 'the principle of double effect'. The Church sees the contraceptive side-effect of condom use against HIV as an objective evil (as explained above, albeit very briefly), and so it is quite negative about the promotion of condoms for HIV/AIDS protection, especially when condoms are the primary focus of a campaign or policy, as often happens. Added to this is the fact that condoms do not give total protection, and HIV is a deadly virus that calls for total protection. It is true, of course, that condoms do give some real protection,[60] and true also that this protection is far better than none, but one major moral question to be asked in individual cases, and regarding policy decisions too, is whether there is a 'best way' of protecting against such a deadly disease. There is a moral and effective way, a 'best way', to protect against HIV/AIDS and the Church wishes to promote this as possible and preferable. One of the programmes often mentioned in this regard is the highly successful ABC approach in Uganda, which counsels abstinence (A) and being faithful in marriage (B), and, only then, using condoms if necessary (C).[61]

Still, it could be argued that in some extreme situations, the contraceptive side-effect of condoms used for HIV/AIDS prevention would be morally acceptable, and even the lack of total protection might be allowed as a pragmatic compromise, whether by individuals or local initiatives or even national programmes. This would be particularly appropriate in cases, for example, where there was evident need for protection for vulnerable women or children from predatory men who were unwilling to listen to any moral message advising abstinence or faithfulness. Even so, the Church so far has mainly treated the situation as one where people should be taught and encouraged to make good free choices rather than accept very imperfect compromises. It may be that such an approach is entirely appropriate for the Church and other religious organisations, concerned as they are with moral ideals and objective principles, whereas the more 'pragmatic' role of the state may be to allow some element of compromise to deal with the less-than-ideal realities (though always guided by moral principle). Also, this may be another example of what we have seen in other parts of this course – high moral ideals and principles being applied to concrete political and social problems in inevitably imperfect ways. Whatever the case, it is worth remembering firstly that this is an emerging area of Church doctrine, so it is not as definitive yet as the teaching on contraception, for example, and secondly that the Church has already allowed that contraception may be used in some circumstances as a form of self-defence or as a medical treatment for health problems, and so it may well come round to allowing the use of condoms as one element in an AIDS prevention programme where it can be prudently judged that an exclusively abstinence-based approach is not fully suitable.[62]

The importance of virtue
The idea of human dominion over nature, which has been the primary focus of this whole section based on the creation accounts in Genesis 1 and 2, also includes man's dominion over himself as an individual who is part of nature. This theme of 'self-mastery' is central to much of the thought of Pope John Paul II, especially his 'theology of the body'.[63] It is a type of virtue ethics focusing on temperance (moderation) and chastity (sexual responsibility). Self-mastery is highly relevant to the discussion above about responsible parenthood and HIV/AIDS protection.[64] As stewards of creation, we are called to look after

ourselves and our moral development prudently, courageously and moderately in order to be able to act towards others justly and lovingly. It could be argued that intemperance in its many forms lies at the heart of our mistreatment of nature. Unless we are able to develop good habits to master our passions, particularly our desire for possessions and for power, we will not be able to give to others what they are due in justice or to see their concerns and needs as our concerns and needs in love. To be a good steward of creation is to be someone who is not intemperate in one's dominion, in one's use of power for other people and for nature, for the sake of the good.

The two remaining religious topics are treated more briefly. Readers are invited to look up the references for more information and discussion.

(iii) Buddhism: Five Precepts of the Buddha

Living in harmony
The Five Precepts of the Buddha are moral principles requiring people not to kill, steal, commit sexual misconduct, lie, or take intoxicants. A peaceful 'living-in-harmony-with' one's body, nature and other people is the ideal. These precepts should be studied along with the eightfold path looked at in 2.3 above. They specify how one ought to follow the paths of right speech, right action and right livelihood (the third, fourth and fifth paths). One primary source on this topic is the Vietnamese Zen Master Thich Nhat Hanh, especially his book *The Heart of the Buddha's Teaching*.

Here is what one leading Irish Buddhist has to say about the Precepts, (following Hanh's teachings):

> There is in essence no difference or separation between the Noble Eightfold Path and the Five Precepts – they both speak about the same thing. Neither is there any

great distinction between Justice (caring for the person) and Environmental Awareness (caring for the earth). Bodhicitta (Sanskrit 'the heart of the enlightened mind') is our essence as spiritual beings and its Wisdom and Compassion shines limitlessly and without impartiality on everyone and everything.

The Five Precepts are guidelines for enlightened daily living:

- Protect life
- Prevent exploitation
- Eliminate all harmful sexual misconduct
- Speak and listen mindfully
- Consume mindfully

Training the mind
In each case we are advised to train the mind to cut through all negative habitual tendencies and wisely offer love and compassion to ourselves and all beings, which is expanded to include all animal and plant life and even minerals – all the various elements which interdependently sustain and nurture this precious human life of ours.

We need to develop our awareness to the level of seeing even in the very page on which these words appear, as Thich Nhat Hanh says, all the causes and conditions which have enabled the paper to manifest in this particular form – the sunshine, the forest, the workers, the food which nourished them, their parents – in fact, we can see all of time and space, weather systems, minerals in the soil, clouds and rivers ...

Without any one of these causal conditions the paper could not exist.

Buddhist logic encourages us to cherish everything we perceive to the point where there is no distinction between the perceiver and what is perceived.

Protecting and nourishing the ecosystem which protects

and nourishes us makes good sense, there is no denying it. We are taught to retrain the mind to see the harm we might do in the world and the potential for real goodness which there is in every action we do.

Some applications to environmental concerns
For cultural reasons not every Buddhist tradition interprets these principles in exactly the same way, but brought to their logical conclusion the precepts call for vegetarianism, mindful farming, fair trade and not exploiting the earth's resources which make it all possible. By 'thinking globally and acting locally' we come to realise that caring for the earth is in every sense caring for ourselves.

From a Buddhist philosophical perspective all phenomena, ourselves included, have the same essence which is empty of self and luminously open and all pervasive.[65]

More details on the precepts
Here is what the 'about.com' site on Buddhism has to say about these precepts:

> On the face of it, [the Buddha] offers five abstentions – things to avoid doing. The first of these is to abstain from killing living beings. This includes human beings, animals and insects. This is why many (but not all!) Buddhists are vegetarians as the eating of meat involves the slaughter of animals. Interestingly, the Buddha didn't forbid the eating of meat altogether. His monks were allowed to eat meat providing it hadn't been killed for them specifically. The second precept is to abstain from taking what is not given – stealing. The third precept is to abstain from sexual misconduct, such as being unfaithful to one's partner, involvement with prostitution or pornography or entertaining lustful thoughts. The fourth precept, abstaining from false speech, includes

lying, tale-bearing, and gossiping. The fifth and final precept is to abstain from intoxicating drinks and drugs – of course, drugs taken for medicinal purposes are perfectly acceptable.[66]

Further resources
Further information about Buddhism and ecology, and Buddhism in general, can be found at the Buddhanet website (www.buddhanet.net).[67] A detailed article specifically on the precepts is Neil Bartholomew, 'Taking the Five Precepts: What does it mean?'[68] Readers might also investigate one or more of the 'Buddhism and Ecology' articles from subsection of the 'Buddhism Today' website at www.buddhismtoday.com /index/ecology.htm. Finally, a feminist Buddhist site ('Skydancer') has some links related to ecological themes (note especially the review by Paul Waldau of the M.E. Tucker and D. Williams book, *Buddhism and Ecology*) at www.loudzen.com /skydancer/links/ecolinks.html

(iv) Islam: Viceregent of the Earth

The central concept
'Viceregent of the Earth' is an Islamic concept that is very similar to the Judeo-Christian concept of stewardship-dominion of the earth (examined above).[69]

> Khalifa – or the role of stewardship – is the sacred duty God has ascribed to the human race. There are many verses in the Qur'an that describe human duties and responsibilities, such as the following which aptly summarizes humanity's role: 'It is He who has appointed You viceroys in the earth' (6: 165). Humankind has a special place in God's scheme. We are more than friends of the Earth – we are its Guardians. Although we are

equal partners with everything else in the natural world we have added responsibilities. We are decidedly not its lords and masters.[70]

The idea here is that human persons are called by God to look after His creation in co-operation with the Lord of creation. This emphasises our need to act responsibly in our personal lives, our social development policies and our environmental strategies. The opposite attitude is one of arrogant domination that disregards any ill effects of our treatment of the environment and neglects our subordination to God and his will. Environmental concern is central to Islam and the Qur'an, though this has been appreciated only recently. As Dr Hasan Zillur Rahim puts it:

> Few know that Qur'anic verses describing nature and natural phenomena outnumber verses dealing with commandments and sacraments. In fact, of more than 6,000 verses in the Holy Qur'an, some 750, one eighth of the Book, exhort believers to reflect on nature, to study the relationship between living organisms and their environment, to make the best use of reason and to maintain the balance and proportion God has built into His creation. The earth's resources; land, water, air, minerals, forests are available for our use, but these gifts come from God with certain ethical restraints imposed on them. We may use them to meet our needs, but only in a way that does not upset ecological balance and that does not compromise the ability of future generations to meet their needs. Because of its ability to reason and think, humanity has been made the trustee or steward of God on earth.[71]

Or, as M. Hope and J. Young say in a *Crosscurrents* article (Summer 1994):[72]

The Qur'an and the *Hadith* are rich in proverbs and precepts that speak of the Almighty's design for creation and humanity's responsibility for preserving it. For many Muslims, citing these is enough to prove that Islam has always embraced a complete environmental ethic. Others are more critical. They readily acknowledge that the guidelines are all there in Islamic doctrine. *Tawhid* (unity), *khalifa* (trusteeship), and *akhirah* (accountability, or literally, the hereafter), three central concepts of Islam, are also the pillars of Islam's environmental ethic. But they add that Muslims have strayed from this nexus of values and need to return to it.

They add:

> To humankind is given the role of *khalifa* (trustee): 'Behold, the Lord said to the angels: "I will create a vicegerent on earth....".' (Q.2:30). But it is a role that each person must perform wisely and responsibly, fully aware of human accountability to the Almighty. 'Do no mischief on the earth after it hath been set in order, but call on him with fear and longing in your hearts: for the Mercy of God is always near to those who do good' (Q.7:56).

Further resources
Some details of the Qur'an verses dealing with environmental matters can be found in J. Abraham 'An Ecological Reading of the Qur'anic Understanding of Creation'.[73] One great website on Islam and ecology, from which the quotation above is taken, and where many other resources and links can be found is: 'The Islamic Foundation for Ecology and Environmental Sciences'.[74] Its 'tutorial' section contains a very attractive visual essay that could be used for a class presentation. 'IslamOnline.net' is another good place to find material. It has a very detailed article, 'Towards an Islamic Jurisprudence of the Environment'

by Prof. Mustafa Abu-Sway,[75] that deals with the Qur'an sources and the *Shariah* and their application to areas of environmental concern such as humans, animals, plants, water, air, and noise pollution. Another article, 'A Wave of Change Required', focuses on Islamic Water Management policy.[76] There is also an interesting article on Mohammed as an environmental pioneer.[77]

Final Overall Comments
One of the most notable things about religion and the environment is how much the different religious traditions share in common. Although they differ in their beliefs and practices in significant ways, Judaism, Christianity, Buddhism and Islam, to mention just the religious traditions studied here, are centrally concerned with the development of personal and social virtue and increasingly concerned with the 'minding of planet earth'.[78] It is possible that the challenges facing us with regard to the various environmental issues mentioned in this chapter, along with the issues of conflict resolution and human rights looked at in chapter two, can motivate the various faiths to join together to co-operate in meeting the challenges. There may be disagreement on what the crises are in exact detail and what we are to do about them practically, but surely it is a very good thing that increasingly we are concerned enough to do the research and engage in the debate, and then to work out policies and procedures and change our behaviour in the light of what we have found in our search for the truth. The new Senior RE syllabus, particularly this section on Issues of Justice and Peace, can constitute a small but significant contribution to that search.

Further Reading
Abraham, J. 'An Ecological Reading of the Qur'anic Understanding of Creation' *Bangalore Theological Forum*, Vol.

XXXIII, No. 1: www.religion-online.org/cgi-bin/relsearchd.dll/showarticle?item_id=1632

Akkara, A. 'The "Social Vaccine"', *Catholic World Report* (October 2004): www.cwnews.com/news/ viewstory.cfm?recnum=33163

Al-Bi'ah fil-Islam, F. 'Towards an Islamic Jurisprudence of the Environment': www.islamonline.net/english/Contemporary/2002/08/Article02.shtml

Bancroft, A. (ed.) *The Buddha Speaks* (Boston: Shambhala, 2000).

Bartholomew, N. 'Taking the five precepts: what does it mean?' www.kwanumzen.com/primarypoint/v14n1-1996-spring-neilbartholomew-takingfiveprecepts.html

Bassett, L. and J. Brinkman and K. Pederson (eds.), *Earth and Faith: A Book of Reflection for Action* (New York: United Nations Environmental Programme, 2000).

Bingham, N., A. Blowers and C. Belshaw (eds.), *Contested Environments*, (Chichester, UK: John Wiley & Sons Ltd./Milton Keynes, UK/ Open University, 2003).

Brand, A. 'The promise of biotechnology', Acton Institute for the Study of Religion and Liberty: www.acton.org/ppolicy/comment/article.php?id=85

Burke, P., 'This is neither scepticism nor science – just nonsense', *The Guardian* (23/10/04) available at www.guardian.co.uk/comment/story/0,3604,1334209,00.html.

Caldecott, S. 'Ecology' at www.tcrnews2.com /ecology2.html

Catechism of the Catholic Church (official edition, 1997), online at: www.vatican.va/archive/ccc/index.htm

Catholic Bishops Conference of the Phillipines, 'What is Happening To Our Beautiful Land?' (1988): www.aenet.org/haribon/bishops.htm

Christiansen, D. and W. Grazer, (eds.) *'And God Saw That It Was Good:' Catholic Theology and the Environment*. (Washington, DC: United States Catholic Conference, Inc, 1996).

Daly, C. Cardinal, *The Minding of Planet Earth* (Dublin: Veritas, 2004).

De Chatel, F. 'Prophet Mohammed: A Pioneer of the Environment':www.islamonline.net/english/Contemporary/2003/02/Article02.shtml

Derr, T.S. 'Animal rights, Human rights' in *First Things* (Feb. 1992) at: www.firstthings.com/ftissues/ft9202/articles/derr.html

Derr, T.S. 'Global Eco-logic' in *First Things* (Feb. 2000): www.firstthings.com/ftissues/ft0002/opinion/derr.html.

Derr. T. 'Strange Science' in *First Things* (Nov 2004): www.firstthings.com/ftissues/ft0411/opinion/derr.htm.

Derrick, C. *Too Many People? A Problem in Values* (San Francisco: Ignatius Press, 1985).

De Vaux, R. *Ancient Israel: Its Life and Institutions*, second edition (London: Darton, Longman and Todd Ltd., 1965; original 1961).

Douthwaite, R. *The Growth Illusion*, revised edition (Gabriola Island BC, Canada: New Society Publishers, 1999).

Epsztein, L. *Social Justice in the Ancient Near East and the People of the Bible*, trans. J. Bowden (London: SCM, 1986, original French edition 1983).

Flanagan, A. 'The Five Precepts' from About.com (Buddhism): http://buddhism.about.com/library/weekly/aa081302a.htm

Gardner, G. 'Engaging Religion in the Quest for a Sustainable World' in Worldwatch Institute, *State of the World 2003: Progress Towards a Sustainable Society* (Earthscan Publications: London, 2003)

Glendon, M.A. 'What happened at Beijing?' in *First Things* (Jan. 1996) at: www.firstthings.com/ftissues/ft9601/articles/glendon.html

Grisez, G. *Living a Christian Life: The Way of the Lord Jesus, Vol. 2* (Illinois: Franciscan Press, 1993)

Hanh, Thich Nhat. *The Heart of the Buddha's Teaching: Transforming Suffering into Peace, Joy, & Liberation : The Four Noble Truths, the Noble Eightfold Path, & Other Basic Buddhist Teachings* (Broadway Books pbk. Ed., 1999).

Hart, J. *What Are They Saying About Environmental Theology?* (New York/Mahweh, NJ: Paulist, 2004).

Hartmann, B. *Reproductive Rights and Wrongs: The Global Politics of Population Control*, revised edition (Cambridge, MA: South End Press, 1995).

Himes, M.J. and K.R. Himes, *Fullness of Faith* (New York/Mahweh, NJ: Paulist, 1993).

Hope, M. and J. Young, 'Islam and Ecology', *Crosscurrents* (Summer 1994): www.crosscurrents.org/islamecology.htm

Hope, M. and J. Young, *Voices of Hope in the Struggle to Save the Planet* (New York: Council on International and Public Affairs/Apex Press, 2000).

John Paul II, *Centesimus Annus* (1991). A full list of papal documents is at www.vatican.va/offices/papal_docs_list.html

Kasun, J. *The War Against Population: The Economics and Ideology of Population Control*, revised edition (Fort Collins, CO: Ignatius Press, 1999).

Khalid, F. 'Guardians of the natural order', Islamic Foundation for Ecology and environmental Sciences: www.ifees.org/jour_art_guard.htm

Keenan, M. *Care for Creation, Human Activity and the Environment*. Pontifical Council for Justice and Peace. (Vatican City: Libreria Editrice Vaticana, 2000).

Keenan, M. *From Stockholm to Johannesburg, An Historical Overview of the Concern of the Holy See for the Environment, 1972-2002*. Pontifical Council for Justice and Peace. Vatican City: Libreria Editrice Vaticana, 2002).

Küng, H. 'Declaration towards a Global Ethic' at: www.cpwr.org/resource/ethic.pdf

Lomborg, B. 'These Hollywood Effects May Cost the World $15 trillion', UK *Telegraph* (9th May 2004) at: www.telegraph.co.uk/opinion/main.jhtml?xml=/opinion/2004/05/09/do0903.xml&sSheet=/portal/2004/05/09/ixportal.html

Lomborg, B. *The Skeptical Environmentalist*, Revised edition, English trans. (Cambridge, UK: Cambridge University Press, 2001).

Lomborg, B (ed.) *Global Crises, Global Solutions* (Cambridge, UK: Cambridge Universtiy Press, 2004).

McCarthy, F. and J. McCann, *Religion and Science*, Into the classroom series (Dublin: Veritas, 2003).

McDonagh, S. *To Care For the Earth* (London: Chapman, 1986).

McDonagh, S. *The Greening of the Church*, (London: Chapman, 1990).

McDonagh, S. *Passion for the Earth* (London: Chapman, 1995)

McDonagh, S. *Greening the Christian Millennium* (Dublin: Dominican, 1998).

McDonagh, S. *Why are we Deaf to the Cry of the Earth?* (Dublin: Veritas, 2001).

McDonagh, S. 'Johannesburg 2002: Few Gains for the Poor and the Environment' at http://eapi.admu.edu.ph /eapr003/ sean.htm

McDonagh, S. *Dying for Water* (Dublin: Veritas, 2003).

McDonagh, S. *Dying for Water* (extract): www.catholicireland.net/pages/index.php?nd=82&art=248

McDonagh, S. *Patenting Life? Stop!* (Dublin: Dominican Publications, 2003).

McDonagh, S. *Patenting Life? Stop!* (online extract): www.catholicireland.net/pages/index.php?nd=193&art=533

McDonagh, S. *The Death of Life: The Horror of Extinction* (Dublin: Columba, 2004).

McDonagh, S. 'A Green Christology' at www.columban.com/ ecorel.htm

National Geographic (September 2004).

Neuhaus, R.J. 'Christ and Creation's Longing', in *First Things* (Dec 1997) at www.firstthings.com/ftissues/ft9712/ articles/neuhaus.html.

Northcott, M.S. 'Ecology and Christian Ethics' in R. Gill (ed.) *The Cambridge Companion to Christian Ethics* (UK: Cambridge

University Press, 2001).
O' Grady, K. 'Contraception and Religion' in Serinity Young et al. (eds). *The Encyclopedia of Women and World Religion* (Macmillan, 1999), online at: www.mum.org/contrace.htm
O' Rourke, P.J. *All the Trouble in the World* (Atlantic Monthly Press, 1995).
Paul VI, *Humanae Vitae* (1968): www.vatican.va/holy_father/paul_vi/encyclicals/documents/ hf_p-vi_enc_25071968_humanae-vitae_en.html
Pieper, J. *The Four Cardinal Virtues* (Indiana: University of Notre Dame Press, 1966).
Pontifical Council of Justice and Peace, *Compendium of the Social Doctrine of the Catholic Church* (Vatican City: Liberia Editrice Vaticana, 2004).
Rahim, H.Z. 'Ecology in Islam: Protection of the web of life a duty for all Muslims', *Washington Report on Middle East Affairs* (October 1991): www.wrmea.com/backissues/ 1091/9110065.htm
Ratzinger, J. *'In the Beginning...' – A Catholic Understanding of the Story of the Creation and the Fall*, trans. B. Ramsey (Edinburgh: T&T Clark, 1995).
Regan, T. *The Case for Animal Rights* (Berkley, Cal.: University of California Press, 1983).
Rhonheimer, M. 'The truth about condoms', *The Tablet* (10th July 2004): www.thetablet.co.uk/cgi-bin/register.cgi/tablet-00914
Royal, R. *The Virgin and the Dynamo: Use and Abuse of Religion in Environmental Debates* (Washington, DC: Ethics and Public Policy Center/Grand Rapids, Michigan; Eerdmans Publishing Company, 1999).
Saint-Paul, B. 'Interview with Bjorn Lomborg', *Crisis* (April 2004); www.crisismagazine.com/april2004/interview.htm
Saleen, A.M. 'A Wave of Change Required': www.islamonline.net/english/Contemporary/2004/01/ Article02.shtml.

Samson, P.J. *6 Modern Myths About Christianity and Western Civilization* (Illinois; Intervarsity, 2001).

Scally, J. 'Healing the Earth' (Interview with Séan McDonagh), *Reality*, March 2002: www.redemptoristpublications.com /reality/march02/earth.html

Schwartz, J.C. *Global Population from a Catholic Perspective* (Mystic, CT: Twenty Third Publications, 1998).

Singer, P. *Animal Liberation* [1975] third edition (New York: Ecco paperback, 2002).

Smith, J.E. *Humanae Vitae: A Generation Later* (Catholic University of America, 1991).

Smith, P. *What Are They Saying About Environmental Ethics?* (New York/Mahweh, NJ: Paulist, 1997).

Splain, T. 'Roman Catholic Religious Orders and Ecology' from B. Taylor and J. Kaplan, *The Encyclopedia of Religion and Nature* (London: Continuum, 2004) at: www.ofm-jpic.org/ecology/relorders/index.html

Thompson, J.M. *Justice and Peace: A Christian Primer* (Maryknoll, New York: Orbis Books, 1997).

Thorngren, J.R. 'Religion and the Environment' at www.thenewenvironmentalist.com/articles_0702/feature/toc_fea2.2.html.

Tucker, M.E. 'The Emerging Alliance of Religions and Ecology', *Changemakers.com Journal* (Feb 2002): www.changemakers.net/journal/02february/tucker.cfm#jump

Twomey, V. 'Experimentation on animals', *Irish Theological Quarterly*, Vol. 69, no. 2, 2004, pp. 157-175.

UK Bishops, 'The Call of Creation: God's Invitation and the Human Response – The Natural Environment and Catholic Social Teaching' at http://217.19.224.165/resource/GreenText/index.htm

United States Catholic Conference, *Renewing the Earth: A Resource for Parishes.* (Washington, DC: United States Catholic Conference, Inc, 1994).

United States Catholic Conference, *Let the Earth Bless the Lord: God's Creation and Our Responsibility, A Catholic Approach to the Environment*. (Washington, DC: United States Catholic Conference, Inc, 1996).

Van Dyke, F., D.C. Mahan, J.K. Sheldon, and R.H. Brand, *Redeeming Creation: The Biblical Basis for Environmental Stewardship* (Donors Grove, IL: InterVarsity Press, 1996).

Waldau, P. 'Review of M.E. Tucker and D. Williams, *Buddhism and Ecology*': www.loudzen.com/skydancer/links/ecolinks.html

Weigel, G. 'What really happened at Ciaro?', *First Things* (Feb. 1995): www.firstthings.com/ftissues/ft9502/articles/weigel.html

White, L. 'The Historical Roots of Our Ecological Crisis' in *Science* 155, no. 3767 (1967: www.bemidjistate.edu/peoplenv/lynnwhite.htm

Woods, C. and D. Philip, *Sustainable Ireland Source Book 2000: Ireland's Social, Environmental and Holistic Directory* (Dublin: United Spirits Publications, 1999).

Websites

Acton Institute subsection on environment and stewardship: www.acton.org/ppolicy/environment/

An Tairseach: www.ecocentrewicklow.com/home.htm

BBC 'Religion and Ethics' site: www.bbc.co.uk/ religion/

Buddha Net: www.buddhanet.net

'Buddhism and Ecology' articles from subsection of the 'Buddhism Today' website at www.buddhismtoday.com/index/ecology.htm

(Buddhist) Sarvodaya movement of Sri Lanka: www.sarvodaya.org/

Catholic Conservation Center: conservation.catholic.org/.

Catholic Educator Resource Center environment page: www.catholiceducation.org/directory/Current_Issues/Environment/

Civic Environmentalism site: www.cpn.org/topics/environment/civicenvironA.html
Competitive Enterprises Institute: www.cei.org/sections/section1.cfm
Columban Fathers: MA in Religion and Ecology: www.columban.com/maecotheo.htm
Copenhagen consensus: www.copenhagenconsensus.com/
Debt and Development Coalition Ireland: www.debtireland.org.
Department of the Environment (Ireland): www.environ.ie
Development Gateway: http://topics.developmentgateway.org /environment/highlights/default/showMore.do
Development Cooperation Ireland [Dept of Foreign Affairs site]: www.dci.gov.ie/
Development Gateway 'topics index' page: http://topics.developmentgateway.org/alltopics/
The 'Earth Charter' website: www.earthcharter.org/
Earth Dialogue Barcelona 2004: www.barcelona2004.org /eng/eventos/dialogos/ficha.cfm?IdEvento=341
Earthwatch international: www.earthwatch.org/
Ecological and Economic Sustainability: www.twb.catholic.edu.au/sose/ecological_and_economic _sustaina.htm
ENFO: www.enfo.ie/
Envirolink: www.envirolink.org/
Environmental directory: www.enviroyellowpages.com/
Environmental Information Centre for Northern Ireland: www.eicni.org/
Environmental News Service: www.ens-news.com/
Environmental Protection Agency (Ireland): www.epa.ie/ www.lomborg.com/
Fertility (UK): www.fertilityuk.org/index.html
Forum on Religion: http://environment.harvard.edu/religion/main.html
Forum on Religion subsection on religions: http://environment.harvard.edu/religion/religion/index.html

GEO 2000: www.unep.org/geo2000/index.htm
Green Cross site: www.greencrossinternational.net/index.asp
Greenspirit: www.greenspirit.com/lomborg/
Greenpeace: www.greenpeace.org/international_en/
Grist magazine (criticisms of Lomborg): www.grist.org/advice/books/2001/12/12/of/index.html.
Harvard Forum on Religion and Ecology: http://environment.harvard.edu/religion/
Integrity of Creation Resources: www.ofm-jpic.org/ecology/index.html
Interfaith Council for Environmental Stewardship www.stewards.net/About.htm
Intergovernmental Panel on Climate Change (a UN body): www.ipcc.ch/.
Institute for Liberal Values: www.liberalvalues.org.nz/
Islam Online: www.islamonline.net/ English/index.shtml
IslamOnline, 'Ask about Islam' [with Qur'anic references to specific items] online at: www.islamonline.net/askaboutislam/display.asp?hquestionID=6238
Islamic Foundation for Ecology and Environmental Sciences: www.ifees.org/.
Jubilee USA site: www.jubileeusa.org/jubilee.cgi
Junk Science website: www.junkscience.com/
Liberation Theology and Land Reform: www.landreform.org/enroll0.htm
Lomborg and The Skeptical Environmentalist website: www.lomborg.com/
New Internationalist index of past issues: www.newint.org/backissue.html
New Scientist climate change page: www.newscientist.com/hottopics/climate/.
One World: www.oneworld.net/
One World AIDS channel: www.aidschannel.org/
Orthodox Union, 'Torah and Tradition': www.ou.org/chagim/shmitah.htm.

Planned Parenthood (on family planning methods' reliability): www.plannedparenthood.org/bc/bcfacts2.html

Regeneration Project: www.theregenerationproject.org/

Religion and the Environment: http://daphne.palomar.edu/calenvironment/religion.htm

Scientific Alliance: www.scientific-alliance.org/index.htm

Smith (Janet E.) articles at the Sacred Heart Major Seminary: www.aodonline.org/SHMS/SHMS.htm [following faculty link].

Shivanandan (Mary) online articles: www.christendom-awake.org [follow link].

Sustainable Energy Ireland [Ireland's national energy authority]: www.sei.ie/home/index.asp

Theology of the Body: www.theologyofthebody.net/index.htm

UNESCO site: 'Culture and religion for a sustainable future': www.unesco.org/education/tlsf/theme_c/mod10/uncom10.htm

United Nations Environment Programme: www.grid.unep.ch/

United Nations Human Development Reports: http://hdr.undp.org/reports/global/2003/

US bishops conference page (with environmental books listed): www.nccbuscc.org/publishing/environment.htm

US Conference of Catholic Bishops, 'Natural Family Planning': www.usccb.org/prolife/issues/nfp/index.htm

US Environmental Protection Agency: http://yosemite.epa.gov/oar/globalwarming.nsf/content/index.html

Voice of Irish Concern for the Environment: www.voice.buz.org/

World Council of Churches (WCC) 'Justice, peace and creation': www.wcc-coe.org/wcc/what/jpc/index-e.html

World Wildlife Fund: www.worldwildlife.org/

Notes

1. A colleague of mine, Fr Paddy Greene, has pointed out in conversation that 'ecology' is a better term than 'environment' as it denotes the fact that the earth is our home, not just our surroundings. The syllabus uses 'environment' and its cognates, however, rather than 'ecology', and this book follows this practice. Further, 'ecology' might be read as a somewhat off-putting technical scientific term. The point about the earth being our home, and the importance of us taking good care of this home, is a valuable one and, hopefully, not one lost with the use of 'environment'.
2. It is worth noting here that the RE teacher is not supposed to be a political campaigner for any particular party. In addition, it should be noted that the 'Greens' do not hold a monopoly on environmental concerns or policies. Also, the specific policies of various 'Green' parties remain debatable even if one agrees with their overall commitment and idealism.
3. See the critical review by Bjørn Lomborg (who will be discussed in detail later in the main text) of the supposed science in this film in the UK *Telegraph* (9 May 2004). Admitting that global warming is a real threat, especially to the developing nations, he says: 'The problem is that if we overestimate the risk that climate change poses, then we will pay less attention to the other challenges that face us. That appears to be exactly the aim of the movie's creators... In an ideal world, we would be able to achieve everything – we should halt global warming and eradicate corruption, end malnutrition and win the war against communicable diseases. Because we cannot do everything, we need sound reasoning and high quality information to defeat the hysteria of Hollywood.' See the complete review online at www.telegraph.co.uk/opinion/main.jhtml?xml=/opinion/2004/05/09/do0903.xml&sSheet=/portal/2004/05/09/ixportal.html.
4. This is not to suggest any rejection of the term or concept of 'integrity of nature', but merely to note some difficulties. A literal or rigid interpretation of our relationship to nature as 'equality' might lead to the idea that we must never harm or interfere with any creature or natural thing or system. It is very difficult to see how this could be a practicable ethic as we must impact on nature to some degree just to survive, not to mention making progress in science and so on. However, the 'integrity' concept is useful in reminding us that

nature ought not be harmed beyond repair or treated carelessly or cruelly. Nature has its own inherent value.

5 See Gary Gardner, 'Engaging Religion in the Quest for a Sustainable World' in Worldwatch Institute, *State of the World 2003: Progress Towards a Sustainable Society* (Earthscan Publications: London, 2003), pp. 152-175 at 154. The phrasing of the five points follows Gardner's original terminology.

6 'Engaging Religion', p. 152.

7 It may be worth mentioning here that it is a basic conviction of this author that there is no ultimate 'neutral' point of view on such matters as whether or not there is a transcendent God. A point of view that sees contradictory positions as possibly true is not neutral, but agnostic. Agnosticism is incompatible with Christian faith, especially that which rejects fideism, and so is hardly neutral. This presents a serious challenge to any teacher of this syllabus, in my opinion. I'm not sure that the challenge is met by emphasising exclusively the good faith of religious believers or the fact that they find meaning and value in their various beliefs, important though these realities are. It is difficult to see how religious schools, including Catholic schools, can accept uncritically any RE course that presents all religions, including their own, as hypothetical, rather than true. Instead of trying to be neutral, it is more realistic and ethical to be honest and fair about what one's point of view is (in harmony with one's school's point of view) and to encourage others by one's teaching to think critically about the issues and to engage with the ultimate question behind every religious and ethical claim. This ultimate question is: 'Is this true?' Although one sometimes ought to adopt a strategy of temporary 'neutrality' in the second-level classroom, to facilitate discussion for example, one ought to avoid giving the impression that the question of religious truth is unanswered or unanswerable. I hope that the introduction of this new syllabus, along with the Junior Certificate, will lead to debate and clarity on these issues.

8 The accusation of anti-environmentalism against the Bible is thought to have originated with a well-known article by Lynn White, 'The Historical Roots of Our Ecological Crisis' in *Science* 155, no. 3767 (1967), 1203-07. This is available online at www.bemidjistate.edu/ peoplenv/lynnwhite.htm or www.zbi.ee/ ~kalevi/lwhite.htm. A clear evangelical Christian answer to White's accusation is found in Philip J. Samson, *6 Modern Myths About Christianity and Western*

Civilization (Illinois; Intervarsity, 2001), ch. 3. See also online the 'Counter Balance' series of articles at www.counterbalance.org/ [following 'Subjects' then 'environment' links]. White's article and the ensuing debate can be seen as a major cultural factor in the greening of religion.

9 See Gardner, 'Engaging Religion', 161.

10 One example, fully cognisant of the controversial nature of the issues, is N. Bingham, A. Blowers and C. Belshaw (eds.), *Contested Environments*, (Chichester, UK: John Wiley & Sons Ltd./Milton Keynes, UK/ Open University, 2003). Many of the references listed in the text above provide detailed information on environmental issues – see for example, the Earthwatch and Greenpeace websites.

11 The full GEO 2000 report is online at www.unep.org/geo2000/index.htm; my quotations are taken directly from the concise 'press release' link at www.unep.org/geo2000/pressrel/index.htm

12 topics.developmentgateway.org/environment/highlights/default/showMore.do

13 The Department of the Environment site is at www.environ.ie and the two publications can be accessed from there [following the 'what we do' then 'environment' then 'Sustainable Development...' links].

14 The Environmental Protection Agency is at www.epa.ie/

15 See www.lomborg.com/ and its internal links. *Crisis* (April 2004) has an informative interview with Lomborg; see www.crisismagazine.com/april2004/interview.htm. Grist magazine: environmental news and commentary (online) devoted several articles to serious criticism of Lomborg in 2001: see the index of articles at www.grist.org/advice/books/2001/12/12/of/index.html.

16 In May 2004, Bjørn Lomborg organised a debate on environmental issues – the 'Copenhagen Consensus'. It ranked the most important projects to solve global environmental/social problems in terms of their cost-effectiveness. Details of the arguments and conclusions (and, interestingly, some counter-arguments) can be found at the official website at www.copenhagenconsensus.com/ and its numerous links. See also B. Lomborg (ed.) *Global Crises, Global Solutions* (Cambridge Universtiy Press, 2004). For a serious criticism of the cost-benefit approach of Lomborg, see T. Burke, 'This is neither scepticism nor science – just nonsense.' in *The Guardian* (23/10/04) available at the *Guardian* site, specificially at www.guardian.co.uk/comment/story/0,3604,1334209,00.html.

17. See McDonagh, 'A Green Christology' at www.columban.com/ecorel.htm
18. The MA in Religion and Ecology web address is www.columban.com/maecotheo.htm (including articles by McDonagh and others).
19. J. Scally, 'Healing the Earth' at www.redemptoristpublications.com/reality/march02/earth.html (originally published in *Reality*, March 2002).
20. The website 'Catholic Ireland' has a section called 'First Chapters' that contains several excerpts from books, including *Dying for Water*. The relevant chapter of McDonagh's book, which is an excellent introduction to his thought on the ethical and theological grounds for environmental concern, is at www.catholicireland.net/pages/index.php?nd=82&art=248
21. McDonagh deals with global warming in chapter three of *Greening the New Millenium* and has devoted a whole book to extinction, *The Death of Life: The Horror of Extinction*. Lomborg deals with global warming in chapter twenty-four, and extinction in chapter twenty-three, of *The Skeptical Environmentalist*.
22. The Wicklow Farm website (an Tairseach) is at www.ecocentrewicklow.com/home.htm
23. This book suggests a few ideas with regard to a Christological focus for environmental ethics in its treatment of the concept of 'stewardship-dominion' in part 3.2 below. It is an area in need of further development.
24. See www.ofm-jpic.org/ecology/relorders/index.html for more details on religious orders and ecology.
25. *Eco-eye* on RTE is one example that would be useful in this regard. Switching media, it is worth mentioning that the *Irish Times* has a regular environmental feature each Saturday in its Weekend Supplement, which gives details of useful websites and discusses specific issues in detail.
26. This section of the text mainly follows Gardner, 'Engaging Religion'; his article also contains examples of Buddhist and Hindu environmentalism in action. See, too, the online site on the Buddhist Sarvodaya movement at www.sarvodaya.org/.
27. More information and hyperlinks to some of the examples mentioned in this paragraph can be found in M.E. Tucker, 'The Emerging Alliance of Religions and Ecology', *Changemakers.com Journal* (Feb 2002) available online at www.changemakers.net

/journal/02february/tucker.cfm#jump. The Harvard Forum on Religion and Ecology is a very useful site, with plenty of articles and information: http://environment.harvard.edu/religion/. See also the WCC (World Council of Churches) page on 'justice, peace and creation' at www.wcc-coe.org/wcc/what/jpc/index-e.html. Finally, the Journal *Daedalus* (Fall 2001) devoted itself to the issue of religion and environmentalism, including an overall-view article by Tucker and Grim at www.amacad.org/publications/fall2001/fall2001.htm

28 'Catholic Conservation Center' at http://conservation.catholic.org/ (highly recommended). Also recommended is D. Christiansen, and W. Grazer, eds. *'And God Saw That It Was Good:' Catholic Theology and the Environment*. (Washington, DC: United States Catholic Conference, Inc, 1996). The final article by the editors, 'Naysayers and Doomsayers: How do We Sort Out the Differences in the Ongoing Environmental Debate?', is especially helpful, advising people to be cautious about environmental issues, taking a risk-avoidance approach generally. Once we are sure that the risks are serious, we do not have to have complete scientific proof before we act to avoid harm or damage to the environment. Pontifical Council of Justice and Peace, *Compendium of the Social Doctrine of the Catholic Church* (Vatican City: Liberia Editrice Vaticana, 2004) has a very interesting paragraph supportive of the 'precautionary principle' that says: 'Prudent policies, based on the precautionary principle require that decisions be based on a comparison of the risks and benefits foreseen for the various possible alternatives, including the decision not to intervene' (paragraph 469). The same paragraph mentions the need for transparent and continuing scientific research in such conditions of uncertainty.

29 The letter of the Philippine bishops is available at www.aenet.org/haribon/bishops.htm

30 I'm particularly grateful to Dr Yaakov Pearlman, Chief Rabbi of Ireland, for sending me some very useful material from the edition of the Pentateuch by the late Chief Rabbi of England, Dr J.H. Hertz.

31 This section draws on R. De Vaux, *Ancient Israel: Its Life and Institutions*, second edition (London: Darton, Longman and Todd Ltd., 1965; original 1961), pp. 481-482.

32 A good article on the specifically Jewish understanding of the Sabbath, though not specifically on the environmental aspect, is found at www.jewfaq.org/shabbat.htm.

33 Léon Epsztein, *Social Justice in the Ancient Near East and the People of the*

Bible , trans. J. Bowden (London: SCM, 1986, original French edition 1983), p. 131, all internal references omitted.
34 Taken from Orthodox Union, 'Torah and Tradition' at www.ou.org/chagim/shmitah.htm
35 De Vaux, *Ancient Israel*, p. 175.
36 An excellent site, containing school material and discussion resources on the topics, is Debt and Development Coalition Ireland at www.debtireland.org. This site has a substantial section on 'Debt and the Environment', containing useful material relevant to this section of the course. Another good site is the Jubilee USA site; its home page is at www.jubileeusa.org/jubilee.cgi.
37 The generic 'he' is mainly used to refer to the human person throughout this section. This simplifies the style and makes the imagery more clearly biblical, allowing for its more direct application to Christ as representative of all human beings, male and female. He is the true *imagio Dei*, the true man, the new Adam, the perfect steward of creation.
38 A particularly good treatment of the Genesis creation accounts is found in Cardinal J. Ratzinger, *'In the Beginning...'* – *A Catholic Understanding of the Story of the Creation and the Fall*, trans. B. Ramsey (Edinburgh: T&T Clark, 1995), especially pp. 33-49.
39 See *The Catechism of the Catholic Church*, pars. 2415-2418, on respect for the integrity of creation, especially the treatment of animals. See also, Grisez, *Living a Christian Life*, pp. 771-788. A particularly good treatment of the issues, including an historical overview of Christian thinking on the topic, is V. Twomey, 'Experimentation on animals', *Irish Theological Quarterly*, Vol. 69, no. 2, 2004, pp. 157-175. The Catholic view is quite different from the radical views of those who argue that animals and humans are equals and that animals have rights. This is a view argued in detail in P. Singer, *Animal Liberation* (1975) third edition (New York: Ecco paperback, 2002) and T. Regan, *The Case for Animal Rights* (Berkley, Cal.: University of California Press, 1983).
40 An idea of the controversy surrounding the area of global warming, from both scientific and ethical perspectives, and an approach for teaching students how to research and debate the issue, can be found by contrasting opposite views on it. Skeptics include T. Derr. 'Strange Science' in *First Things* (Nov 2004) at www.firstthings.com/ftissues /ft0411/opinion/derr.htm; Lomborg's approach in chapter 23 of *The Skeptical Environmentalist*; the 'Junk Science' website at

www.junkscience.com/ and 'The Scientific Alliance' site at www.scientific-alliance.org/index.htm. More positive approaches can be found in *National Geographic* (September 2004); the US Environmental Protection Agency at yosemite.epa.gov/oar/globalwarming.nsf/content/index.html; the very detailed reports of the Intergovernmental Panal on Climate Change (a UN body) at www.ipcc.ch/; and the *New Scientist* site at www.newscientist.com/hottopics/climate/.

41 The secular, libertarian approach of the Institute for Liberal Values is a good example of one non-Catholic approach on this issue: see www.liberalvalues.org.nz/ [following 'library' and then 'The Third World' links]. A short article on contraception and the world's religions is Kathleen O' Grady, 'Contraception and Religion' from Serinity Young *et al.* (eds). *The Encyclopedia of Women and World Religion* (Macmillan, 1999) available online at www.mum.org/contrace.htm

42 Pope Paul VI, in his encyclical *Humanae Vitae* in 1968, gave a concise definition of 'responsible parenthood': see n. 10 (and also n. 13). He made the point that responsible parenthood could include a couple deciding to limit the number of their children for serious reasons, taking into account the 'physical, economic, psychological and social conditions'. It is left to the prudent and generous decision of the couple themselves what this means in specific situations. The Church is wary of the official state authorities interfering in the personal decisions of families, especially in such intimate matters as the size of one's family; see nn. 17 and 23. The document is available online at www.vatican.va/holy_father/paul_vi/encyclicals/documents/hf_p-vi_enc_25071968_humanae-vitae_en.html

43 'Prudence' refers to the virtue whereby one is able to apply moral principles to concrete situations with wisdom and knowledge. To say that couples should make the decision about how many children to have prudently and generously is no more than to say that they should decide the matter wisely and lovingly, in light of their specific situation. Other than this, the Church says very little in the way of specific direction regarding the number of children one ought to have, though it has generally encouraged couples to be very positive about procreation and children.

44 P.J. O'Rourke puts it humorously in the chapter title regarding population issues – 'Just enough of me, way too much of you!' in ch. 2 of *All the Trouble in the World* (Atlantic Monthly Press, 1995).

45 See Lomborg, *The Skeptical Environmentalist*, p. 47, citing the UN's medium variant forecast from the year 2000.
46 According to Lomborg, citing a UN Population Division report from 1999, global infant mortality rates have been declining steadily in the last few decades. In the developing world there was a quite dramatic decrease from eighteen per cent in 1950 to six per cent in 1995; even in sub-Saharan Africa, where the AIDS epidemic has had devastating effects, there has still been an overall decline in infant mortality rates, though at a much slower rate than elsewhere. See *The Skeptical Environmentalist*, pp. 53-54, and figure 19 on p. 55.
47 On this point see John Paul II, *Centisimus Annus* (1991), especially parts IV and V. This encyclical can be found at the full list of papal documents at www.vatican.va/offices/papal_docs_list.html .
48 The Church's position on this issue has been strongly expressed in the recently published *Compendium of the Social Doctrine of the Catholic Church*, paragraph 234.
49 C. Derrick, *Too Many People? A Problem in Values* (San Francisco: Ignatius Press, 1985), pp. 99-100. Emphasis in original. Derrick makes a fascinating argument in this short book that behind all talk of population control lie deep philosophical and religious questions about the purpose of human beings, the value of human life and the meaning of happiness – questions that render highly problematic the assertion that there are too many people. These questions certainly cannot be answered by mere utilitarian calculus or scientific studies.
50 Readers may wish to consult two very informative articles on this area, focusing on two important UN conferences and the Church's role therein, which will flesh out the details of what is discussed in the text: G. Weigel, 'What really happened at Ciaro?', *First Things* (Feb 1995) at www.firstthings.com/ftissues/ft9502/articles/weigel.html and M. A. Glendon, 'What happened at Beijing?', *First Things* (Jan 1996) www.firstthings.com/ftissues/ft9601/articles/glendon.html
51 It is important to mention here that pro-life people do not generally look for punishment of women who choose abortions, even though they see abortion as always wrong, but rather for the prevention of legalised abortion clinics and for various actions to help bring down the incidence of women choosing abortion. One important reason for this is that there are strong mitigating circumstances that often rightly lead society to look leniently on a woman who chooses abortion. This would especially be the case if abortion was chosen

after rape. The situation is quite different with regard to rapists, who are generally looked on as people deserving harsh punishment. The fact that both abortion and rape (and contraception) are described in the text as 'intrinsically evil' should not be misconstrued as implying that they are identical in this respect.

52 On this idea of a 'moral ecology' paralleling nature's ecology, see *Centisimus Annus*, no. 38: 'In addition to the irrational destruction of the natural environment, we must also mention the more serious destruction of the *human environment,* something which is by no means receiving the attention it deserves. Although people are rightly worried — though much less than they should be — about preserving the natural habitats of the various animal species threatened with extinction, because they realize that each of these species makes its particular contribution to the balance of nature in general, too little effort is made to *safeguard the moral conditions for an authentic "human ecology".* Not only has God given the earth to man, who must use it with respect for the original good purpose for which it was given to him, but man too is God's gift to man. He must therefore respect the natural and moral structure with which he has been endowed' (emphasis in original). In the next paragraph, the Pope applies this to the family and issues of sexuality.

53 On the effectiveness of NFP as a method of family planning, see the US bishops conference site on NFP with links www.usccb.org/ prolife/issues/nfp/index.htm and the UK site, 'Fertility', at www.fertilityuk.org/index.html. These sites are very positive about NFP's reliability. Others are more negative about its effectiveness, citing user failure rates of up to 20 per cent or so (see the Planned Parenthood at www.plannedparenthood.org/ bc/bcfacts2.html). The difference in the evaluations could be due to the lumping together of various natural methods in some statistical analysis, with no advertence to the admitted fact that not all natural methods are equally reliable. The older 'rhythm method', which relied on average cycles and guesswork, was not reliable, but more modern 'sympto-thermal methods' are.

54 Regarding another environmental issue: The Church is not in principle against genetically modified food, either, because it is 'unnatural'. The Church would support it if it can be proven to be safe for humans and the environment and its distribution fair and just. This is an area of ongoing debate. A negative judgement on the advisability of relying on genetically modified food is found in J.

Joseph, *Food, Christian Perspectives on Development Issues* (Dublin: Trocaire, Veritas, Cafod, 1999). See also the online excerpt from Seán McDonagh, *Patenting Life? Stop!* at www.catholicireland.net/pages/index.php?nd=193&art=533. A. Brand, 'The promise of biotechnology" at www.acton.org/ppolicy/comment /article.php?id=85 is more positive.

55 It should be clearly noted that the treatment of contraception's wrongness here is *not* a claim that people who use contraception are necessarily personally guilty of wrongdoing or of sin. Someone who follows his last and best moral judgement in this area (i.e. follows his conscience) is blameless, once he has done his best to form his judgement as well as he can. The Church proposes its teaching on this issue as an invaluable aid for the formation of correct conscience, which is why Catholics ought to look to the Church for guidance for conscience. Further, the objective wrongness of contraception is not seen by the Church as intentional selfishness, malice, or promiscuity. (Nor is it primarily a matter of disobedience, though this is one aspect of it.) According to Church teaching, even a person who means well, and acts from a completely loving motive, can do what is objectively wrong. Good intentions are not enough; a good end does not justify a bad means. The means chosen must be objectively good. One must aim not only to act personally 'in good conscience', but to act according to a correct conscience that grasps the objective good.

56 Fertility awareness can be used to help couples conceive children by choosing sexual intercourse during the fertile period of the cycle. By contrast, couples who want to conceive children and who have been using contraception have to stop using contraception before choosing sexual intercourse. This is another sign of the difference between the two methods.

57 Interestingly, although sex is not always naturally fertile, couples who choose to use contraception can only choose it because they see sex as possibly or probably fertile. In other words, the biological fact that sex does not always achieve conception does not affect the Church's teaching at all, because people can only choose contraception when they disregard this fact, which is totally irrelevant to their concerns, and focus on the fact that sex *does* sometimes achieve conception. For those considering contraception, sex is always considered a procreative type of act, and their choice of contraception is a means to deliberately make it non-procreative. The Church's position is not

based on an out-moded biology that sees all sex as procreative; in the intentionality of the couple choosing contraception, sex is procreative, and it is this that matters morally. The fact that sex is naturally infertile is relevant to those using NFP, however, as they can know which times are naturally infertile.

58 To find out more about the Church's sexual ethics and related matters see Janet E. Smith's articles at the Sacred Heart Major Seminary at www.aodonline.org/SHMS/SHMS.htm [click on her page on the 'faculty' link or, alternatively, type 'Prof. Janet E. Smith' into Google or another search engine and follow the links]. Her book *Humanae Vitae: A Generation Later* (Catholic University of America, 1991) is the most thorough treatment of the Church's position on contraception and a brilliant analysis of the encyclical. Also worth looking at is Mary Shivanandan's work, which can be accessed from www.christendom-awake.org. By way of contrast, a detailed argument for the Church to reverse its teaching on contraception and embrace population reduction is made in J.C. Schwartz, *Global Population from a Catholic Perspective* (Mystic, CT: Twenty Third Publications, 1998).

59 Contraception can also be a side-effect of the use of 'contraceptives' in other situations, such as protection against the effects of rape or medical treatment for menstrual problems. Provided that the normal principles for accepting bad side-effects are applicable (e.g. no alternative effective choice is available), accepting the side-effect is compatible with Catholic doctrine.

60 Condom effectiveness in preventing pregnancy is rated as between 2 per cent and 15 per cent by Planned Parenthood; see www.plannedparenthood.org/bc/bcfacts2.html. One can assume that the effectiveness in preventing HIV will be similar, or maybe slightly less (as the level of risk regarding HIV will be constant throughout the menstrual cycle, in contrast to the potential to become pregnant, which is non-existent the majority of the time).

61 See Anto Akkara, 'The "Social Vaccine"', *Catholic World Report* (October 2004), where an account is given of the 15th International AIDS Conference (IAC), held July 11th-16th, 2004 in Bangkok. This article reports on the increasingly positive response there to 'faith-based' action to cope with the AIDS problem. One speaker highlighted is the Ugandan President, Yoweri Museveni, who 'spoke of the great success achieved by an abstinence-based program to counter AIDS in his country... Uganda's aggressive effort to promote

abstinence outside marriage, and fidelity within, has become Africa's only success story in fighting AIDS. While the HIV virus continues to spread unchecked across the rest of sub-Saharan Africa, in Uganda the rate of HIV infection has dropped from 18 percent in 1991 to 6 percent in 2001.' This report is online at www.cwnews.com/news/viewstory.cfm?recnum=33163

62 Fr Martin Rhonheimer, an orthodox Catholic theologian who fully accepts the Church's teaching on contraception, has argued that the Church does not teach that condom use for HIV/AIDS prevention is necessarily wrong; see his article in *The Tablet* 10th July 2004, online at www.thetablet.co.uk/cgi-bin/register.cgi/tablet-00914. It has yet to be seen if this kind of argument becomes the more official position of the Church.

63 The 'theology of the body' refers to a body of teaching by Pope John Paul II in the mid 80s about the symbolism of the human body, especially with regard to sexual ethics. It started with a reflection on the Genisis creation accounts. It is regarded by some as a hugely positive development in the Church's theology of sex. One author who has tried to bring the pope's thinking to a wider audience is Christopher West; see www.theologyofthebody.net/index.htm.

64 The statement in the text is not saying that all aspects of the issues of population, responsible parenthood and HIV/AIDS are to be seen as caused by intemperance or unchastity. In some cases, people are potential or actual victims of *others'* intemperance and therefore self-defence measures for these victims, perhaps including condoms, may be appropriate. Nevertheless, an exclusive focus on the need for protection in such cases may preclude us from seeing the fuller picture that includes the lack of virtue of those who are the true causes of problems such as the spread of AIDS and the unjust distribution of resources in developing countries. The classic virtues of prudence, justice, fortitude and temperance are well analysed in J. Pieper, *The Four Cardinal Virtues* (Indiana: University of Notre Dame Press, 1966). I have tried to reflect to some extent in this book a recent renewed interest in virtue ethics amongst ethicists, seen in the work of such writers as Servais Pinckaers and Stanley Hauerwas.

65 I am again grateful to Bruno Breathnach, Director of Rigpa Dublin, Tibetan Buddhist Meditation Centre, for reading the sections on Buddhism and providing material.

66 From buddhism.about.com/library/weekly/aa081302a.htm

67 At the www.buddhanet.net site, following the 'e-book library' menu at the top of the page, the following can be found: Philip Kaplau, *To Cherish All Life*; K Sri Dhammananda, *What Buddhists Believe*, 4th expanded edition; Pategama Gnanarama, *Essentials of Buddhism*. Following the 'file library/resources' menu, then 'general buddhism', a number of excellent zipped articles can be found, including Phil Brown, 'Buddhism and the Ecocrisis', 'Buddhist ethics – the precepts', and Ven. Professor Dhammavihari, 'Progress, Development of Survival of Man'. (The web addresses of the various documents tend to be very long so I've suggested an easier way to access them!)
68 See the website at www.kwanumzen.com/primarypoint/v14n1-1996-spring-neilbartholomew-takingfiveprecepts.html
69 It is interesting, for example, to compare and contrast the Islamic concept of 'vice-regent' with the Christian concept of sharing in Christ's kingship, as seen in Pope John Paul II *Christifideles Laici* (1988), nn. 14 (kingship) and 43 (ecology), available online at the papal documents index at www.vatican.va/offices/ papal_docs_list.html#C. Of course, Islam does not see Christ as divine and so it associates the concept of vice-regent with Allah, not Christ.
70 Fazlun Khalid, 'Guardians of the natural order' from 'Islamic Foundation for Ecology and environmental Sciences' online at www.ifees.org/jour_art_guard.htm
71 'Ecology in Islam: Protection of the web of life a duty for all Muslims' from *Washington Report on Middle East Affairs* (October 1991) online at www.wrmea.com/backissues/ 1091/9110065.htm
72 Available online at www.crosscurrents.org/islamecology.htm
73 The quote is taken from *Bangalore Theological Forum*, Vol. XXXIII, No. 1, published by the United Theological College, Bangalore, India, 2001 – online at www.religion-online.org/cgi-bin/relsearchd.dll/ showarticle?item_id=1632
74 The Islamic Foundation for Ecology and Environmental Sciences: www.ifees.org/
75 This article is at www.islamonline.net/english/Contemporary/2002 /08/Article02.shtml
76 Amjad Mohammad Saleen, 'A Wave of Change Required' [includes detailed application of principles] at www.islamonline.net/english/ Contemporary/2004/01/Article02.shtml
77 Francesca de Chatel, 'Prophet Mohammed: A Pioneer of the Environment' at www.islamonline.net/english/Contemporary/ 2003/02/Article02.shtml

78 The phrase is taken from the title of a recent book by Cardinal Cahal B. Daly, *The Minding of Planet Earth* (Dublin: Veritas, 2004). It deals concisely and inspiringly with many of the themes of this section of the syllabus.

Appendix One: Outline of the Course

On the following two page spread is my own outline of section F: *Issues of Justice and Peace*. This is a 'bird's eye view' of the section as a whole and should be read in conjuction with the official syllabus and this book. It is not a substitute for the syllabus. The wording here is taken from the official syllabus, but it is written in notes format, based on the 'stated outcomes' section of the syllabus. This is not meant to imply that the teacher should teach only the specified outcomes mentioned in the syllabus and this outline. Good education goes beyond such a minimilist approach. One should be mainly guided by the aims of the syllabus and should teach to these. As stated at several points in this book, this teaching should be in harmony with the ethos of the school.

Having an outline such as this can help the teacher and student to get an overview of the whole course at a glance. This can help one to understand the structure of the course, to see what follows on from what, and how there might be a logic to the flow of the parts. It is important for teachers and students not to see the course as simply one thing after another, fragments of interesting items about justice and peace with no relationship between them.

I used this outline in the writing of this book and I hope it will prove helpful to readers as they navigate through it. The book follows the syllabus structure exactly – and so this outline is a kind of detailed contents page too.

Course Aims
To teach the principles and skills of social analysis.
To encourage their application in local, and some national and global contexts.
To identify and analyse the links between religious belief and commitment and action for justice and peace.
To explore the relationship between justice and peace, and how to sustain it, especially in the Irish context.

Part one: Reflecting on Context (Stated Outcomes)

Social Analysis
Identify the most significant economic, political, social and cultural structures within their own context that:
- Influence availability and allocation of resources
- Determine the type and sources of power
- Shape various relationships
- Determine people's accorded meaning and value

Social Analysis in Action (using the principles from 1.1)
HL choose two; OL choose one of the following:
a. *World hunger* (one country's experience; two causes at national and international level)
b. *Poverty in Ireland* (relative and absolute; one group affected; two structural factors that affect this group)
c. *Discrimination in Ireland* (two examples of one form of it; two structural factors contributing to this form of discrimination)

Part two: The Concept of Justice and Peace

2.1 Visions of Justice
Describe these understandings of justice and identify their strengths and weaknesses:
- Right relationship
- Retribution
- Fair play
- The promotion of equality
- The upholding of human rights

2.2 Visions of Peace
- Explain and illustrate the relationship between justice and peace
- Define two types of peace, (with an example of each)
- Differentiate between non-violence as lifestyle and as protest

- Present one model of conflict resolution and apply to one local or global situation
- Define dialogue within the context of conflict resolution

2.3 Religious Perspectives on Justice and Peace
Making reference to one scripture/source and one example of current thinking: outline two of the following:
- The Judaeo-Christian vision of justice
- The Zakat of Islam
- The Four Varnas of Hinduism
- The Eightfold Path of Buddhism

2.4 Violence
- Outline two causes and two effects of personal violence and structural violence
- Identify the key principles of the "just war" theory
- Illustrate it by applying it to one contemporary example
- Taking one example of personal and one example of structural violence, 'show how someone might legitimise this violence'

Part Three: The Religious Imperative to Act for Justice and Peace

3.1 Religion and the Environment
- Explain the 'greening' of religion
- Give three factors that contributed to this process
- Outline the biography of a commentator on religion and the environment
- Present a summary of his/her main ideas
- Explain how religious beliefs impact on the environmental lifestyle of 1 religious group/organisation

3.2 Religious Traditions and the Environment
- Explain the Jewish concepts of Sabbath, Schmittah and Jubilee and their relationship to the environmental crisis
- Relate the concepts of stewardship and domination as found in Genesis creation texts to one current environmental crisis [in this book I have focused on the issue of population control]
- Explain the Five Precepts of the Buddha and show how each is acted out in the lifestyle of Buddhists today
- Explain the concept of Viceregent of the earth as found in Islam and show how it impacts on two aspects of Islamic lifestyle

Appendix Two: Concerning the Use of Websites and Other Resources

This book is happy to present many internet references because the internet is so accessible for teacher and student alike. Books can be expensive and are not always available, whereas the internet is relatively cheap and only a click away. There is a great deal of material related to issues of justice and peace available online. That said, there are problems. Anyone can publish material on the internet. You may not know if the author of the site you are visiting is merely pretending to be the expert he or she claims to be. There are extremist views expressed online. Most importantly, it is relatively easy to 'cut and paste' material from websites to make up essays or projects without much in the way of personal understanding, assessment or integration. This last point is an increasingly serious matter for teachers' evaluation of students' continuous assessment work.

What follows are my own listing of criteria to help a teacher or student to evaluate the reliability of a site and its contents. They are mainly common sense principles and can guide one's prudent use of other resources too. It is an important aim of this course to teach students how to judge accurately and fairly the material they come across when researching topics on the internet. Many of the same problems arise in reading printed books or articles too – an established publisher may cut out some of the more amateur or extremist material, but not all published books or articles are therefore reliable or accurate. Not everything in the reference materials mentioned in this book is of the same standard; nor does the present author agree with everything asserted in every site or every book. Actually, some of the references mentioned or listed are for comparison and contrast purposes – presenting students with widely divergent articles or views can be an excellent way to encourage and provoke learning. The teacher should use all materials carefully and make sure that students do not simply find items on the internet and take them for Gospel truth just because they are there, or they agree with the students' own prejudices/views, or because they disagree with the teacher's views and so forth.

Seven Criteria for Evaluating Websites and Other Sources

(1) *Known Authority:* The first thing to bear in mind is whether you know the author or organisation behind the site. A site run by a Government Deptartment or an established charity such as Trócaire or a justice organisation such as Amnesty International will be much more trustworthy than one run by an obscure person or organisation. Even still, one should think critically about all material found online and elsewhere even if it is found on a good site. Sites that are new or unknown may of course be reputable, but should be handled with extra care.

(2) *Internal Logic:* A second thing to bear in mind is that one should be concerned with the coherence and clarity of the material. Ask questions such as: Is it intelligible? Is it logical? Does it contradict itself? And so on. (This book indicates, for example, several common fallacies and weaknesses in the justice and peace area. Sites that suffer from them should be avoided.)

(3) *External Backup:* A third thing to bear in mind is whether the claims made are backed up by references and publicly accessible reliable sources. One needs to be critically aware of websites' sources of information. Claims that contradict known facts or established information should not be accepted.

(4) *Distorting Bias:* Fourthly, one can ask the questions: Who benefits from this point of view? Who pays the cost? These questions may uncover bias in the website. One need not avoid all perspectives that are biased, however, but one should always deal critically with biased reporting and commenting. Sometimes it is a 'biased' point of view that will see the truth most clearly and honestly – if the bias is appropriate to the subject matter.

(5) *Varied Sources:* Having said this, the fifth point is to recommend the use of many and varied websites, rather than just one or two. Comparison of sites and their content is a good way to develop critical awareness and informed discrimination.

(6) *Extremism:* One will probably be most impressed by a consensus of views, by the mainstream in opinion. Extremist minority views are suspect, especially if they are aggressive or uncivil. That said, one should not necessarily reject views that criticise the mainstream in a civil manner or approaches that disturb the consensus by reasoned argument. Some seemingly 'extremist' views may be true; the consensus may be wrong.

(7) *Religious Faith:* Believers ought to evaluate things from their faith perspective. Christians believe that God has revealed his truth, which we accept in faith, and this revelation is the primary point of reference regarding knowledge and wisdom for us. This means that any website content that contradicts a truth of faith will not be accepted as true. A Catholic ought always be open to learn from truth wherever it is to be found, of course,

and such open-mindedness ought to be a hallmark of anyone involved in education. The Christian always judges from within the light of faith, however, in confident trust that one's religious tradition is the most reliable source of principles and knowledge concerning matters of good and evil, truth and falsity, justice and peace. Only the Gospel is 'Gospel truth'. Test everything else.

Finally

Two final points remain. Firstly, most of the web addresses in this book were checked in July and August 2004, and a few late entries in November 2004. Secondly, if a reference is no longer available when you attempt to access one from this book, or if the address given is too laborious to copy, one can always try typing the title or author's name into a search engine to find the original reference.

Appendix Three: A Shorter Bibliography

Books and articles

80:20 Development in an Unequal World (England: Teachers in Development Education, 2002).

Gardner, G. 'Engaging Religion in the Quest for a Sustainable World' in Worldwatch Institute, *State of the World 2003: Progress Towards a Sustainable Society* (Earthscan Publications: London, 2003).

Glendon, M.A. *A World Made New: Eleanor Roosevelt and the Universal Declaration of Human Rights* (New York: Random House Trade Paperbacks, 2001).

Grisez, G. *Living a Christian Life: The Way of the Lord Jesus, Vol. 2* (Illinois: Franciscan Press, 1993).

Himes, K. *Responses to 101 Questions on Catholic Social Teaching* (New Jersey: Paulist, 2001).

Holland, J. and P. Henriot *Social Analysis: Linking Faith and Justice*, revised and enlarged edition, (Washington, DC: Orbis Books/The Center of Concern, 1983).

Lebacqz, K. *Six Theories of Justice* (Minneapolis: Augsburg Publishing House, 1986).

McDonagh, S. *Greening the Christian Millennium* (Dublin: Dominican, 1998).

Pieper, J. *The Four Cardinal Virtues* (Indiana: University of Notre

Dame Press, 1966 – including the original book on *Justice* of 1955).

Pontifical Council of Justice and Peace, *Compendium of the Social Doctrine of the Catholic Church* (Vatican City: Liberia Editrice Vaticana, 2004).

Simon, R.L. (ed.), *The Blackwell Guide to Social and Political Philosophy* (Oxford, UK: Blackwell, 2002).

Singer, P. (ed.), *A Companion to Ethics*, Blackwell Companions to Philosophy (Oxford: Blackwell, 1993).

Smith, P. *What Are They Saying About Environmental Ethics?* (New York/Mahweh, NJ: Paulist, 1997).

Websites

Acton Institute subsection on environment and stewardship: www.acton.org/ppolicy/environment/

An Tairseach (Dominican Co. Wicklow Ecological Farm): www.ecocentrewicklow.com/home.htm

Archdiocese of St Paul and Minneapolis Office of Social Justice: www.osjspm.org

Buddha net: www.buddhanet.net

Cardinal Ratzinger Fanclub archive on just war: www.ratzingerfanclub.com/justwar/index.html

Catholic Conservation Center: www.conservation.catholic.org/

Combat Poverty Organisation: www.cpa.ie/

CORI (Conference of Religious of Ireland) Justice site: www.cori.ie/justice.

Development Gateway: http://home.developmentgateway.org/

Development Education Ireland: www.developmenteducation.ie/home.php

Equality Authority official site: www.equality.ie/

Food First – Institute for Food and Development Policy: www.foodfirst.org/progs/

GEO 2000: www.unep.org/geo2000/index.htm

Harvard Forum on Religion and Ecology: http://environment.harvard.edu/religion/

Hindu Resources Online: www.hindu.org/
Islamicity: www.islamicity.com/mosque/Zakat/
King Center: www.thekingcenter.org/tkc/index.asp
Trócaire: www.trocaire.org
UN Declaration of Human Rights: www.unhchr.ch/udhr/lang/eng.htm
University of Colarado online conflict resolution programme: www.colorado.edu/conflict/peace/overview_pg.htm
Vatican Archive [Bible, Catechism, Vatican II, Code of Canon Law]: www.vatican.va/archive/index.htm